GAME PLANS

Sports Strategies for Business

Robert W. Keidel

BERKLEY BOOKS, NEW YORK

to Carole

Some of the material in this book originally appeared in slightly different form in "Baseball, Football, and Basketball: Models for Business," by Robert Keidel, in *Organizational Dynamics* (Winter 1984).

This Berkley book contains the complete
text of the original hardcover edition.
It has been completely reset in a typeface
designed for easy reading and was printed
from new film.

GAME PLANS: SPORTS STRATEGIES FOR BUSINESS

A Berkley Book/published by arrangement with
E. P. Dutton

PRINTING HISTORY
E. P. Dutton edition published 1985
Berkley edition/October 1986

ISBN: 0-425-09394-8

GAME PLAN: Have an idea of where you are going and how you intend to get there.

—WAYNE LOCKWOOD, "The Anatomy of a Game Plan," in John Thorn, ed., *The Armchair Quarterback*

CONTENTS

PREFACE

I've identified with sports for as long as I can remember. In so many ways, the world of sports is a mirror of the world we live in, but not until about five years ago did I begin to appreciate the depth of the parallels between sports and business. The connections began to form in my mind in the fall of 1980, as I was teaching a class of university students. The course was a business school staple: organizational behavior. Unfortunately, much of the subject matter turned out to be indigestible. Theory came off as boring and irrelevant—especially to a group of students who were varsity athletes. In order to make the material come alive for these students—and to make the course lively for me—I began almost instinctively to couch questions in terms of local professional sports teams—specifically the Philadelphia Phillies (baseball), Eagles (football), and 76ers (basketball). Was player (employee) loyalty more important for the Eagles than for the Phillies? For which team was the game plan most essential? Would a group bonus system make more sense for the Phillies or for the 76ers?

We then generalized from team to sport, and between sports. Did different factors separate winners from losers in each sport? Could a football team tolerate an eccentric owner like Charlie Finley of the Oakland Athletics or George Steinbrenner of the New York Yankees (both of whose teams won multiple World Series during the 1970s)? Would top football coaches like Don Shula or Tom Landry make equally good pro basketball coaches?

Could a smoothly functioning, all-star basketball team be put together as easily as a comparable, all-star baseball team?

These questions led inevitably from sports to business. What business situations most closely resembled baseball? Football? Basketball? Could specific parallels be drawn between the structure of these sports and different types of business organization? The more we probed, the richer and more animated our discussions became.

With encouragement from some colleagues, I started to develop theoretical configurations of baseball, football, and basketball—profiles that contrasted the sports across several dimensions. I then began to use these profiles as a diagnostic tool in several companies to which I was a consultant. I quickly learned that the sports idiom could provide a systematic way to analyze a business organization. Corporate responses were just as encouraging as my class's had been; in fact, it was these responses that convinced me that there was more to sports analogies than anyone had yet shown—enough to make a book that would be practically useful to a wide range of people, not just business people. After eating and sleeping *Game Plans* for the last year and a half, I am more certain than ever that team sports have much to tell us about how our nonsports organizations work.

ACKNOWLEDGMENTS

My Wharton colleague Bruce McWilliams linked me with literary agent Peter Livingston, who then placed my book with E. P. Dutton. It's been a good match. And Bruce's and Peter's assistance proved invaluable. Bill Whitehead, Dutton's editor-in-chief, very skillfully helped shape *Game Plans* and rid it of jargon; in the process, he gracefully taught me a lot about writing. But even more important, Bill never lost confidence in my ideas, or in my ability to develop them.

I owe a significant intellectual debt to Russ Ackoff, whose concepts continue to enable me to make sense of complexity. Peter Davis, Director of the Wharton Applied Research Center, generously supported my work. Other Wharton colleagues who provided constructive feedback at various stages are Frank Farrow, Bill Gavelis, Tom Gilmore, Peter Heyler, Susan Hyman, Mark Levenson, Lynn Oppenheim, and Greg Shea. I also want to recognize the help of colleagues from outside Wharton—in particular, Gerry Zeitz, Bruce Grigg, Art Hochner, Dick Koenig, Steve Porth, and Paul Simmonds.

I should like to acknowledge the contributions of my client companies, which have helped me to refine the sports-models scheme in the course of our work together. Charlie Schroeder, in particular, has pointed out many nuances that had escaped me, and has sharpened my thinking about the differences among sports. Jack Charron, Tom Costello, Rich D'Amato, Al DiLascia, John Dorsey, John Flannery, Milt Havens, Tom

Kolasinski, Karl Kraske, John Letherland, Norb Machamer, Ed Sullivan, and Frank Welsh—and many others—have improved my understanding of the role that metaphor can play in real-life organizational change.

Several persons have given me new perspectives from business and/or sports; they include Jim Borden, Irv Cross, John Eldred, Frank Farrell, Bill Giles, John Good, Bill Graham, Wayne Hardin, Kurt Kendis, Hans Koehler, Ed Kuljian, Alan Livingston, Stan Lundine, Patrick McGinity, Bill Orr, Carl Peterson, Don Tuckerman, and Pat Williams.

Thanks are also due Jeff Kernan of the National Baseball Hall of Fame, Anne Mangus of the Pro Football Hall of Fame, and June Seitz of the Basketball Hall of Fame for responding promptly and cheerfully to series of requests for information.

Three individuals deserve special recognition. I am deeply grateful to Eric Trist, who has been my mentor for more than eleven years; once again, Eric has helped me go from kernel to construct. Vinnie Carroll, Associate Director—and resident baseball guru—of the Wharton Applied Research Center, has provided me with a continuing flow of insights into the whole sports:business nexus. And fellow consultant Michael Umen has not only shown me new applications of the sports models, but has been an unfailing source of encouragement from the very start.

Most of all, I want to thank my wife, Carole, who has been with me all the way on this. Her substantive help and emotional support have made all the difference. *Game Plans* would not have happened without her.

Finally, to Andy and Carly: Dad has time to play now.

INTRODUCTION

The worlds of sports and business have been closely linked for as long as anyone alive today can remember. Major sports are big business, involving big cities, big egos, and big bucks. On the other hand, big business—indeed, all business—can be viewed as sport. Scan any popular business periodical and you will find at least one article or advertisement about coaching and teamwork in business. Or listen to the sportslike language used by people in business. Increasingly, companies and individuals are players, in one or another game, who must defeat their opponents in a league known as the marketplace. In the words of Andrew Grove, president of Intel: "Turning the workplace into a playing field can turn our subordinates into 'athletes' dedicated to performing at the limit of their capabilities—the key to making our team consistent winners."

Every business organization is a team—or a team of teams. But how different some teams are from others! Incredibly, for all that has been written about the relevance of sports to business, no one has systematically contrasted the structures of various team sports to find out what is distinctive about the different games. Analysis has almost always dealt with sports in general, not in particular. Until *Game Plans*.

This book shows that different team sports have very different requirements for teamwork and coaching—and these differences have close parallels in business. More specifically, the three major team sports in the United States—baseball, football, and basketball—represent generic organizational forms common in business (and other sectors of the economy). By studying these models and understanding their differences, you will gain new insight into how your own organization works.

Every company is a lot like a baseball, football, or basketball team—or some combination of these. If it is like a baseball team, then the players are using their own initiative, pretty much independently of each other and the manager. If it is like a football team, then the manager (the coach) is calling all the shots for everyone else. And if the organization resembles basketball, then the players are coordinating themselves as a group, with the manager (coach) acting as a catalyst.

As some clients of mine have learned, matching up a given organization with the appropriate sport is critical. One case involved the president of a high-technology marketing firm. This chief operating officer had wanted to encourage close, voluntary teamwork among all organizational units in his company, but his firm was organized in a way that discouraged such collaboration. Units were geographically scattered across the country, and each operated highly autonomously. They rarely interacted and, in fact, perceived themselves (accurately) to be in competition with each other for corporate recognition and resources. Hence, attempts to inspire a sense of "all-for-one" were set up to fail, and so they did. The president admitted in retrospect: "I didn't see this until I thought about the different sports. I was expecting my units to play basketball with each other when what I really had designed was a baseball team."

Another client—an entrepreneur/manager—*had* wanted individual autonomy in his organization. His was an embryonic firm that depended on several individuals to act on their own initiative. But after a year and a half of lackluster performance by his company, the manager was perplexed; he simply could not figure out what was wrong. Only after thinking metaphorically in terms of sports did he come to realize that he had hired people with strong needs for direction, instead of the self-starters his organization required: "Now it's clear to me why we've struggled. We brought in football players to play baseball; they kept waiting for me to call the plays. There's no way it could have worked."

The baseball, football, and basketball models are an exciting way to understand and improve the performance of your own organization, regardless of how big or small it is. Recently, in a daylong workshop with the top ten managers of a $4 billion

corporation, I used the sports models to lay out the organizational effects of different corporate strategies. This analysis helped the senior management team to clarify which games the company was in—and which it was not in.

The very next day, in a $4 *million* unit of a different company, I was asked to explain to a group of twelve skeptical production workers what *employee involvement* meant. These workers were to begin to operate a new production process in a new plant in a few months. Management had been unable to impress on them the need for flexibility—and the increased opportunities for worker decision making—the new facility would bring with it. The workers were still psychologically, as well as physically, stuck in the old process. But when we examined old and new systems in terms of the sports models, it became obvious that the name of the game was changing. Workers'—and management's—behavior would have to change dramatically for the plant to function smoothly. The workers immediately grasped this point and, from then on, referred to the new facility in terms of the game it called for: basketball.

The bottom line for people in business? To make sure you're in the right game—and then to be sure you're playing it right. This book will show you how to determine what game your organization is playing, what game it should be playing, and how to play to win.

1

The Corporate Team

What is Organizational Design?

Few things have greater impact on corporate performance than
organizational design: literally, the way a company is put together. But too many businesses are unaware of their design
options, and the strengths and weaknesses of each. To understand organizational design we need concrete models, and there
may be none better than team sports. This realm is not only
concrete, it is also accessible to everyone, familiar to almost
everyone, and deeply meaningful to many. Most important,
team sports can reduce the complex issue of organizational
design to a simple question: What kind of teamwork is required?

Baseball is a highly individualistic sport that calls for only
occasional or *situational* teamwork. Scoring plays are not hierarchically planned, and players interact only minimally. Coordination is achieved through the design of the game. Football
demands *systematic* teamwork. Plays are meticulously crafted
ahead of time, and players interact according to the script.
Coordination is thus accomplished through managerial planning. Basketball requires *spontaneous* teamwork. The speed of
the game precludes the kind of top-down direction characteristic
of football. Instead, coordination in basketball is through mutual adjustment by the players themselves.

Team Sports as Models

Baseball. In baseball, team-member contributions are relatively independent of each other. In the words of Pete Rose, "Baseball is a team game, but nine men who reach their individual goals make a nice team." Player interaction is minimal. When it does occur, usually only two or three players (on the same team) are involved—for example, pitcher-catcher, shortstop-second baseman-first baseman, batter-base runner. Rarely are more than a few of the players on the field involved directly in a given play—outside of making adjustments in fielding positions in anticipation of a play (or to back up a play).

Baseball is also the least dense of the three sports; the players are widely dispersed geographically. Nine (defensive) players are spread across a wide playing area, especially the three "outfielders"—a wonderfully descriptive term. Spatial separation is mirrored by the relation between offense and defense: They are totally separate. The contest is stopped while one team leaves the field and the other takes over. Of the three sports, only baseball is without a game clock; in the words of Yogi Berra: "The game's not over until it's over."

The basic unit in baseball is the individual. Overall performance in baseball approximates the sum of the team members' performances. This is vividly demonstrated by the way offense works: Players come up to bat one at a time. In this respect, as several sportswriters have pointed out, baseball is the only sport (of the three) in which the players "take turns." Although it is true that scoring often involves a sequence of actions, such as walks, hits, and sacrifices, the most dramatic method—and what many baseball statisticians believe to be the crucial method—is the home run. This is the supreme individual act; one powerful hitter does it alone. The home run underlines the discreteness and importance of individual offensive contributions in this sport, just as pitching does with respect to defense.

Coordination in baseball is achieved through the design of the sport itself. Because the sport is so deliberately paced, even parsed—"take turns at bat, take turns playing offense and defense"—there isn't a whole lot of coordinating left for the manager to do. His primary game task is to "fill out the lineup card," that is, to determine who will play when (in the course of the game) and where (in the batting order on offense, and in the field on defense).

One of the most familiar examples of a baseball-like organization in business is the sales force made up of high-performing soloists who require little direction and who only occasionally need to work together. Similarly, an aggregation of basic researchers, whether making up their own firm or part of a larger firm, has much in common with a baseball team. The individuals constituting such an organization pursue their own lines of inquiry independently. A similar pattern describes organizations in which the task is to discover something: energy company units prospecting for new oil deposits, venture capitalists searching for innovative concepts to back, book publishers looking for promising authors. The players on such teams are relatively independent operators. The same is true of the units comprising a conglomerate or holding company, a large-scale baseball analogue. But regardless of size or nature, all organizations that resemble baseball teams have this common feature: Their players enjoy considerable autonomy with respect both to supervision and to their relations with each other.

Football. In football, every player is directly involved in every play. And although individual execution is important in football, the sport demands a good deal more player interaction than baseball. The dispersion of the players in football is denser than in baseball. Football involves about twice as many players on a smaller playing field. Most players—the lines, offensive backs, and, to an extent, the linebackers—are usually clustered together.

Moreover, in football, a team is not guaranteed a certain number of offensive tries. And offense can become defense, and vice versa, at any time as a result of a turnover (a fumble or an interception). Apart from turnovers, the normal transition game has become a third component of football, linking offense and defense. Transitions are frequently played by specialists, members of "special teams" who may have made the squad solely on the basis of their play in this facet of the game.

The basic units in football are the large group, or platoon (offense, defense, and transition), and, to a lesser extent, the small group (linemen, linebackers, backfield, and so forth). Overall performance is basically the sum of the platoons' performances. Each platoon's challenge is to be as machinelike as possible—a metaphor that is especially apt for this sport. George Allen, former head coach of the National Football League's Washington Redskins, has made this comparison to the team as a whole:

> A football team is a lot like a machine. It's made up of parts. I like to think of it as a Cadillac. A Cadillac's a pretty good car. All the refined parts working together make the team. If one part doesn't work, one player pulling against you and not doing his job, the whole machine fails.
>
> Nobody is indispensable.... We try to improve and replace some of the parts every year.

To carry the metaphor one step further, it is instructive to picture the football field as a factory, with the moving ball/line of scrimmage representing product flow through the workplace. Different players and plays are required at different points in this sequence, based on several interrelated variables: the location of the ball on the field, the yardage required, the number of downs (chances) that remain to gain that yardage, defensive alignment, weather, and so on. Factory equivalents to these variables are different performance standards, workers, machines, work centers, and processes.

Coordination in football is achieved through planning and hierarchical direction by the head coach and his staff. The head coach's composite game task is to prepare a comprehensive game plan, exhaustively rehearse it, and then implement it. There is clearly a similarity here to programming a machine and then running it according to the program.

Football-equivalents in business tend to have "long-linked" technologies; that is, their production processes involve a complex of discrete steps, tightly coupled in serial (and sometimes parallel) order. A familiar example is the steel company that carries out an entire chain of operations, all the way from mining its own ore (producing raw materials) to distributing its final products to customers. Another analogous activity is the management of large-scale construction projects (power plants, ships, high-rise buildings, and so on). Perhaps the most common example of a football-like company is the high-volume manufacturer that relies on an assembly line—often the equivalent of a giant conveyor belt. Fast-food chain restaurants with tightly controlled—even programmed—technologies are also conceptually similar to assembly-line manufacturing. Whatever the scale or variety, effective performance in a football-like company depends on the top-down orchestration of a complicated but predictable set of sequential activities.

Basketball. Basketball exhibits a high degree of player interaction, as demonstrated by the back-and-forth movement of the ball among team members. Plays that lead to baskets frequently involve every player (on offense) handling the ball. The intensely interactive character of the sport is also evident in the often-frenetic movement up and down the court—a far cry from the measured advance of a classic football scoring drive.

Basketball is the most dense of the three sports, with players crowded into a playing area one-fifteenth the size of a football field. Whereas football players are connected to their individual roles as though programmed, basketball players are connected to all their teammates in a fluid manner. Every player must be able to play offense, defense, and transition; each must dribble, pass, shoot, and go for rebounds. The basic unit in basketball is the team. With only five players on the court, an intermediate grouping between the team and the individual is unrealistic.

If offense and defense are "linked" in football, they are overlapping or "intersecting" in basketball. A team on the offensive may instantly be put on the defensive as a result of a steal or a blocked shot. The transition game between offense and defense is not separate, with separate players, as it is in football; it is continuous, a part of the flow. Indeed, a fast-breaking basketball game—particularly at the professional level—closely resembles an electronic video game.

Because of the speed and flexibility required in basketball, coordination has to come from the players themselves, as a group. They must be able to function as a unit without precise direction by their coach—especially as most plays are not punctuated by official time-outs (in contrast to football) or by pauses between batters and innings (as in baseball).

Basketball analogues in business include firms that are highly integrated across products, markets, technologies, and/or other dimensions. Such firms are *synergistic:* Their several units work together closely—often reciprocally—so that the combined effect is greater than the sum of the separate initiatives. One of the best examples of a basketball-like company is the innovative computer company that, even though often large in size, is able to remain nonbureaucratic and nimble. Smaller examples range from think-tank consulting firms to creative advertising agencies (or departments). An analogue within more conventional organizations is the ad hoc task force that cuts across levels and functions, in which all members interact with each other in virtually all aspects of problem solving. In general, such basketball-equivalents as task forces are self-organizing and highly flexible.

The means/end structures of the three sports are depicted graphically in the following chart.

THREE MEANS/END STRUCTURES

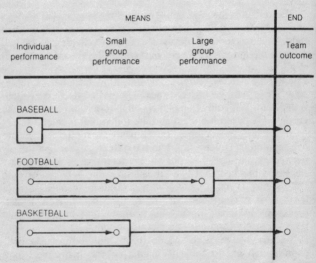

In baseball, team outcome—a win or a loss—is the aggregate of individual efforts. It is predominately the sum of individual versus individual (pitcher versus batter) confrontations. In football, team outcome is a function of large group performances. The dominant competition is platoon versus platoon (offense versus defense, special team versus special team), where each platoon requires intensive coordination of individuals and small groups. And in basketball, team outcome is a function of small group (= team) performance—player actions and, especially, interactions. The dominant competition is team versus team (encompassing offense, defense, and transition).

Another way to summarize the differences among baseball, football, and basketball is to contrast scoring patterns. Scoring in baseball is concentrated; scoring in football is sequential; and scoring in basketball is continuous.

The individual player in baseball can have a more significant offensive impact at any point in the game than his counterparts in either football or basketball because he can produce more than one run at a time. The most dramatic example of this is the grand-slam home run, which is worth four runs. In the other sports, a player can score only one goal—a touchdown, a field goal, or a basket—at a time.

On top of this, scoring in baseball does not have to stop once it has started. In football and basketball, after a team has scored, it surrenders the ball to its opponent and goes on the defensive. Only in baseball can a team continue to score—until it accumulates three outs. It is for both these reasons—individual leverage and the opportunity to score in clusters—that the Big Bang theory of scoring makes sense for baseball. This theory argues that concentrated bursts of scoring are critical, because in a large percentage of cases, the winning team scores more runs in one inning than the loser does in the entire nine-inning contest.

In baseball the name of the offensive game is power through individual sluggers. In an analysis covering 1970 through 1983, Peter Pascarelli found that only four of the twenty-eight teams playing in the World Series during those fourteen years were not among their league's top five in home-run production. Pascarelli concludes that "in world diplomacy and baseball, there is one overriding constant. For better or worse, the big stick approach almost always wins out."

Many baseball experts are acknowledging that game-related decisions dealing with one-base-at-a-time possibilities are not all that important—and are sometimes even dysfunctional. The problem with such decisions—which involve sacrifice bunts, sacrifice flies, hit-and-run plays, and base-stealing—is that they depend on the occurrence of a *sequence* of improbable events. Baseball statistician Bill James discovered that the teams with the higher batting averages during the regular season usually lost the World Series. James explains this apparent anomaly as follows:

Why do teams with high batting averages do poorly in World Series play? A simple reason: it takes them too many hits to score. . . .

High-average offenses score by stringing sequences together. To get a three-run inning, it might take them five or six hits. Every one of those hits gets harder to come by. If each one of them becomes 10% more difficult to get, how much more difficult to get are *all five* of them? You've got five chances to stop that inning.

With the three-run home run, on the other hand, you've got only three chances to stop it. As each element of the offense becomes 10% less common, the 5-element offense is damaged much more than the 3-element offense is.

Now contrast baseball with football. In football, intelligent offense is eminently sequential. The difference is that the sequence is made up of *probable* events or elements. A football scoring drive typically involves linking together several "first downs" across the field. To make a first down, a team must advance the ball ten yards. But it has three or four opportunities to do this. It doesn't take a genius to see that gaining three or four yards per play is easier than gaining ten, and that achieving a first down with a few plays is easier than scoring a touchdown. In relating his pro football experience to business management, former quarterback Fran Tarkenton claims that "If football taught me anything about business, it is that *you win the game one play at a time*." Tarkenton goes on to scorn big-play thinking:

don't go for 15 risky yards when you can get 5 sure ones. It is a principle of the marketplace that you will never fail if you take your gains modestly but consistently. . . .

When in doubt, remember that in football an 80-yard drive is better than an 80-yard "bomb." The bomb—the long pass that scores a touchdown—can be dismissed by the other team as a lucky, one-time fluke, which it probably is. The sustained drive that systematically pushes the other team back over its own goal line shows them that you play sound, unbeatable football, and is far more demoralizing to your opposition.

I believe that Fran Tarkenton's advice is quite sensible for the game of football, but less so for baseball. In baseball, big plays *are* a high-percentage way to score—and to win.

Baseball simply is less controllable by the manager. The defense puts the ball into play, and the probability of a hit is roughly one in four to one in three. Extended sequences cannot be counted on, much less scripted, under such conditions. In football, by contrast, the odds favor cumulative, incremental gains—"three yards and a cloud of dust" or four yards and a swatch of Astroturf. Thus, in the words of coaching great Bud Wilkinson, "statistically speaking, the team that controls the ball for the longer time is usually victorious. The quarterback should think of maintaining control, making first downs, keeping the ball. If he thinks exclusively in terms of scoring, he loses his perspective." And as Wilkinson intimates, stringing plays together eats up the clock—wearing out the opponent's defense and keeping its offense off the field. In baseball, time is irrelevant.

Scoring in baseball occurs in a relatively few uncontrollable bursts in the course of a game; in football, scoring typically follows sustained "drives" made up of sequences of intended plays. Basketball differs from both these sports. Scoring in basketball is nearly continuous—especially in the pro game. The National Basketball Association (NBA) rules require a team to attempt a shot within twenty-four seconds; on average, a shot is put up every fifteen seconds.

Basketball requires a sustained mix of intensity and flexibility that sets it apart from the other two sports. Basketball very much resembles the process of brainstorming, in which all members of a group contribute—in a nonprogrammed, back-and-forth manner—to produce insights that eventually will accumulate as a "win." The basketball coach lacks the overarching control of his football counterpart, but he can have a greater influence over the flow of the game than can the manager in baseball.

Applying the Sports Models

You can use the sports models to make sense of any kind of organization, of any size: from just a handful of people to a gigantic multinational corporation. The "players" that you identify may be individuals or they may be organizational units (in the latter case, player:team is equivalent to unit:organization).

These models have helped a pharmaceutical research and development (R & D) manager interpret the organizational milieu in which he operates. By applying the sports models to the drug discovery and development process, he was able to identify three distinct phases—each corresponding to a different model. As the manager later admitted, "I never understood the process so clearly as I do now. It's like going from baseball, to football, to basketball."

In the *first stage,* basic research, scientists work more or less independently, like baseball players. Medicinal chemists produce new molecules for biological testing; biochemists and pharmacologists develop evaluation methods for detecting potential new drugs; and pharmacy researchers devise new dosage forms and drug-delivery methods. The product of all these efforts is an increased pool of knowledge about how to discover a drug. It is the sum of individual contributions—as in baseball.

The *second stage,* "lead development," begins once a promising drug has been identified. Things move in train. First, developmental chemists engineer an economical process to manufacture enough of the drug for further testing. Then the drug is sent to pharmacy researchers, who develop specific dosages, and to toxicologists, who test the drug's toxicity in cultures and/or animals. Next, after government approval has been secured, clinical trials are performed. The new drug is evaluated in healthy humans for side effects and later in patients with the disease the drug is intended to treat. The sequence is cumulative, like a series of first downs in football.

Not until these steps have been completed successfully— and the company is convinced that the drug is safe, effective, and salable—does the *third stage,* aimed at developing a "new drug application" (NDA), begin. In this stage, relevant groups of specialists (physicians, statisticians, pharmacists, pharmacologists, toxicologists, and chemists) work together closely and intensely, like a basketball team, to win approval of their NDA from the Food and Drug Administration.

To succeed, whatever its game, a team must effectively carry out three related sets of tasks: staffing, planning, and operating. *Staffing* is deciding which players will be on the team and in the game; *planning* is specifying in advance how the game should be played; and *operating* has to do with influencing the process or flow of the game. The dominant challenges, however, are not identical for each sport. They are as follows:

- Baseball: Get the *players* right;
- Football: Get the *plan* right;
- Basketball: Get the *process* right.

Of course, all these challenges are important in each of the sports, but the number-one priority differs. The best teams understand their dominant challenge and organize to meet it. Business can learn from them. For corporations, the above "challenges" represent partially opposing pulls (as diagrammed below).

Obviously, no company is a pure type. And in some cases,

ORGANIZATIONAL DESIGN PRIORITIES
AS COMPETING PULLS

BASKETBALL
(process)

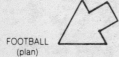

FOOTBALL
(plan)

BASEBALL
(players)

a change from one model to another over time may be the rule, not the exception. The sports models do represent organizational alternatives: All three pulls cannot be maximized at once. Deciding which pull(s) to favor is up to the corporation.

Design requires trade-offs. The local autonomy inherent in a baseball design is in conflict with the global perspective demanded by football; the coordination made possible by a football design is in conflict with the flexibility required in basketball; and the individualistic character of a baseball design is in conflict with the group bias of basketball. In all, the sports models will help you to

1. Understand generic organizational design options;

2. Appreciate the strengths and weaknesses of each option;

3. Relate sports design concepts to your own organizational world; and

4. Implement change successfully, and reinforce current practices, as appropriate.

Whether in sports or in business, the most effective systems are those in which their designs reflect their purpose. This correspondence was popularized in architecture by the German Bauhaus School (and more recently by the U.S. Cranbrook School) with the dictum "Form should follow function." The organization-theory equivalent has long been the injunction "Structure should follow strategy." First figure out what you want your strategic competence—competitive advantage—to be and then create a structure to make it happen.

No organization can do everything superbly. But once it knows which criteria really matter, a corporation can find in the appropriate sports model a practical design guide. In other words, once you know *what* your company *should* win at, the sports models will show *how* to organize so you *will* win.

2

---

*Filling Out
the Lineup Card*

BASEBALL

> *Baseball is the American success story. . . . It is, more-over, a great common ground on which bartenders and bishops, clergymen and bosses, bankers and la-borers meet with true equality and understanding. The game has proved in everyday language that democracy works.*
>
> —J. G. TAYLOR SPINK

> *Baseball is almost the only orderly thing in a very unorderly world. If you get three strikes, even the best lawyer in the world can't get you off.*
>
> —BILL VEECK

> *Whoever wants to know the heart and mind of America had better learn baseball. . . .*
>
> —JACQUES BARZUN

GEORGE PLIMPTON HAS observed that the volume of writing about a sport varies inversely with the size of the ball used. There is a lot more on baseball than on football, and reams more on either than on basketball. In general, the smaller the ball, the more dead time in the game; hence the more opportunities—and even the need—for reflection. Words, like base hits, are made for the gaps. Although much baseball writing has not been analytical, if the literature, and the game, are viewed through an organizational lens, the structure of baseball becomes clear. Equally clear, then, is the relevance of this structure to business.

Baseball is derived from the English game "rounders." Rounders pitted each batter against a defensive team made up of a pitcher, a catcher, and two or more fielders. After hitting the ball, a batter had to circle or "round" two base posts in order to score. Baseball as we know it today—three bases and home plate, nine players on a side, nine innings to a game—took shape during the middle of the nineteenth century. Despite the rather recent appearance of artificial turf, flamboyant uniforms, and the American League's designated hitter (who bats in place of the pitcher), baseball has changed remarkably little since 1871 when, according to historian Stuart Berg Flexner, it had become "America's first mass spectator sport and sports industry."

Baseball-organizations come in a wide array of sizes and styles. At one end of the spectrum, such a "team" is made up of a handful of individuals—like a small clothing store with three or four salespersons. At the other end, the multinational conglomerate employs tens or even hundreds of thousands of people. Skill levels are also diverse. The tasks of people in a baseball-organization may range from inventing new technologies to providing personal service. Similarly, individual performance criteria may vary from highly specifiable (dollars of sales) to virtually nonspecifiable (working on the cure for a rare disease).

Despite this diversity, all baseball-organizations have several properties in common. The most basic property is individual autonomy. Persons (roles) or organizational units are relatively independent. Each has considerable elbowroom and, in fact, is expected to take a lot of initiative—to be a self-starter.

Another common property is the absence of a known or predictable "long-linked" sequence of tasks. The work of many baseball-organizations and their players is nonsequential. Thus, neither bank tellers nor travel agents contribute in a serial way to a larger task that culminates in an end product; rather, they carry out a variety of independent tasks, the order of occurrence of which is often impossible to predict.

In those cases when the work of a baseball-organization does unfold in sequence, this sequence typically cannot be mapped beforehand. Neither can the character of the end state be specified in any detail. Clarity of process (and often outcome) appears only in retrospect. For instance, consider the task of conducting research. Clearly, there are different phases that must take place: literature reviews, problem formulation, hypothesis testing, experimentation, and so on. But these phases cannot be delineated the same way a manufacturing process can. The researcher will not know ahead of time how long he or she must spend in each phase or when it will be necessary to cycle back through an earlier phase. Thus, the actual process of this work is hardly more predictable than its outcome—the research product. It is just like the process and outcome of a baseball game. As Stanley Cohen has pointed out, "a baseball game follows no predictable pattern. Its turning can come at any moment, and today's game will offer little suggestion of what one might expect tomorrow when the same two teams meet. Other sports, in which size and power count for more than they do in baseball, adhere to form more closely, and none more so than football."

Baseball is further characterized by infrequent—and brief— interactions among team members. "Players" in a baseball-organization interact with each other only minimally and contribute to the organization independently. Finally, many baseball-organizations are geographically spread out, which further reduces the likelihood of interaction.

All these properties are embodied in the scouting organization of an actual baseball team. A scout's work does not unfold in programmed sequence. Each scout is an independent prospector who must organize his own day and put himself on the line—figuratively swing or hold back. The Phillies' scout Gary Nickels describes his own initiation into the profession:

What I thought scouting would be when I was in the office wasn't what scouting really is. . . . In the first place, you have to push yourself. It's not a job where you punch in or where someone's always looking over your shoulder. You're on your own for a week, two weeks at a time, and it's up to you where you should go. It wouldn't be that hard, if you wanted to, to fool your boss with your reports and expense account, and if you weren't a self-motivated person you could slide by for a while.

But the biggest surprise was that I had to make clear-cut decisions under tough circumstances.

Your boss calls you about a player and you've got to say yes or no; you can't sit on the fence.

Baseball is designed to contain discrete individual (unit) initiatives. *Sports Illustrated,* under managing editor Andre Laguerre in the 1960s, was a good example of a baseball-organization* in which the players were individual writers. Writer Dan Jenkins admits that Laguerre gave him nearly un-limited freedom to write his own way: "When I arrived, Andre told me he had four rules: 'You cannot spend too much money. You cannot get enough people angry with you. You cannot get too much hate mail. And if any editors fool with your copy, tell me and I'll kill them.'"

General Signal Corporation, a $1.6 billion (1983 sales) man-ufacturer of instruments and controls, is a case of a baseball-organization in which the players are units (and unit top managers). This company encompasses forty-four acquired businesses, each of which operates autonomously; each, for in-stance, retains its original name, is run by its former manage-ment, and continues its previous personnel policies and benefits programs. Yohan Cho, the head of a firm acquired by General Signal in 1982, claimed two years later that he had all the dis-cretion he could want: "We are operating exactly as an inde-pendent . . . company."

In baseball, strategy is *What players do I want on my team?* It is rational for a baseball team to maximize its number of star performers because one player's statistics normally do not come at the expense of another's. Batters take turns batting, and pitchers take turns pitching. No club has ever had too much hitting or too much pitching. In contrast, football and basketball teams can suffer from too many stars—especially in glamour positions (the equivalent of slugger or pitcher)—because there may not be enough opportunities for every player to run with or pass or shoot the ball.

Mary Kay Cosmetics, Inc., is a baseball-organization that clearly tries to increase its number of individual stars. In 1983,

*From this point on, "baseball-organization," "football-organization," or "basketball-organization" will refer to the business equivalent of that particular sport.

Mary Kay had 190,000 independent salespersons, known as beauty consultants, who operate as independent contractors. Whereas each consultant may set her own pace, the company reinforces individual effort. Says founder Mary K. Ash, "I think the competition we have at Mary Kay Cosmetics is very healthy. . . . I do believe in encouraging a person to compete with herself—here at Mary Kay Cosmetics, we've made that philosophy a company policy." For those who can compete, the money is there. More women earn in excess of $50,000 a year at Mary Kay than at any other company in the world, and many sales directors earn more than $100,000. In fact, top sales directors at Mary Kay also are given pink Cadillacs, symbols that they are star players on a winning team. Mary K. Ash finds a direct parallel with baseball:

> The New York Yankees baseball team has a well-earned reputation for excellence. I've heard it said that when a player dons the Yankees' striped uniform he plays better ball. Why? Because he's proud to be part of a team with a winning tradition.
>   Similarly the Cadillac is considered the hallmark of quality in the American automobile industry. For this reason we award pink Cadillacs to those directors whose sales units have attained a certain sales volume. Whenever people see a pink Cadillac, they know it's being driven by someone very important to our organization.

If strategy in baseball revolves around the question of what players I want on my team, then the core tactical decision is *What players do I want in the game?* (For our purposes, *tactics*—in all three sports—will refer to game-related decisions, and *strategy* to more general decisions involving anywhere from several games to several seasons.) Few, if any, managers were more competent strategically or tactically than former Baltimore Orioles manager Earl Weaver, whose career winning percentage (.596) is the third highest in major league history.

INTERVIEWER: What's the secret to managing?
WEAVER: Get the guy up there you want.

Weaver responds to charges that he was a "push-button manager":

I have nothing against being called a push-button manager. Early in my career it might have bothered me. But
think about it. What else does a manager do but push
buttons? He doesn't hit, he doesn't run, he doesn't throw,
and he doesn't catch the ball. A manager has twenty-
five players, or twenty-five buttons, and he selects which
one he'll use, or push, that day. The manager who presses
the right buttons most often is the one who wins the most
games. When a manager has been pushing the same
buttons day after day and losing, he'd better start pushing
some different ones. The key to managing is player evaluation, which is another way of saying that you must
know which buttons to push and when to push them.

More than either football or basketball, baseball is a game of
situations. Earl Weaver was appropriately named. He was able
(1) to weave together "a unit that would include a man who
could fill every conceivable role at any time all season" (a
strategic skill) and (2) to weave into a game exactly the player
required, situation after situation (a tactical skill).

Weaver was able, in other words, to select and deploy individual players. Such tasks are what player-management in
baseball is all about: It is the management of individuals—of
independence. The extraordinary player can have a greater independent effect in baseball than in football or basketball. This
is probably most apparent with respect to pitching—which
accounts for anywhere between 45 to 90 percent of the game,
depending on whom you listen to. Much of the remaining 10
to 55 percent (or whatever it is) consists of slugging—especially if the Big Bang theory of scoring is valid.

Bill James, in analyzing the Phillies' 1980 World Series
championship season, assigns the credit to three players: pitchers Steve Carlton (a starter) and Tug McGraw (a reliever) and
slugger Mike Schmidt: "I still think it was the worst 22-man
championship team that I ever saw and the best 3-man combo
that any team has had at least since World War II." As always,
Earl Weaver generalizes the point economically: "Baseball is
pitching, three-run homers, and fundamentals."

So baseball-organizations go for stars. This bias is nowhere
more evident than in high-powered sales. Consider Julien J.
Studley, Inc., a commercial real estate broker in Washington,
D.C. Rookie brokers, who are housed in an area called "the
bullpen," are paid no salary, have no "company" medical in-

surance, and receive no paid vacations or holidays. Their income is strictly a function of what they bring in. More than 25 percent do not make it through two years with the firm. But for those who do succeed, the commissions can be enormous— even into the high six figures. What is it like to manage such high-fliers? Says founder Julien Studley: "Sometimes I feel like I'm running a film studio. I have stars here to contend with."

But with stars comes idiosyncrasy. In baseball this expresses itself in many ways, from the bizarre behavior of "flakes" like Jimmy Piersall (who once circled the bases running backward) and Mark "The Bird" Fidrych (a pitcher fond of talking to the ball) to such loners as Ty Cobb, Joe DiMaggio, Ted Williams, Sandy Koufax, and Steve Carlton—immortals of baseball. Sportswriter Jimmy Cannon observed that Cobb, for one, seemed to take pride in his loneliness, "as if it were a reward for perfection." This kind of personality finds a welcome home in baseball. John Updike has written that "of all team sports, baseball, with its graceful intermittences of action, its immense and tranquil field sparsely settled with poised men in white, its dispassionate mathematics, seems to me best suited to accommodate, and be ornamented by, a loner. It is an essentially lonely game."

Psychologically, baseball, more than either football or basketball, seems to tolerate personality extremes—extroverts and introverts. Yet the game is grounded in averages. Of the three sports, only in baseball are the players of generally "average" size. And as much as baseball can tolerate deviance in personality, it seems unalterably opposed to deviance in statistics. Marvin Cohen has written that "Any deviation from the 'usual' is noted, since every baseball-knower knows what the usual is, and has that same 'usual' in common with all other baseball fans—as a standard, a framework, a reference, from which to judge each new play, game, or season's performance."

One of the best examples of a baseball-organization in the corporate world is the *conglomerate*. The pure form of a conglomerate is called a "holding company," which is little more than a financial structure overlaid on a set of unrelated businesses. The various businesses, often referred to as "profit centers," are supposed to contribute profits to the financial entity, which, in turn, allocates financial resources among them.

The logic for a conglomerate approach to organizational design is twofold. On the up side, a corporate structure should do a better job of allocating capital among several businesses than the marketplace can. On the down side, the unrelated character of these businesses should make it possible to pool risks among them and thereby enable the corporation as a whole to weather downturns in the business cycle. Conglomerates thus attempt to have the best of two worlds: high return and low risk.

Conglomerates clearly have a lot of baseball characteristics. As is a baseball team's coaching staff, the corporate administrative structure is sparse. Indeed, this must be so because the marginal advantage a conglomerate enjoys over marketplace mechanisms is not that great. But even if it were, the expertise at the corporate level will always be limited. It usually will be confined to financial, legal, and planning areas. Expertise in marketing, manufacturing, engineering, and research and development will be lacking because these functions will differ so widely among the unrelated businesses making up the conglomerate.

Operating units "on the team" typically have a great deal of autonomy—with respect both to corporate headquarters and to each other. These units are likely to be geographically scattered, and their contributions are almost always discrete. Measuring the contributions of each unit in a conglomerate is the same as measuring the contribution of each player on a baseball team. In baseball, according to Thomas Boswell, "almost every act has an accountability. The box score must add up with each run, hit, and error charged to someone." Boswell elaborates: "Other sports have an impenetrable mystique. Baseball offers insights. Even as we are watching it, we can dissect the game, then reassemble it to a better-understood whole—with the simple scorecard." The key words are *dissect* and *reassemble*. For in baseball, more than in the other two sports, the whole is roughly the sum of its parts. Translated, team performance is roughly the sum of the individual players' performances. Branch Rickey, who broke baseball's color barrier by signing Jackie Robinson in 1946, declared that "Only in baseball can a team player be a pure individualist first and a team player second, within the rules and the spirit of the game."

Royal Little, who founded Textron, the first conglomerate, says that "The key to running a conglomerate well is to give the division [unit] managers the authority to run their own shows—but to make sure they are motivated." One conglomerate that does exactly this is the Marmon Group, a closely held set of seventy operating companies and ten affiliates with annual sales of $2.8 billion (1984). The Marmon Group has been assembled and managed by brothers Jay and Robert Pritzker. Jay has played the role-equivalent of a baseball team general manager by acquiring the units; Robert has been the (game) manager, directly concerned with operations. As do his counterparts in baseball, Robert relies heavily on the managers of the operating units (the "players") to make their own decisions. According to David Gardiner, manager of one of these units, "You run the show, or they will put someone else in to run it. It's like running your own company without your own money."

Conglomerates typically grow by acquiring existing companies, rather than by developing from within. They are eager suitors of free (and sometimes not-so-free) agent-firms. The relative ease with which conglomerates add or subtract (acquire or divest) operating units parallels the flexibility that baseball teams have in making player transactions: just like kids swapping bubble-gum cards. In each case, the core strategic question is "What players do we want on our team?" The "players," of course, are operating units (facilities, divisions, groups—or the heads of these units); the "manager" is the conglomerate's corporate management, which almost invariably includes its chief executive officer.

A contemporary conglomerator who has received a good deal of attention in the press is William F. Farley, a former encyclopedia salesman who now owns Farley Industries—a collection of low-technology companies—and 3 percent of the Chicago White Sox. General Electric Credit Corporation, which underwrote Farley, ran an advertisement in *Forbes* with this title: "How Bill Farley could *swing* a $123 million buyout with a $4 million investment" [emphasis added]. In the center of the advertisement sits Farley, in a White Sox T-shirt, atop the caption, "William Farley—Part owner Chicago White Sox and a big leaguer in leveraged buy-outs."

Baseball-organizations tend to be risk-takers. This is especially true of what I call *independent production* organizations, in which *production* has mainly to do with discovery, invention, creation, or design, and the *production system* is an individual or an autonomous organizational unit that requires minimal coordination with other units. Indeed, although the sport of baseball showcases individual achievement, it is rigidly unforgiving of failure. And baseball provides plenty of that. To wit: Quarterbacks in pro football complete about half their passes; pro basketball players score on about half their shots;

the batter in pro baseball, however, gets a hit only once in every three or four at-bats. And the numbers are never hidden from public view. According to Bill James, "A baseball field ... is so covered with statistics that nothing can happen there without leaving its tracks in the records. There may well be no other facet of American life, the activities of laboratory rats excepted, which is so extensively categorized, counted and recorded."

The exploration activities of oil companies are a clear example of risk-taking. In an article titled "How Amoco Finds All That Oil," *Fortune*'s Donald Holt writes that "When the Baltimore Canyon offshore tracts went on the block in 1976 ... Exxon and Mobil, seeking a big U.S. strike, bid like roughnecks in a Saturday night poker game." Amoco's "manager" at the time was former CEO John E. Swearingen. Said a former executive who was close to Swearingen, "He lets you run, 'and that makes it a very good place to work.'" Actually, Swearingen had two sets of "players": his direct subordinates and outsiders to the company who collaborated on joint ventures: "[Amoco] likes to drill as many wells as possible. 'Most of the favorable results we've had were completely unforseen [sic]—by us or anybody else. That happens *if* you drill a lot of wells,' says George Galloway, president of Amoco Production. Having more prospects than money, [Amoco] farms out acreage and participates in hundreds of joint wildcat ventures."

In fact, the company as a whole has two additional sets of "players": its young field managers (who "work with a passion seldom seen outside of combat, sometimes staying on the job for days, sleeping in their cars or on rigs," and its geologists and geophysicists. About the latter: "The company's biggest problem is finding enough good geologists and geophysicists, and then hanging on to them. So strong is Amoco Production's reputation that independents are tripping over one another in their efforts to hire away the company's young hotshots."

A problem analogous to discovering oil confronts another kind of independent production baseball-organization: commercial developers. In each case, the primary concern is location, location, location. A baseball approach characterizes Trammell Crow Company, a Dallas-based developer owned by eighty partners in forty regional offices. The regional partners are highly autonomous; they make their own decisions about what, where, and how to build, as well as whom to hire or to contract with.

Self-reliance is a prerequisite for working at Crow. According to the chief financial officer, Joel Peterson, "There's no training. . . . [New employees] have to learn the business on their own. People have to be self-disciplined and self-motivated." But this presents no difficulties for Crow players, who thrive in an open-ended environment. In the words of Ned Spieker of the San Francisco office, "The kind of people who are good at real estate don't respond well to structure." Trammell Crow himself puts it this way: "Most real estate judgments are made on the basis of instincts—not analysis. . . ."

Book publishers are still another variety of "independent production" baseball-organization. It's a real crap shoot to pick winners, and especially big winners, in this game. William Jovanovich of Harcourt Brace Jovanovich breaks books into binary categories: those that are profitable and all others: "If I knew how to distinguish between those two kinds . . . let alone a third kind that might be called 'making a *little* money,' then publishing would be easy. About 70 percent of our adult trade books [those aimed at general readers and sold in bookstores] lose money." Still, he's batting .300. William Morrow's Lawrence Hughes affirms that "the joy and the frustration are that each book is an individual act of publishing. Except for ground-out category books, each book is an individual problem to be solved in reaching an audience." A publishing firm actually includes two sets of baseball players: its editors and the authors whose work it publishes. Editors thus may have a dual role: players within their firm's hierarchy and managers of authors. In a sense, editors are player-managers.

Managing a baseball-organization means managing *individuals,* just as the sport itself is made for soloists—virtuosos. There is no clearer evidence of this individualistic bias than the behavior of venture capitalists, who will lay out millions for a compelling concept, as long as it is being championed by the right person. Take the case of Metaphor Computer Systems, which in 1983–84 attracted $15 million on the basis of an idea and a business plan. "'In this business, we basically back people,' admits William R. Hambrecht, president of Hambrecht & Quist Inc., the investment bank that in 1982 helped raise Metaphor's first $5 million. . . ." The venture capitalist is the manager; the venture, the player. (In fact, venture capital firms themselves typically resemble baseball teams, with key players acting autonomously. In such cases, one baseball-organization is effectively backing another.) In a recent cover story on entrepreneurs, *Time* profiled a venture capitalist under the following title: "Arthur Rock: 'The Best Long-Ball Hitter Around.'" The story begins with this paragraph:

When the San Francisco Giants play in windy Candlestick Park, a man with owlish spectacles, tight lips, an aquiline nose and a stern gaze usually sits in a front-row seat, 70 ft. from home plate. Arthur Rock, 57, has been a Giants fan for 25 years, watching batters try to sort curve balls from sliders and change-ups from screwballs. Since the late 1950s, Rock has been carefully scrutinizing pitches of another kind—start-up bids by young technology companies—and when he goes for one of these, he rarely misses. Says San Francisco Venture Capitalist Thomas Perkins: "Arthur Rock is the best long-ball hitter around."

A number of major corporations have tried to foster invention within their ranks by setting up small organizational units staffed with entrepreneurially inclined people—dubbed *intrapreneurs*. How to manage them? A familiar answer. From his own experience, Innotech's Don Gamache believes the formula is simple: "There are only a few rules in managing new ventures, inside or outside a company: Pick the right people, give them broadstroke performance goals and leave them alone."

IBM, for one, has its IBM Fellows program, which was started in 1963. In an advertisement titled "Dreamers, Heretics, Gadflies, Mavericks, and Geniuses," IBM describes its Fellows (players) and their charter:

They earned the title by having ideas that made a difference. Their job is to have more ideas like that, but under a very special condition.

It's called freedom.

Freedom from deadlines. Freedom from committees. Freedom from the usual limits of corporate approval.

For a term of at least 5 years, an IBM Fellow is free to pursue any advanced project of value to IBM, even if chances for success may seem remote.

As a result, some of the great innovations of our time have come from IBM Fellows.

We may not always understand what they're doing, much less how they do it. But we do know this:

The best way to inspire an IBM Fellow is to get out of the way.

In effect, the IBM Fellows program is an attempt to promote basic research and development (R & D) within a corporate context. As defined by the National Science Foundation, the term *basic research* refers to "original investigations for the advancement of scientific knowledge not having specific commercial objectives." Basic researchers typically work independently, or with a very few others. Their autonomy mirrors that of university professors. The classic large-scale example of this kind of operation is Bell Labs, AT&T's R & D unit, which employs some 18,000 people. Despite Bell Labs' size, the organization has much in common with a university research center. According to research vice-president Arno Penzias, "One of the things that people are constantly amazed at in this place is just how little short-term management there really is."

There is increasing evidence that short-term management—in the form of game tactics (apart from substitutions)—is not especially important in baseball and may, in fact, be dysfunctional. Boswell describes the penchant for analysis of Gene Mauch, one of the keenest tacticians in recent years: "Mauch lives the game at a level of detail perhaps never before reached—some would say which never *needed* to be reached. He has pitch-by-pitch records, box scores and personal notes on every game he's managed back to 1961."

But Mauch's lifetime win/loss percentage through the 1983 season was only .473. Twenty times in his twenty-three-year career, his teams finished fourth or lower. Earl Weaver's response to Mauch's approach? "Play for one run, lose by one run. . . . Over a season, three-run homers beat 'inside' baseball every time."

The herculean homer—that really big score—is exactly what Bristol-Myers is looking for under chairman Richard Gelb. Gelb's idea of this is a "blockbuster drug"—such as an effective treatment for cancer. The means to this end is research. In Gelb's words, "Our goal is to be seen as a world-class research organization. . . . One way to do that is to spend money and hope that it bears fruit."

Independent producers—prospectors, writers, entrepreneurs, basic researchers, whatever—thrive on independence. Monitoring them too closely is likely to be counterproductive, just as in baseball. You do not "supervise" Nolan Ryan's pitching or George Brett's hitting. Rather, you do everything you can to get these players on your team and into the game. Then you let them play.

Because the crux of baseball is the pitcher-batter confrontation, with the pitcher (defense) initiating play, the game has a fundamentally uncontrollable character; it's partly random in nature. Various observers have suggested that baseball, much more than football or basketball, involves competing against nature. For apart from the central pitcher-batter contest, the game is less a matter of head-to-head competition than either football or basketball. This feature distinguishes another large class of baseball-organizations in which the players are out there dealing with situations that are unpredictable and often uncertain: individual-based service organizations with tasks that range from investment analysis to field engineering.

Traditional organizational theory has concerned itself primarily with production or manufacturing firms. The heart of this genre is the sequential conversion process: Known inputs are acted on through a preestablished, step-by-step procedure to obtain known outputs. Anybody who has ever worked in a factory knows that the fewer the interferences and interruptions from the outside, the better. Factories are designed for efficiency, and efficiency is obtained by avoiding distractions from the task at hand. The challenge to management is to minimize these distractions. In other words, to live a life of "no surprises." Academics call this "sealing off the technical core." By such logic, the more isolated the production process is from changes provoked by suppliers, customers, competitors, regulators, and local communities, the closer to the ideal it is. Such isolation may be appropriate for football-organizations in the goods-production game. It is not only inappropriate, but also impossible, for baseball-organizations in the service-delivery game.

Individual-based service calls for the reverse strategy: opening up, not closing off, the "production" process. Those who provide services are "where the rubber meets the road." Two implications follow from this. First, customers or clients may contribute to the conversion process; they may supply solutions that become part of the service technology. This is something that Tom Peters clearly has in mind when he preaches the virtues of being "close to the customer." Second, the conversion process, which is centered on information exchange, is nonlinear. It often follows an errant trajectory, as customers back off, reconsider, abort, seek more information, solicit a second opinion, and so on.

What all this means is that the service-based player who competes on the basis of individual skills must, while alone, be able to cope with a high degree of ambiguity and unpredictability. A service baseball-organization that exemplifies risk-taking—at least at high levels—is Citicorp, the giant bank and holding company. In fact, Citicorp could also be classified as a financial conglomerate, given the wide range of financial services and markets it is into—as well as its global reach. Citicorp employs 63,000 people in ninety-five countries. But it is as individualistically intensive as it is geographically extensive. Citicorp is a superstar's bank, committed to "meritocracy":

> Behind locked doors in the fifteenth floor of Citicorp's Park Avenue headquarters sits [*sic*] a room devoted to what's called "Corporate Property." Pinned on a board in the office are the photos and biographies of about 75 managers, considered to be the bank's up-and-coming superstars. The only people permitted entry into the room are the bank's top two dozen senior executives. They make sure the superstars get special attention. . . .

For as in the real game of baseball, no managerial skill is more precious than player evaluation. Says Bill James:

> A manager's job isn't to decide when to hit-and-run. A manager's job is to look over three kid pitchers who were 15–6 at Toledo last year and figure out which one of them deserves the fifth spot in the starting rotation. You make the wrong decision there and it can cost you a whole bunch of ballgames. A manager's job isn't to know when to pull the infield in and when to keep it back. A manager's job is to know whether the 35-year-old shortstop batting .119 in April is in a slump or over the hill.

Shortly before announcing that John S. Reed would be his replacement, Citicorp chairman Walter Wriston commented in April 1984: "I think the most important thing is to take a chance on people. Somebody took a hell of a chance on me." A senior executive at another leading bank gave his explanation for

Reed's selection: "Reed would bet the bank, and that is just what Wriston would do." Irving Shapiro, a Citicorp board member—and former CEO of du Pont—reduced the decision to baseball statistics: "in a practical sense, he [Reed] was batting .350 and the other two guys [Reed's competitors for the top post] were batting .340."

Delegation of authority is essential in a service baseball-organization. Thus, Jerry Reinsdorf, chairman of Balcor/American Express, Inc. (a real estate syndicator he cofounded and later sold to American Express, Inc.) *and* chairman of the Chicago White Sox, claims: "I never even hear about most of the little problems, like a fire at a property. My management style is to hire good people and develop a relationship with them so that 95% of the time they'll know what decision I'd make and go ahead without asking me."

Having the right players (skills) is essential in any service that is not automated. Fred Carr, who led First Executive Corporation from being a loser in 1974 to one of the insurance success stories of the 1980s, certainly believes that. He goes with long-ball hitters all the way. According to *Fortune*, "First Executive's staff is the trimmest of any major underwriter's. With just 394 employees, the company writes as much insurance as outfits with ten times the work force. It has wooed 400 top independent agents, who concentrate on selling large policies to rich individuals."

Another successful baseball-organization is Visa International. Much of the credit goes to its former CEO, Dee W. Hock, whom *Business Week* has described as an "iconoclast." Hock shuns bureaucratic trappings—job descriptions, procedures manuals, dress codes, and the like. In the words of Executive Vice-President Charles T. Russell, "What Dee has done is make this a place where people experiment with ideas." Not only did Hock give his subordinates a long tether, he also steadfastly resisted becoming involved in solving the problems of Visa-member banks, even when they appear to need help: "he adamantly refuses to cater to the individual problems, financial or otherwise, of member banks. . . . Hock insists that Visa members run their own operations and that Visa has little responsibility for their red ink." In a sense, Hock seemed to be managing two baseball-organizations: Visa and Visa's banks.

A stock brokerage firm, like an investment banking firm, contains many baseball players. Perhaps no individual is better qualified for this designation than E. F. Hutton broker Gerald

Hannahs. Hannahs joined Hutton in 1982 after spending eight years in professional baseball with three different major-league teams. When he was forced to the minors after an injury, Hannahs opted for another career. How did he perceive the move to E. F. Hutton? "I looked at it as just like going to another ball club. . . . I've had to put my numbers on the board for a long time before this."

By no means are the only service baseball-organizations those organizations involved in financial services. A good example from retailing is Dayton Hudson, which has some 90,000 employees spread across almost every state in the country. According to Robert Levering and his coauthors, Dayton Hudson is

> looking for people who are self-starters and sensitive to changes in the marketplace—and society. A Dayton Hudson manager is measured on his or her community involvement as well as his or her financial performance.
>
> The different chain operations are given considerable autonomy. For example, they don't have to buy corporate services (legal, research) offered by headquarters staffers in Minneapolis. They can go to outside suppliers and compare prices and other factors. However, all the statistics on how you're doing come to roost in Minneapolis, where they are scrutinized carefully. If you do well, you are likely to be tapped for a higher position, maybe in another location. And you may even be asked to move your skills to another part of the *retail ball field*—say, switch from discount stores to bookstores [emphasis added].

A different variety of service baseball-organization is US WEST, the parent company of Mountain, Northwestern, and Pacific Northwest Bell. The autonomy required for effective service is poignantly expressed in a *Forbes* advertisement placed by US WEST. The ad, which appeared just before (and after) AT&T's breakup, was titled: "When you ride alone you have to sit tall in the saddle." Playing on the Western frontier theme, the message (in part) goes as follows: "Each of the subsidiary companies of US WEST is autonomous. . . . Each must earn its own way. . . . We are ready. Three technologically advanced Bell operating companies, a growing number of unregulated subsidiaries and open trail as far as the eye can see." This advertisement is the portrait of a baseball-organization—or at least a would-be baseball-organization: geographically separate, streamlined, self-contained structures (the "players"), each more concerned with exploiting the opportunities presented by nature (the "open trail") than with simply meeting competition.

A baseball-organization in which the players quite literally confront nature is Schlumberger Limited, a multinational provider of oil-field services. The heart of Schlumberger's field operations is its highly competent contingent of engineers who help drillers determine the production prospects of their wells:

> In most corporations, the superstars are firmly ensconced in the executive suite. But at Schlumberger Ltd., the oil services giant, the superstars are in the field. A cadre of 2,000 or so highly trained field engineers—cited by others as Schlumberger's best asset—labor from the jungles of Indonesia to wind-ripped North Sea oil rigs to provide a difficult but indispensable service to oil drillers: a series of sophisticated measurements, called logs, that help show whether and how much producible oil and gas can be tapped by a given well. "To me, Schlumberger is the fellow who goes out to the well a bit anxious, provides good answers for the customer, and drives away believing he's King Kong," says D. Euan Baird, head of the logging operation. "The rest of the company is devoted to making that happen."

The staff of a classic, luxury hotel provides another example of a service baseball-organization that, although far different in content, is similar in form. Take New York's Algonquin Hotel, for instance. Managing director Andrew A. Anspach insists that "We don't think in terms of efficiency. We think in terms of maintaining a civilized, literate, comfortable, inn-like hotel. We are well aware we spend more than we might, but we are family-run and don't have to worry about the budget." The emphasis here is on value added (quality and responsiveness), not cost reduction (efficiency). This bias is common to individual-based service baseball-organizations, which, by definition, are person-intensive as opposed to production-intensive equivalents (which will be discussed in Chapter 3).

Jim Murray of the *Los Angeles Times* has suggested that "Baseball is not precisely a team sport. It is more a series of concerts by the artists." The players on a baseball-organization may range from one, two, or a few individuals to corporate divisions employing thousands of people. And the players may be outside the focal corporation—as are authors under contract to a publisher, independent partners on a joint oil-prospecting venture, and member banks of a financial services firm. In general, however, the players on a baseball-organization rarely interact with each other, are likely to be geographically dispersed, and render discrete, quantifiable contributions to the whole. They relish being on their own and being evaluated for their individual performance—like the batter challenging the pitcher, and vice versa.

3

Preparing the Game Plan

FOOTBALL

> [I]t's a world in itself, designed in a way that condenses most of the things you hate to see coming in this life into a very short period of time: decision, pain, fear, embarrassment, confrontation, spit hanging from the bars of your face mask.
>
> —PETE DEXTER

> The game proceeds in short bursts of synchronized combat broken by pauses to regroup. At each break, the stakes escalate. The strategy is enormously complex and the execution brutally simple. The object is to dominate.
>
> —DAVID HARRIS

> It is not just violence we like in football. . . . It's that meeting of violence and artistry, the tension between the two, that so appeals. It's that instant when ball, receiver, and defender converge, when artistry is threatened by violence and the outcome is in doubt, that epitomizes the game's attraction.
>
> —MICHAEL ORIARD

PERHAPS NO OTHER sport has been used so often to characterize contemporary America as football. Football has become a metaphor for the factory, for the corporation, and, indeed, for industrial society. It is also a metaphor for the military and for war. The thread connecting all these images is *organization*—specifically, hierarchically controlled organization. It is a sport made for top-down direction.

American football's origins are traceable to England in the first century A.D., when a brutal game was developed after the Roman conquest of A.D. 43–47. This game, which resembled a mass riot, was first called "kicking the bladder." Centuries later, after the eleventh-century Danish invasion, the sport became known as "kicking the Dane's head"; the "ball," according to legend, was once the skull of a Danish soldier.

English "football" ultimately led to three distinct modern sports: soccer, rugby, and American football. When the English game was first played in the United States, it closely resembled soccer. In fact, the first intercollegiate "football game," Rutgers versus Princeton in 1869, actually was a form of soccer. But this version of the sport was soon replaced in America by a rugby-like game in which players could run with the ball as well as kick it. Gradually the game evolved into the highly structured sport that is contemporary American football.

Football is designed to reward comprehensive planning, coordination, and execution. It is what might be called a "business textbook" sport. For the past three decades, the typical management texts used in collegiate business schools in the United States have been organized around basic functions or "principles" of management. According to John Ralston, who coached at the major college level as well as the pro, "When you talk about the functions of management you talk about planning, direction, organizing, and controlling, something we as coaches have been doing for years but never with any formal training. The problems of industry are no different than those of a football coach." Or, at least, some industry. In spite of the conventional textbook wisdom, only certain corporations are really football-organizations.

Like baseball-organizations, football-organizations come in many varieties, ranging in size from the group level (for example, a local construction firm that specializes in small developments) to the international corporation with annual sales in the billions (for instance, a major steel company). Some have to do with engineering and systems development (for example, the construction of a dam, a tunnel, an urban sewage system, or a power plant); others are concerned with repetitive production routines (for example, the technology of manufacturing portable radios).

Although most football-organizations produce tangible goods, some offer system-based services. Examples range from data- and word-processing contractors to automatic car washes. But regardless of the nature of their output, all football-organizations are characterized by the central coordination of people and/or technology. This is because their task is complex enough to require orchestration from the top, yet predictable enough to be understood in detail.

Complexity stems primarily from interaction. The work of most football-organizations involves the interaction of several roles or units (or system operations) in a specific sequence. Subtask or decision A must be successfully carried out before B, B before C, and so on. If tight sequencing were not required—or if significantly fewer roles/units were involved— there would be less need for central coordination. But because the scheduling or system design task *is* intricate, it must be carried out at a level that has "the big picture," a view of the whole.

One more requirement for a football-organization is stability. It makes little sense to invest in complex production/decision technology if the environment in which it will be applied is not stable enough to accommodate it. The coaching staff of a professional football team has a week to prepare for each game. During the game, it has a thirty-second pause before each play. If these opportunities—before the contest and during it—were not available to the head coach, pro football would be a far different sport. It would be far less centrally coordinated, more like rugby or soccer—or, according to my categories, basketball.

In a nutshell, football-organizations must develop effective and efficient *plans* that specify who, what, when, where, and how. The plan may be a unique set of instructions, to be used only once (for example, the engineering of a prototype recovery vehicle for one phase of the nation's space exploration program). Or the plan may be essentially a production program, that is, a detailed protocol meant to be used continuously (for example, an automobile assembly line that programs the piecing together of 10,000 parts to yield a car, then another car, then another, every few minutes).

Football is a coach's sport. The popular and serious literature on football is predominately about coaches, and, to a lesser extent, quarterbacks—their surrogates on the field. Neither baseball nor basketball presents the variety of decision areas football does; and neither demands such up-front, overarching coordination as football. Consider the number of players who have to be managed in each sport. In baseball it is essentially nine (in the field) versus one, the batter; in basketball it is five versus five. But in football it is eleven versus eleven, times two—offense and defense—not counting special teams. Small wonder, then, that the football coach has to deal with more complex trade-offs than his counterparts in either baseball or basketball.

Strategy in baseball is What players do I want on my team? Strategy in football is *How do I organize my team?* If success in baseball depends on individual players, success in football turns on organizational planning. The planning preoccupation of coaches is nowhere more in evidence than in the way they approach a season. The late Carroll Rosenbloom, owner of the Los Angeles Rams, interviewed several candidates for the head coaching position before the 1973 season. The successful applicant turned out to be Chuck Knox. Rosenbloom had asked Knox "to outline each day's work for an entire football season and the man did just that, day-by-day, prospective opponent-by-prospective opponent."

Don Shula of the Miami Dolphins is, by any measure, one of the very best head coaches in professional football. Shula's dedication to planning is seen in the way he organizes his staff's work schedule. Every day is mapped out well in advance. According to former assistant coach Howard Schnellenberger, "Don can look at the schedule, then at the progress we've made and tell exactly at a specific time of the year where we are. He can measure his team's progress and stay atop any situations that might develop."

Winning football-organizations are also superior organizers and planners; at the corporate level, they are superior *long-term* planners. Thus, Lee L. Morgan, former CEO of Caterpillar Tractor Co.—a firm with several football characteristics—has declared that "in our business the lead times are long. It takes 10 years or more to develop and introduce a new product. To us, short-term planning means the next five years."

Another distinctive example of a planning-intensive football-organization is Joy Manufacturing Company, a producer of machinery for the petroleum, coal-mining, and other industries. Joy's planning is rooted in the "long-wave" theory developed by Russian economist Nikolai Kondratieff. According to this theory, general economic conditions follow a long-term pattern consisting of growth waves and decline waves. Joy's chairman, Andre R. Horn, "believes that the world economy is in a 10-year transition period between two 45- to 60-year growth cycles. . . . Moving in step with those cycles, Joy laid out a strategy to survive early in the transition by pruning overhead dramatically, then to reposition itself for the next upturn by increasing its presence in capital goods."

The tactical complement to team organization in football is game preparation: *How do I plan for the game?* Football is front-end intensive. Carl Peterson, president of the 1984 United States Football League champion Philadelphia (now Baltimore) Stars, believes that managing a football game is 75 percent preparation and only 25 percent adjustment.

Of the three sports, professional football is the most tactically demanding—both because of the relative importance of each contest and because of the nature of the sport. The NFL's regular season consists of 16 games, as compared with 82 in the National Basketball Association and 162 in major league baseball; hence, the average football game has five times the significance of a basketball game and ten times the significance of a baseball game. Moreover, in the postseason play-offs, a football team is eliminated by a single loss, whereas at each step in the elimination process, baseball and basketball teams play the best of a series.

Football's complexity shows in the sport's organizational structure. Unlike baseball and basketball, modern pro football features separate groups (units) for offense, defense, and the transition game. Further, within offense and defense, there are smaller groups that often must function as units (for example, linemen and backs on offense and linemen, linebackers, and backs on defense), as well as parts of the larger platoon.

In a trivial sense, a game plan is "no more than a list of plays to be used during a given game." But arriving at these plays and specific decision rules about when to use which is no easy matter because of the number of players to be coordinated and the variety of plays possible. For example, San Francisco 49er scout Neal Dahlen may analyze up to forty different variables on a single play. The coaching task is further complicated by the fact that through the years the sport has become ever more specialized. Thus, Woody Widenhofer, former defensive coordinator of the Pittsburgh Steelers, boasts that "we can use up to 20 different players on one series [a set of four plays]." Without question, the coaching staff of a football team has an enormous integrating task, for it is only at these overarching levels that all the players and parts can be meshed.

If player-management in baseball is the management of *independence*, in football it is the management of *dependence*. Many aspects of the sport work together to reinforce an asymmetrical relation between coaches and players—planners and doers, managers and workers.

Paul Wiggin, an all-pro who had played for Brown's Cleveland Browns in the 1950s and 1960s, had this to say about his former mentor:

> People say he's a patterned coach and they're right. . . .
> That's why he was so successful. His players always
> knew what to expect and they knew he wouldn't deviate
> from his plan. There is a certain sense of security in that
> a player can prepare himself each day for something and
> know that it will happen. Look at the effect in concen-
> tration that stems from this.

On his part, Vince Lombardi saw his players as "an extension of my personality." Biographer Robert Wells describes a revealing incident just before the start of the first football season after Lombardi had retired as head coach of the Green Bay Packers. Lombardi found it impossible to stay away from the Packers' practice field. During one visit he ran into tackle Henry Jordan, whose less than deferential attitude often had prompted him to respond sarcastically.

> Over the years, however, big Henry had developed a
> fondness for Lombardi and now he had a question to
> ask. It went directly to the heart of the matter that was
> bugging Vince, and it was made partly in jest and partly
> in earnest.
> "Coach," Jordan said, looking down at the stocky man
> on the sidelines, "wouldn't you like to chew us out just
> once more for old time's sake?"
> Lombardi managed a laugh. But the question had
> come uncomfortably close to the truth.

Finally, the Cowboys' Tom Landry sees a close correspondence between conforming and performing: "Players talk about individualism, but I believe they all want to live and work under a single standard. If a player is contributing and performing the way he ought to, he will conform. If he's not performing well or conforming to team standards, he ought not to be around."

The best pro football teams do not try to get rich quick—to "buy a championship." In some cases, their offensive or defensive systems are just too complicated to be assimilated in short order. The Dallas Cowboys' "flex" defense, for instance, requires linemen to resist the temptation to react immediately, but, rather, to wait and defend a particular area. It may take a player up to three years before he is comfortable with this procedure.

The Cowboys have always taken the long view with respect to player selection and development. The Oakland/Los Angeles Raiders are another good example of a long-term view toward personnel. The Raiders draft a player not to fill an immediate need but, rather, to contribute over an eight- to ten-year period. The trick, according to John Madden, who coached the team to the Superbowl championship in 1977, is to maintain a balance of young, middle-aged, and older players. Said Madden:

> Our team never will be too old, nor [sic] will it ever be too young. If a team becomes too old at the same time, the next step is that it becomes too young at the same time. It's been proven too often that top clubs that merely stand still soon find themselves slipping back into the middle of the pack. I know that a great reason for the success of this organization is that it never has stood still in its personnel development.

As important as player continuity is, there is evidence that ownership/management/coaching staff continuity may be even more critical. A 1983 study reported that the top five teams in the National Football League (NFL) over a thirteen-year period (1970—the year the National and American Football leagues were merged—through 1982) had all enjoyed "the same owners and substantially the same managements for years."

Managerial and personnel continuity is no less characteristic of football-organizations. Caterpillar, for instance, has been described as "an inbred, promote-from-within organization where executives and workers alike often walked to their first jobs from one of the many small farming communities that surround Peoria. They still climb the ladder by keeping their noses clean and working hard—almost no one leaves" [voluntarily]. The story is similar for a different company whose game—until recently—resembled football: Rochester-based Eastman Kodak. A 1984 *Forbes* article notes that historically, "People went to work for Kodak straight out of school or college—as did both Chairman Colby Chandler and President Kay Whitmore—and expected to remain until they retired. . . . [The company] has commanded extraordinary loyalty from its employees."

Football is a sport fraught with contradictions. To begin with, the pace of the game is staccato: periods of inactivity punctuated with bursts of unbridled action—not unlike the way combat veterans often describe war. In fact, war is the favorite metaphor for many close to the sport. Forrest McDonald, a historian at the University of Alabama, advanced the following concept in describing the late Bear Bryant, then head coach at Alabama: "The Southerners are naturally violent, and football is the idealized ritual substitute for actual warfare. If you happen to be 10 years old, or 30, when a war breaks out, instead of being lucky enough to be 20, the Southerner . . . will feel deprived of his manhood. Football can fill that void. For Alabama, The Bear is the Robert E. Lee of this warfare."

Football combines the cerebral with the physical. In fact, it counterposes these demands. Football places intellectual demands on the coach and physical demands on the players. And football appeals not only to a player's physical courage, but also to his emotional dependency. As tough as the players must be, the sport brings out deep feelings of vulnerability.

Prior to the 1982 strike, former all-pro defensive back Irv Cross ventured that one force against the players going out was their need for "the womb," as many had come to view their teams. In light of this feeling, it is small wonder that many players maintain a love-hate relationship with their coaches. Neither is it surprising that there is often a wider gap between manager and managed in football-organizations than in either baseball- or basketball-organizations. Football-organizations—like football teams—tend to be structured as neat, rather steep, hierarchies.

Many football-organizations exhibit *vertical integration:* the combination of different economic processes within a company.

The processes that are integrated may include any mix of discovery, procurement, production, distribution, promotion, and selling. In other words, the chain of activities along which vertical integration can take place starts with the discovery/identification of raw materials and ends with a completed sale—or even service after the sale. The vertically integrated firm is to football what the conglomerate is to baseball.

A major advantage of vertical integration is efficiency. By combining operations, a firm can reduce costs—in production, in transportation, in buying and selling, and in other areas. A further advantage is the assurance a company gains in having a source of supply and/or demand for its products. Vertical integration also enables a firm to coordinate production and inventory across different phases better. You can plan it all internally—and not have to worry about meshing with an outsider's plan.

Cooper Industries, Inc., a manufacturer of hand tools, electrical equipment, and energy equipment, is a company that recently vertically integrated for all these reasons. Cooper started up a $7.5 million rolling mill in Alabama to provide the steel that goes into its Nicholson files. By having this processing capability in-house, Cooper saves money on overhead and materials, simplifies the task of scheduling operations, and reduces its dependence on Japanese steel.

Caterpillar Tractor's huge dealer network (213 dealerships as of 1984) is a kind of substitute for vertical integration. Even though the dealers are independent operators, their taut linkage to Caterpillar provides the company with many benefits of ownership. In fact, Caterpillar plans globally for them:

> Caterpillar goes out of its way to make sure dealers' inventories are at the right level. There is a national computer network linking all dealers to the Morton (Ill.) distribution center, enabling them to order any part they need for delivery the next day. The company will buy back parts the dealers do not sell. And it tries to pace its introduction of new products according to dealers' capabilities.

Companies that are heavily vertically integrated exhibit an extreme bias for coordination and control. The name of the game here is orchestrating, synchronizing, and linking multiple processes and technologies. As a rule, such coordination has to be done top-down, from a corporate perspective, because of the enormous complexity involved. This translates into a sizable corporate staff—a far cry from the almost skeletal corporate staff of a comparably sized conglomerate. At the same time, the various units making up the vertically integrated firm necessarily surrender autonomy. All play roles for which the boundaries are carefully specified by senior management.

Examples of extensive vertical integration in industry abound. Most of the major oil companies, for instance, are highly integrated across the following spectrum: crude oil discovery/ production, transportation, refining, and marketing. The nation's largest chemical company, du Pont, made headlines in 1981 when it integrated backward by acquiring Conoco, Inc., for $7.3 billion. Why such a big purchase? So that du Pont would have a captive hydrocarbon feedstock source, according to chairman Edward Jefferson.

Historically, perhaps the most striking example of vertical integration has been the steel industry. Paul Lawrence and Davis Dyer trace this tendency back to

> [Andrew] Carnegie [who] adopted a strategy of vertical integration early on. He built the Lucy furnace in 1870 to supply another of his companies which fabricated iron bridges. A few years later the Lucy furnace supplied iron to his steel plant at Homestead, Pennsylvania. In the 1880s Carnegie integrated backward into production of coke and in the 1890s he bought into the fabulous ore deposits of the Mesabi range in Minnesota. He announced the intention in 1900 to integrate forward into manufacture of finished steel products. Thus Carnegie gained control over his business from the mining of raw materials through the production of steel itself.

Have things really changed over the last century? Not in all quarters. Despite the recent tendency of steel companies to diversify—heralded perhaps by U.S. Steel's acquisition of Marathon Oil in 1982—vertical integration is a game that many are still playing. Consider the 1984 merger of J&L Steel and Republic Steel, in which Republic became a subsidiary of LTV Corporation. Republic's CEO, E. Bradley Jones, justified the proposed merger by citing redundancies that could be eliminated, and a chain of anticipated "realignments," or cost-efficient vertical linkages, involving such things as "sourcing of coal

for cokemaking operations and of iron ore for certain of the
steel plants."

Long-linked production *within* a factory unit is analogous
to vertical integration *between* factory (and other) units. In fact,
as I use the term here, *long-linked production* refers to construction as well as manufacturing and, therefore, may take
place outside the factory as well as inside it.

For our purposes, long-linked production systems break down
into two broad types: high volume and low volume. Problems
of sequencing tasks must be solved in both types. The high-
volume variety is symbolized by the mass assembly line. Because of the pervasive influence of mass assembly—its logic
still dominates most organizational thinking in the Western
world—it is important to understand how this mode of production developed.

In their book, *Industrial Renaissance,* William Abernathy
and coauthors (1983) trace the evolution of manufacturing/
assembly systems through several stages. Making the transition
to stage one—rudimentary assembly—was like going from
baseball to football. Subsequent stages only reinforced this
basic shift. The catalogue of those associated with fine-tuning
the assembly line reads like a "Who's Who" of American invention.

Eli Whitney, inventor of the cotton gin, played the most
prominent role in bringing about the first stage. Until his time
(1800), manufacturing had been a craft activity in which each
worker made an entire product by himself. Quality levels were
uneven, and output severely limited. Against this backdrop,
Whitney prepared to take on a government contract to produce
10,000 complete stands of muskets within two years.

Whitney spent a whole year preparing his factory for high-
volume manufacture. He placed machines, fixtures, parts, and
workers necessary to ensure an integrated flow of production
at each work station. In essence, he made a machine out of his
factory of machines and, in so doing, redefined the manufacturing task: "No longer was it to coordinate the efforts of individual virtuosos; now it was to solve the technical problems
of process organization. . . . The concept of progressive work
flows placed the responsibility for product quantity and quality
on the internal coherence of the manufacturing system—and
not on the whims of individual craftsmen."

Stage two was initiated by Isaac Singer, the sewing machine
manufacturer, who pioneered "the use of families of specialized

and standardized technological components, the application of time and energy to product design, and the careful organization of the production system as a vertically integrated whole." Stage three is most closely identified with Samuel Colt, who is famous for the pistol bearing his name. Colt demonstrated the importance of planning product change and developing new products.

Stage four, according to Abernathy and his coauthors, was marked by manufacturers' increased reliance on outside suppliers. By not trying to produce everything themselves, manufacturers were able to become specialists in what they did produce. Stage five was the product of Henry Ford. Ford organized operations "strictly in terms of the necessary flow of work, by using separate production lines for each component to reduce process bottlenecks, by applying conveyors and other techniques of line-flow management, and by driving inventories down to the lowest acceptable level. . . ." Henry Ford's innovation represents the best and the worst in mass assembly. From a technical standpoint, Ford's construct was brilliant; from a human standpoint, it was delinquent. As we will see later, more advanced production systems have taken the best of Ford's thinking (manufacturing discipline) and combined it with a sensitivity to human needs (Ford's omission).

As Abernathy and his coauthors noted, Henry Ford's real contribution lay in his grasp of the complexity of auto manufacturing and the tasks that it entailed: "he saw that the sheer magnitude of the undertaking (providing on demand to many thousands of workers thousands of complex parts made to exacting specifications) created unprecedented challenges to production planning and control."

In auto assembly and other high-volume manufacturing, a critical problem is "line balance." *Line balance* has to do with organizing tasks so that all work stations have an equal amount of work to perform in terms of time. A well-balanced production process, or "line," flows smoothly and produces quantities that match its maximum potential. An unbalanced process has an interrupted flow, with the total line's output limited by the slowest operation—in the same way that the strength of a chain is limited by its weakest link. Vertically integrated firms have exactly the same problem *between* economic stages (procurement, production, distribution, and so on): if all stages are not synchronized, then some will be overloaded and others underloaded.

Because the sport of football requires similar precision, it is understandable that not only the game plan but also the individual plays are decided by the head coach. Few quarterbacks in professional football call their own plays. They may call "audibles"—last-moment adjustments at the line of scrimmage to take advantage of something they notice in the defense's alignment. But even these decisions typically take place within a framework of options prescribed by the coaching staff. Paul Brown probably spoke for the coaching majority:

> There are a lot of times a team will go into a game with a perfectly solid plan of attack and the quarterback will go out there and start changing everything around. I want to keep control of the game and I want my quarterback in control of the game. With all that is going on around him on the field, all that he must think about, he can't give as much thought to our plan as people can do on the sidelines with all the information in front of us at all times.

The head coach's control over his players ranges from the philosophy and emotional tenor of a team (cool or hot) to the preparation of game plans (that often emphasize *"ball"* control") to the selection of individual plays. Especially for the offensive platoon—and most especially the offensive line—plays are quite literally choreographed. Former Baltimore Colts' center Bill Curry once described the process this way: "An offensive lineman is programmed. I move my right foot and the offensive guard next to me puts his left foot where my right foot was. Everything is done in concert."

If high-volume manufacturing, which we have been discussing, is football-like, so is low-volume manufacturing. The lowest possible volume, of course, is a single-unit—as in much construction. The parallel between football and construction is clear to Billy Joe DuPree, a former all-pro tight end with the Dallas Cowboys who heads CWC Construction, Inc., a North Dallas construction company. DuPree started his own firm so that he could be the head coach: "There's nothing like having control. It beats running somebody else's plays." Says DuPree: "I think about what I've seen in the Cowboys' system—how they move players around to get the results they want, how they plan on people having 10-, 12-year careers, how they don't bring in a new coach and a whole new playbook every two years—and realize it's been like a business-school education for me." For DuPree, the Cowboys' head coach Tom Landry is the perfect role model:

> two qualities stand out: his absolute control and his absolute honesty. When Tom Landry says something is so, it's true today, it's true tomorrow, and it's true until he says it isn't. He gives his players very defined responsibilities on the football field and leaves it up to them to execute them. Really, it isn't even Landry any more but Landry's system that runs the Cowboys. It's a very comfortable, very flexible system for coming up with new plans of attack, and it's the way I want to run my business.

Sequencing in construction is absolutely crucial—as anyone who has ever tried to build a house knows. Construction's equivalent to line balance is "critical path." The *critical path* is the longest time path through a sequence of tasks required to complete a project. Stated another way, "the critical path is the bottleneck route. Only by finding ways to shorten jobs along the critical path can the over-all project time be reduced; the time required to perform noncritical jobs is irrelevant from the viewpoint of total project time."

If doing things in the right order is critical in constructing a simple building, it is absolutely essential in carrying out the large-scale projects that firms like Bechtel, Fluor, and Parsons are known for—including the building of a new, multibillion-dollar industrial city in a developing country. Specifying the steps required in construction is conceptually similar to planning the work flow of a manufacturing process. Each activity is long-linked, and the central task is to plan the correct sequencing. This is the limiting factor for all manufacturing systems; if the "plan" is deficient, no amount of managerial acumen or energy downstream—short of revising the plan itself—is likely to overcome its limitations.

An analogous kind of planning underlies *system-based service* football-organizations. The core logic is well expressed in two *Harvard Business Review* articles by Theodore Levitt: "Production-Line Approach to Service" (1972) and "The Industrialization of Service" (1976). In Levitt's view, this kind of service means systematically substituting technology and equipment for people. As a result, individual discretion is virtually eliminated.

The archetype of system-based service is McDonald's, in which restaurant technology has been meticulously engineered. Raw meat patties are premeasured and prepacked; storage and preparation space are dictated by the predetermined product mix; the french fries preparation process is rigorously specified; the paper in which each sandwich is wrapped is color-coded to indicate condiments; pre-prepared sandwiches are held in heated reservoirs; and so on. The idea is to approximate a machine (MacChine? Big MacChine?): "Through painstaking attention to total design and facilities planning, everything is built integrally into the machine itself, into the technology of the system. The only choice available to the attendant is to operate it exactly as the designers intended." Programming such a machine-equivalent is no different from devising an intricate plan: "The substitution of technology and systems for people and serendipity is complex in its conception and design; only in its *operation*, as at McDonald's, is it simple."

A related brand of football is global marketing—using the same approach to selling a product everywhere in the world. Global marketing is another system-based service intended to achieve economies of scale. Thus Coca-Cola's push toward "one sight, one sound, one sell" has enabled that firm to save an estimated $8 million annually "in the cost of thinking up new imagery." According to *Fortune*'s Anne Fisher, Remington Products has also used a global marketing approach to dramatically lower advertising costs and boost sales: "The shaver company's chairman ["head coach"], Victor Kiam, makes all his own commercials—the same pitch in 15 languages—in his Bridgeport, Connecticut, office. Since he started his star turn five years ago, Remington's unit sales have gone up 60% in Britain and 140% in Australia."

Yet another realm of system-based service (that may also represent vertical integration) is logistics—controlling material and transportation—and personnel—flows from the top down. An example from retail is Hechinger Company, a group of do-it-yourself home and garden stores in the middle Atlantic states. Each Hechinger store contains some 40,000 items—more than three times the number in Hechinger's largest competitors' stores. How to manage this volume? Historically, Hechinger limited its expansion to areas within one-day delivery from a single distribution complex in Landover, Maryland, the firm's base of operations. Each store was therefore an extension of a centralized inventory system. Although the company recently has expanded beyond this (200-mile) radius, a global approach to inventory management remains critical, given Hechinger's variety and volume of units stocked.

Or consider the programming of the 1984 Summer Olympics in Los Angeles. In addition to their awesome task of distributing 10,000 athletes (before the boycotts by certain nations) across 370 events, the Games' management had to arrange for a plethora of support services. For instance,

- 21,000 vehicles had to be provided (by Hertz) for rent;
- 500 buses were purchased by the Southern California Rapid Transit District to move 350,000 people back and forth;
- 17,000 law enforcement personnel had to be mobilized to ensure maximum security; and
- 2,500 television staff personnel were required by ABC to handle its 185(+)-hour telecast.

Moreover, the Olympics opened with the simultaneous release of 5,000 pigeons from 160 crates. This event depended on the precise coordination of thirty people, who simultaneously opened all of the crates—as if on a quarterback's snap count.

Football-organizations reward global coordination. Their core task is to design and operate a team that is as machinelike as possible. In football, the game belongs to the coach. This cardinal fact was lyrically expressed by Bum Phillips in his tribute to fellow NFL head coach Don Shula: "He can take his'n and beat your'n, or he can take your'n and beat his'n." So it is with the best head coaches of football-organizations— the planners, system architects, and/or senior managers. Their players—whether organizational units in a vertically integrated chain, assembly-line workers, or programmed hamburger flippers—are part of a tightly joined technology choreographed from the top.

4

Managing the Flow

BASKETBALL

> *The game is simple. . . . But its simple motions swirl into intricate patterns, its variations become almost endless, its brief soaring moments merge into a fascinating dance.*
>
> —PETE AXTHELM

> *The thinking parts of basketball, in actual play, are like combining the lightning attack and response of an épée duel with finding the optional solutions to a sequence of variable algebraic-geometric problems.*
>
> —NEIL ISAACS and DICK MOTTA

> *The game is unified action up and down the floor . . . it is five men playing as one.*
>
> —JACK RAMSAY with JOHN STRAWN

THERE IS A flow and a rhythm to basketball that separates it from football's staccato pace and baseball's discontinuities. At the same time, the game is nothing if not a disciplined display of cooperation and teamwork. Basketball is, in the view of concert pianist Russell Sherman, an ongoing tension between style and efficiency.

Unlike baseball or football, which evolved from earlier English games, basketball was invented in the United States to meet the need for an indoor sport to bridge the fall season (which was devoted to football) and the spring season (baseball) at a YMCA school in Springfield, Massachusetts. The game, conceived by Dr. James Naismith in 1891 and first played professionally in 1896, however, was a far cry from the sport as we now know it.

Basketball began as a relatively deliberate, low-scoring game, with final scores like 20-15 not uncommon. Dunking was unheard of. Until 1937, a jump-ball took place after each basket. The real stars up to that point—and in fact, until the coming of the six-foot, ten-inch center George Mikan in the 1940s—were the smallest players on the court, the guards. Today there are guards who are nearly Mikan's height. In fact, the average player in the National Basketball Association (NBA) stands six feet, seven inches. A field goal is attempted every fifteen seconds, and teams regularly score more than one hundred points a game. Everyone can dunk. In short, basketball has become both electric and crowded. The players—in size, speed, and overall athletic ability—have transcended the physical limits of the sport.

If anything, this dynamic density has rendered cooperation ever more important. Professional basketball at its best is the quintessential display of patterned, yet spontaneous teamwork. Bill Russell, one of the greatest players in the history of the game, and an NBA championship coach, put it this way:

> In each split second a basketball game changes as fast as ten rapidly moving objects can create new angles and positions on the floor. Your game plan may be wiped out by what happens in the first minute of play. The coach can't be out there; the player has to see what's going on. More, he has to predict where a pattern of action will lead, and then act to change that pattern to the advantage of his team. Teams that can do this under the greatest pressure will win most of the time.

The tasks of basketball-organizations range from the simple to the complex: from the family restaurant, in which everyone cooks, serves, washes dishes, and acts as cashier, to the interdisciplinary consulting firm, which brings together market researchers, demographers, economists, and statisticians. Although basketball-organizations tend to be small in size, some are large—for instance, many high-technology corporations. The organizational structure of the latter often resembles sets of smaller, linked basketball-organizations.

Basketball-organizations may be found at the very top of a company (in the form of a closely knit senior management staff) or at the bottom (in the form of a self-managing work team) or anywhere in between. They may represent permanent structures, expected to endure indefinitely—such as a liaison department between basic research and manufacturing. Or they may be temporary—put together to accomplish a particular goal, after which they will be dissolved—as an ad hoc task force to develop a program to halve the scrap rate.

In every case, however, basketball-organizations rely on peer relations. It is the frequent, often intense sharing of information back and forth among "players" that makes this kind of organization work. Basketball-organizations function with minimal supervision; the management guidance they do receive is more enabling than controlling—in academic jargon, more facilitative than authoritarian.

A good example of a basketball-organization is Philadelphia-based Elkman Advertising, whose clients, fittingly enough, include the Philadelphia 76ers. Elkman views the process of managing an ad campaign as directly analogous to playing basketball. "We have five departments [research, creative, production/traffic, media, and account services] which are similar to the five players on a basketball team," says president Don Tuckerman. "After a job is logged, all of the players get involved. There's a tremendous amount of passing ideas back and forth between departments, with everyone coordinating their part of the game plan. . . . Whenever it's appropriate, we also bring in our public relations people. They're like a sixth man." Tuckerman concludes: "Our environment changes so fast that we have to work together closely and flexibly—just like the Sixers."

The universal property of basketball-organizations is their integrative nature. They not only bridge different disciplines or competencies, they also bring together the worlds of planning and doing—worlds that, for football-organizations, especially, remain worlds apart.

Basketball-organizations are uniquely suited to change. They can survive in a dynamic milieu because they can adapt to unforeseen conditions. In an uncertain, rapidly changing environment, the central planning of a football-organization is often of limited usefulness. Things just change too quickly. The more long term the plan, the more quickly it will decay, as events unfold that undercut its assumptions. Such conditions favor a basketball-organization, which has the resources and flexibility to plan as it goes.

Strategy in basketball is *How do I develop my team's ability to coordinate itself?* In baseball, coordination is achieved by the design of the sport, which minimizes the need for player interaction; in football, coordination is the result of hierarchical planning and direction. But basketball requires much more teamwork than baseball; and a basketball game is a flow of plays that cannot be "programmed" to the extent a football game can. Basketball teams do not pause and regroup after each play. The boundaries between offense, transition, and defense are not clear cut, and teams quickly pass in and out of these modes. Hence, basketball coaches cannot concentrate on matching players with individual roles and situations, as baseball managers can. Nor do they have the opportunity their football counterparts enjoy to script a set of precise instructions for the whole team.

Consider, too, how a professional team's season unfolds. In football, a team has a week to prepare for its next game—ample time for planning. In baseball, although a team rarely has more than a day or two to prepare for a contest, it plays a series of games with each opponent so it can adjust between games—a kind of substitute for planning. But in basketball, a team plays several different opponents each week. Basketball teams thus have neither the time to plan nor the chance to become familiar with an opponent—all the more reason for developing the team's ability to coordinate play under varying conditions.

Cooperation is more discretionary in basketball than in either baseball or (especially) football. Players continually face situations in which they can either go it alone or work cooperatively with other players. The former course often brings individual glory (in the form of points scored); the latter course always requires sacrifice. There is no better evidence of unselfishness than an effective passing game. This aspect of the sport requires continuous movement by all, not just by the player with the ball. A strong passing game diminishes the

need for outstanding shooters or (offensive) rebounders because
it leads to dunks and lay-ups—relatively easy shots.

One of the most basketball-like of all established U.S. manufacturers is Donnelly Mirrors, Inc., a family-owned maker of
rearview mirrors for automobiles. Donnelly employees work
in small teams that interlock to form larger teams throughout
the organization. The teams establish their own production
standards. Team members allocate work among themselves,
routinely cover for each other when necessary, and review each
other's performance. This work team structure is complemented
by the Donnelly Committee, a company-wide personnel forum
made up of elected employee representatives. The Donnelly
Committee makes policy recommendations on pay, fringe benefits, and related matters that are then voted on annually by
the entire work force. One Donnelly employee referred to this
committee as the "heart of the company. That's where very big
decisions are made and where we've got management people,
production people, office people—everyone—represented. The
company *is* everybody, you know."

The discretionary character of teamwork in basketball makes
special demands on a coach's human relations skills. He must
be able to induce his players to want to cooperate, as well as
to show them how to. That is, he must integrate the interpersonal and the technical. For only when this integration has
occurred will a team realize its potential, because only then
will it have the ability to respond to the nearly infinite variety
of situations that each game presents.

Dick Motta, generally considered one of the most insightful
of all active pro coaches, contrasts basketball and the other
sports, as follows:

> Scouting reports and statistical studies in basketball
> do not determine precise courses of action as they do in
> baseball, but they do suggest probabilities for success in
> determining a style or tempo or general plan of play.
> Unlike football, a basketball play is a pattern with mul-
> tiple variations, with each variation having a number of
> options measurable only by the number of moves each
> player can make, times the moves of his teammates,
> times the possible defensive adjustments.

The man who probably achieved the best blend of interpersonal and technical competence is the legendary Red Auer-

bach, who as coach and/or general manager led the Boston Celtics to eleven NBA championships in a thirteen-year stretch (1957–69). In fact, Auerbach's technical "system" was remarkably uncomplicated. According to Bob Cousy, Auerbach's philosophy was "'Keep it simple and execute properly.' I don't think we used more than six plays in my thirteen years as a Celtic." When hall-of-famer-to-be John Havlicek joined the team in 1962, after the Celtics had won four straight NBA championships, he discovered that the Celtics did not even have a playbook. "Auerbach would introduce a play, and Havlicek would write it down and memorize it."

What made Auerbach so effective was his ability to instill in his team a powerful sense of family—off the court as well as on. Tommy Heinsohn, who played under Auerbach and later coached the Celtics to two NBA titles, tells the following story of Celtics cohesiveness:

> In the 1961-62 season, we played a game in Marion, Ind. They gave us a banquet and keys to the city. After the game, a bunch of us were eating in some greasy spoon. In walked [Bill] Russell and K. C. Jones. The place wouldn't serve them because they were black.
>
> Another teammate, Carl Braun, came over to our table, ripping mad.
>
> "Some place this is," he shouted. "Let's find out where the mayor lives and give him back his keys."
>
> And we did.

Tactics in basketball, as in baseball and football, has to do with game management. But the core issue in basketball is not decision-rule-based lineups, substitutions, or plays. It is rhythm: *How do I influence the flow of the game?* Former NBA all-star guard Gail Goodrich expresses it this way: "The tempo, the essential beat of the game, ultimately will be controlled by one team—the winning one."

Whereas his counterpart in baseball must make a *flow of adjustments* to specific game situations, the basketball coach must make *adjustments to the flow* of the overall game. He does this by calling time-outs in order to break the opponent's momentum, by resting/reactivating key players, and by making match-up changes.

Ironically, one of the most powerful ways a coach can influence the rhythm of a basketball game is to get kicked out of it—and thereby force leadership to emerge from the team.

Red Auerbach was a master at this. Bob Ryan of the *Boston Globe* tells of the time Auerbach had to take over for then-head coach Tommy Heinsohn (who had fallen sick) in 1974:

> It was the first time he had coached in an emergency capacity in five years. Early in the fourth period the club had fallen behind by 11 points, when suddenly Auerbach was involved in an incident with veteran referee Richie Powers, an old antagonist. He drew a first technical for his all-too-vivid description of a three-second call against the Celtics. Then he said to Powers, "You still have rabbit ears." The key word, obviously, was "still." "You're absolutely right," replied Powers, slapping him with a second technical [and automatic ejection]. Red stomped off to the locker room.
>
> The team responded with 10 points in the next 1:20 and went on to win the game on a last-second basket by John Havlicek, who had served as chairman of a committee that ran the club for the last eight minutes. Auerbach denied he had gotten himself thrown out deliberately, but it was hard to belive him. He had been seen in action too many times.

Douglas Strain, chairman of Electro Scientific Industries, Inc. (ESI), a high-technology basketball-organization that makes laser trimming devices and testing equipment, could relate to Auerbach's methods. Strain believes that the conventional "distinction between management and employee is far too sharp and not very productive. . . . The real problem is the function of management. Most management gets in the way." Strain has translated his philosophy into a decision-making process at ESI that relies on group consensus.

Harry V. Quadracci, founder and president of Quad/Graphics, a printing firm, has institutionalized a process that *Inc.* calls "management by walking away." Each May, Quadracci and his entire management organization go offsite for their "Spring Fling"—a daylong, strategy-and-social affair. While the managers are gone, the workers take over full responsibility for production. Says Quadracci: "Spring Fling gives many of our people their first chance to take the initiative—to get involved, and see what responsibility feels like. By putting the employees in charge, even for a day, we show them that we mean what we say—that we trust them and that we're willing to give them the freedom to make mistakes." Spring Fling is but one expression of Quadracci's guiding organizational philosophy: to be a "company built by employees for employees, instead of a company run by a management class against a counterclass."

Player-management in baseball is the management of *independence;* in football it is the management of *dependence;* in basketball it is the management of *interdependence*. Consider the coach's (manager's) part in influencing play. In baseball, each play is determined by what the pitcher and batter do—in large part independent of the manager. In football, each (offensive) play is meticulously crafted in advance, so the players' roles are highly dependent on the coach's plan. In basketball, plays are a combination of patterns directed by the coach and improvisation on the part of the players; the initiative goes back and forth. The coach:player relation in basketball is thus interdependent.

These differences are reflected in the physical location of the manager or (head) coach during a game. In baseball, the manager is below ground level in the team's dugout—although presumably on his feet (former Phillies manager Paul Owens once claimed that "The toughest thing about managing is standing up for nine innings"). The head coach in football is standing on the sidelines and is, in fact, aided by spotters high in the air, overlooking the entire field. This vertical presence is a physical reminder of the strongly hierarchical character of football. (It was perhaps best symbolized by the tower used by the late Bear Bryant to oversee practices of his University of Alabama football team.) The pro basketball coach is right next to the out-of-bounds line near center court. Basketball coaches routinely communicate with their teams while play is in progress and, in fact, are in a position to touch players as they run up and down the court.

In neither baseball nor football is chemistry so important—between games as well as during games. "Spending 82 games plus pre- and postseason with a group of players is an unbelievably demanding relationship," says Golden State Warriors coach John Bach. Because a basketball team has so few members, there is really no place the player or the coach can hide. A high-performing team is a sensitive mix of personalities that can easily be knocked off balance. Consider Kareem Abdul-Jabbar's reaction to the trade of teammate Greg Smith (and one other player) for Curtis Perry:

I was very upset. I'd never had a friend forcibly re-
moved before by some management whim. It was typical, wrong-headed owner thinking: Somebody tells you
that Curtis has more of the basketball skills necessary to
play the position, so get Curtis. What they didn't understand was that Greg was a key ingredient in the special
chemistry that had made us champions. His selflessness,
his continual movement, his leaping and defense, all
were blended into a team that knew exactly how to win.
We had become close as a team on and off the court
largely because of his bright and affable personality. We'd
just become champs, why break us up?

Former Princeton All-American (and today U.S. Senator
from New Jersey) Bill Bradley, who helped lead the New York
Knickerbockers to NBA titles in 1970 and 1973, believes that
"An exceptional player is simply one point on a five-pointed
star. Great individual players may earn dollars for the owner
just as a sideshow does for the circus, but stardom is if anything
a deterrent in the pursuit of a championship."

The five-pointed star image is apt, particularly if all points
are connected, as shown in the following diagram. This diagram symbolizes ball movement among all the players on the
team; more generally, it symbolizes communication, decision-
making, and cooperation patterns. Because team performance
in basketball depends so much on player *inter*actions, it is
nearly impossible to distinguish individual contributions.

A compelling business analogue of flexible, shared contributions is Data General's development of the Eagle computer
—the subject of Tracy Kidder's Pulitzer Prize-winning book,
The Soul of a New Machine. Tom West, the engineering manager overseeing the project, clearly was coaching a basketball-
organization: "The entire Eclipse Group, especially its managers, seemed to be operating on instinct. Only the simplest
visible arrangements existed among them. They kept no charts
and graphs or organizational tables that meant anything. But
those webs of voluntary, mutual responsibility, the product of
many signings-up, held them together." In his epilogue, Kidder
affirms "that the building of Eagle really did constitute a collective effort, for now that they [the Eclipse Group] had finished, they themselves were having a hard time agreeing on
what each individual had contributed."

When individual scoring statistics on a team repeatedly stand

PLAYER INTERACTION IN BASKETBALL

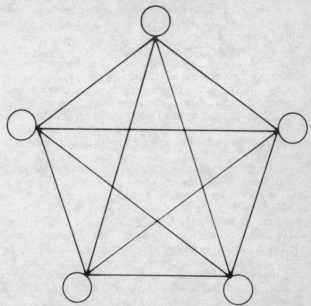

out, team performance may suffer. The classic example of this point is the Wilt Chamberlain-Bill Russell rivalry. Chamberlain's lifetime scoring average was over thirty points a game; until the 1983/84 season, he was the NBA's all-time leading scorer. Russell, by contrast, averaged fifteen points a game— only half as many. But whereas Chamberlain's teams won only two NBA championships during his fourteen seasons, Russell's won eleven. Although it can be argued that Chamberlain had weaker supporting casts, most observers believe that Russell simply was a better team player. Auerbach saw it this way: "I'm not taking anything away from Chamberlain's one-man offense. It was something to behold. The question is, can you win with it? Can you use the rest of your stars as nothing more than a bunch of highly paid errand boys? . . . Maybe you can, but the records tell you what happens in the process." The process indeed!

Significantly, at this writing, only once since 1950 has the

NBA champion contained the league's leading scorer: Lew Alcindor (now Kareem Abdul-Jabbar), in 1970/71, with the Milwaukee Bucks. Bill Bradley was on the mark when he said of a professional championship, "One man alone can't make it happen; in fact, the contrary is true: a single man can prevent it from happening."

More than either baseball or football, basketball illustrates group dynamics. To begin with, basketball underscores the close connection between individual roles and group norms. In Bradley's experience, "a player can play an on-court role only if everyone agrees. Roles don't come from a job description sheet. There is more to them than physical skill. They must evolve within the context of the team so that creative spontaneity is preserved while at the same time self-sacrifice is volunteered."

Of the three sports, basketball is the most integrative. It bridges many realms that are otherwise opposed. It not only fills the seasonal gap between the fall and the spring, it also combines football's emphasis on the team with baseball's emphasis on the individual. And if baseball is a player's game and football is a coach's, then basketball belongs to both. Player and coach overlap in basketball—sometimes literally, in the form of a player-coach—just as offense and defense do. Finally, in neither of the other sports are ability and sociability so closely joined. Bill Bradley has expressed this fact concisely: "Teams develop when talents and personalities mesh."

Writing about network television's snubbing of pro basketball in 1977, David Halberstam acknowledges that despite the sport's artistic beauty and the skills of its athletes, "professional basketball had not entered the national psyche or become part of the national myth. It remained . . . a sport of some isolated urban areas and some rural areas struggling for national acceptance." The sport thus linked geographical and cultural opposites—ghettoes and farms—but not the great big in-between. This is the remaining bridge. For although pro basketball may not yet enjoy the popularity of either baseball or football, it is, as I argue later, the most relevant of the three to future corporate effectiveness.

Many basketball-organizations display *horizontal integration:* the nonhierarchical linking of their various parts. Conglomerate baseball-organizations have virtually no linkage between their parts, whereas vertically integrated football-organizations have tight, sequential linkage, which is managed top-down. Horizontally integrated basketball-organizations are companies in which the parts (divisions, facilities, departments, individuals) interact with each other closely but fluidly.

Horizontally integrated firms may produce either a single product or multiple products. In the latter case, however, all products tend to be strongly related in terms of such things as function, material, technology, manufacturing process, customers/markets served, or distribution system.

Some of the best examples of horizontally integrated basketball-organizations are high-technology (hereafter "high-tech") companies. These firms operate in fast-changing environments that demand innovation and flexibility. A football-organization approach of relying on hierarchy—the chain of command—for integration does not work because too many things are happening at once; the hierarchy is easily overloaded. Alternatively, the baseball-organization approach, of disregarding integration, is simply too expensive because it duplicates resources. Only a basketball-organization can achieve real-time integration in a dynamic environment. As technical writer Michael Wolff has observed, with respect to high-tech electronic instrument companies, "the technology lends itself—indeed, requires—the collaborative efforts of relatively small teams of technical specialists."

Tandem Computer, a California-based manufacturer of failsafe computer systems (which connect central processors so that if one fails, another takes over), is a prototypical basketball-organization. Tandem's integrative bias stems from the philosophy of its founder and chief executive officer, James G. Treybig: "Creativity comes from sharing ideas. An idea may be sparked by an individual, but then it must be built on and modified and improved by the group until it becomes something really significant. That's why I say the environment nurtures creativity."

Seemingly every facet of the Tandem organization works to reinforce horizontal integration. Not only do most employees have computer terminals at their work stations that are connected to the firm's mainframes, Tandem's major facilities are also linked by an electronic teleconferencing system that allows all employees to express themselves through electronic memos visible to everyone in the company. Bureaucratic and status trappings have been done away with. The firm does not publish an organization chart. There are no reserved parking spaces, no time clocks, and no badges. Stock options are available not just to managers, but to every employee. This benefit, coupled with the company's growth, has riveted everyone's attention on corporate performance. In response, "Tandem now posts the stock price three times a day on its work-station screens: formerly too many people were monopolizing the telex machines to find out."

The company is careful about the people it hires. Managers do not rely on administrative personnel, but rather do their own hiring—with input from prospective co-workers. According to a programmer, "A manager will never hire somebody his people don't think is good. Basically, he says will you work with this person, and you say yes or no."

When they come on board, employees receive an indoctrination that includes some basketball numbers: an overview of the company's five-year plan and exposure to Treybig's five guiding principles for running the business:

1. All people are good;

2. People, workers, management and company are all the same thing;

3. Every single person in a company must understand the essence of the business;

4. Every employee must benefit from the company's success; and

5. You must create an environment where all of the above can happen.

Finally, Tandem helps many of its employees achieve an internal form of integration: a reconciliation of the tension "between the claims of openness, spontaneity, nonjudgmental acceptance, brotherhood, freedom, and expressiveness on the one hand, and technical proficiency coupled with personal ambition on the other. Tandem, with its youthful style, beer-bust rap sessions, high-flown egalitarianism, engineering excellence, and hefty financial incentives, resolves that conflict."

Basketball-organizations like Tandem Computer go to great lengths to minimize hierarchy—that is, to flatten the pyramid. Few companies have been more explicit in this regard than Versatec, Inc., a maker of electrostatic printers, plotters, and dual-function printer-plotters. Renn Zaphiropoulos, co-founder and former CEO of Versatec, argues as follows: "When the general idea is that people should be put in an environment that encourages free communication, there is a de-emphasis of levels and status. We do this here merely by being the kind of people who are comfortable being close to others." Zaphiropoulos conceives of the corporation as a series of concentric circles, with the chief executive at the center (just like the "center" of a basketball team, who occupies the central or "pivot" position): "The trouble with the pyramid is that it accents up and down, and we attach values to up and down. Up is good, down is bad." By contrast, Zaphiropoulos's circular design emphasizes the horizontal and the fact that *all* employees' efforts relate directly to the firm's survival.

In pursuit of democratization, another basketball-organization, Tektronix (a manufacturer of oscilloscopes and other electronic display and control instruments), does not even provide its top managers with private offices. Instead, they work in a large room broken up by four-foot-high dividers. Such an arrangement encourages reciprocal exchanges between people—just like the back-and-forth movement of basketball players. Stimulating this kind of interaction between people and technology (as well as between people) has been a conscious goal of still another company with many basketball features, Digital Equipment Corporation (DEC), the second-largest computer manufacturer in the United States. According to DEC's founder and CEO, Kenneth Olsen, "From the beginning, at MIT in the 1950s, we wanted to be interactive—instant back-and-forth between man and machine."

Japan's NEC Corporation is a good example of playing basketball in a large company (1984 sales: $7.8 billion) that is involved in several business areas—computers, communications, electron devices, and home electronics. To begin with, NEC is horizontally integrated through common technologies, products, and markets. But the company goes much further. It has forty-four corporate committees, many of which cut across business areas. One of these committees, "C & C," has the express task of "identifying and exploiting the potential interrelationships created by the convergence of computers and communications." In fact, C & C has become a unifying corporation-wide theme at NEC; it is reinforced in top-management speeches, management forums, and the company's annual report. Even in international advertising, NEC proclaims that "the new information age is built on C & C, the merging of computers and communications."

Long-linked production—the football variety we discussed in Chapter 3—is based on the central planning and direction of discrete tasks, each to be carried out in a tight sequence by a different individual (unit). In contrast, *composite production*—a basketball-like alternative—is based on the capacity of groups of individuals to allocate and accomplish composite sets of tasks flexibly. Although still sequential at a general level, composite production is *less rigidly sequential* than long-linked production; when possible, serially ordered tasks are redesigned so that they can be completed at the discretion of the worker, not the production line architect.

The origin of composite production is a series of field studies in underground coal mining conducted by Eric Trist and his colleagues at the Tavistock Institute of Human Relations in London, from 1949 on. Before World War II, *single-place* coal mining had been the standard method: a group of miners completed the entire cycle of mining activities with only minimal supervision. After the war, a more mechanized, "long-linked" form of mining (called, appropriately enough, the *longwall* method) was introduced. This method broke down the mining cycle into three sequences, each to be carried out by a different (and isolated) shift. Tasks were "rationalized" so that each miner had a single, narrow responsibility. Tight supervisory controls were installed to coordinate the overall operation.

The mechanized method of mining had a severe negative effect. Productivity fell, turnover and absenteeism increased, and other indices of psychological health declined. As Trist and his colleagues studied this situation, they learned about a spontaneous experiment by a group of miners that blended characteristics of single-place mining with the longwall method. As Trist put it, "Now they had found a way at a higher level of mechanization of recovering the group cohesion and self-regulation they had lost and of advancing their power to participate in decisions concerning their work arrangements." The new way increased productivity and worker satisfaction. It later gave rise to the concept of *sociotechnical systems* and the notion that optimal performance depends on getting the best match of a system's (organization's) social (human) and technical components.

Sociotechnical systems theory became expressed in the concept of *self-managing* work teams, often referred to as (semi)autonomous work teams. In such teams, employees effectively manage themselves; at the limit, they hire, fire, train, evaluate, and promote as a group. The supervisory role, if any, is to facilitate self-management. Self-managing work teams are at the heart of composite production. The difference between the composite production method (basketball) and long-linked production (football) is summarized in the following illustration. In composite production (a), a group of employees—at any level—assigns a variety of tasks to members of the group and regulates performance; in the more common, long-linked method (b), each employee is responsible to a supervisor for a discrete serial task that he or she has been assigned.

A growing number of companies in the United States and abroad have designed new facilities that organize work in a composite production manner. Perhaps the best-known U.S. example is the General Foods Corporation's Topeka, Kansas, dog food plant, which was conceived in 1968 and started up in 1971. The work flow at Topeka was divided into two segments: front-end "processing," and back-end "packaging." Each shift consisted of two self-managing teams, one for processing and the other for packaging. Decisions had to do not only with scheduling and allocating work; they also involved such responsibilities as maintenance, quality control, industrial engineering, and personnel. Operators were encouraged to learn as many skills as they could. The greater their knowledge, the more they were paid. Because everybody was eligible to earn increased amounts based on learning, no one would be hurt by sharing knowledge. As a result, the workers trained each other.

Richard Walton of Harvard, an early consultant to Topeka, notes that operators were provided with the information to make decisions usually reserved for higher-level people in the organization; the role of the first-line supervisor, called a team leader, was defined as helping the team make its own decisions; status symbols were kept to a minimum; no plant rules were published in advance (the intent being to let rules develop as needed over time); and the plant's architecture and technology were designed to encourage informal exchanges among team members.

Volvo's Kalmar, Sweden, plant has proven that even the automobile assembly line can be reorganized for composite production. The Kalmar facility, completed in 1974, is arranged into twenty-person working groups. Each group is responsible for a particular portion of the car—wheels and brakes, doors, electrical system, and so on. The work groups divide the tasks

COMPOSITE VERSUS LONG-LINKED PRODUCTION

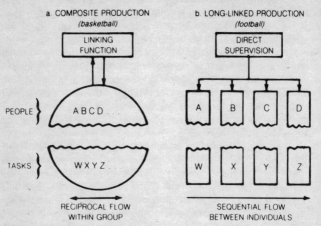

a. COMPOSITE PRODUCTION
(basketball)

b. LONG-LINKED PRODUCTION
(football)

LINKING FUNCTION

DIRECT SUPERVISION

PEOPLE } A B C D ...

TASKS } W X Y Z ...

A B C D

W X Y Z

RECIPROCAL FLOW WITHIN GROUP

SEQUENTIAL FLOW BETWEEN INDIVIDUALS

Source: This exhibit is adapted from M. E. Emery, *QWL FOCUS*, Ontario Quality of Working Life Centre (February 1983): 4.

among members, control their own pace, and inspect their own work. Says Volvo president Pehr Gyllenhammar: "In essence, our approach is based on stimulation rather than restriction."

The new Toyota–General Motors joint venture at Fremont, California—New United Motor Manufacturing Inc. (NUMMI)—also incorporates many features of composite production. All assembly workers fall within a single job classification and are assigned to small (five- to seven-person) work teams. Each worker will be trained to do every job within his team and, eventually, in neighboring teams. Skilled trades workers are covered by only three classifications, and maintenance workers, as members of teams, are expected to provide whatever competence a job requires.

General Motors' new Saturn Corporation subsidiary, which will manufacture subcompacts, will go even further in the composite direction. Early reports suggest that the Saturn organization will have much in common with Volvo's Kalmar design. One expected payoff is a quicker response to dealers' orders. Today's six- to eight-week lag should be reduced to a matter of days when the Saturn plant is on-line in 1988 or 1989.

Several major corporations have created internal basketball-organizations to design and develop new products. The computer industry offers a host of examples, one of the most famous of which is IBM's personal computer (PC). *Business Week* reports that IBM developed the PC in a way that is far from business as usual in a large, highly structured corporation. "IBM designers worked 80 to 100 hours per week under spartan conditions for a year to bring the machine to life. 'If you're going to compete with *five men in a garage,* you have to do something different . . . ' says David J. Bradley, one of the designers of the PC" [emphasis added].

Creative filmmaking likewise has significant parallels to basketball. Alan Ladd, Jr., who left Twentieth Century-Fox in 1979 to found The Ladd Company, recalls earlier personal relationships: "One thing that characterized us at Fox . . . was that we ran it much like a family. Our personalities, thoughts, and ideas intertwine. This is a business of collaboration. . . . The creative side is a business of input, discussion, and attitude." In describing his relationship with colleagues Jay Kanter and Gareth Wigan (both of whom had worked with him at Fox before coming to The Ladd Company), Ladd is emphatic: "One thing that has made all this teamwork succeed is that none of our egos are involved. Nobody's ever said, 'This is mine.' Everything is everybody's. We all share."

Wigan echoes this sentiment with respect to others: "I've always made a practice of talking about people working *with* me and not *for* me. That prepositional change is very important. If it's a reasonable portrayal of an attitude, it carries through into your work." Interestingly, Wigan—like Renn Zaphiropoulos of Versatec—uses the circle as a metaphor to characterize organizational structure:

> It's a small culture, but it's curious that it's also pervasive. I think one of the enormous errors that Fox made in considering letting Ladd go, and in what was done at Fox after his departure, was the purblind inability to recognize the depth to which his inspiration had permeated the company. I think Fox management thought that if the three of us went, we would go and that would be it. But apart from Jay and myself, there was another inner circle of maybe 12 more people, then other circles beyond that. The sense of confidence in and tremendous affection for him had gone very deep.

According to Eileen Morley (a psychologist) and Andrew Silver (who has both taught film and made films), there are essentially two kinds of film director: those who work everything out in their heads in advance and those who prefer to let much of the conceptualization evolve in concert with actors and technicians as the film is produced. For the second type, Morley and Silver suggest that "the making of a film is a search. They do not know exactly what they will do, but in production they find it."

Clearly, actors and actresses who collaborate with this second type of director—an Ingmar Bergman or an Arthur Penn, in Morley and Silver's opinion—are part of a basketball-organization. But even those working with a more front-end-loaded director (like the late Alfred Hitchcock) are playing basketball—but for an authoritarian "coach," like the New York Knicks' Hubie Brown. They still need to interact spontaneously because so much of what happens cannot be programmed.

One of the most telling comments about the similarity between filmmaking and basketball comes from a pro basketball player. Mark McNamara, a seven-foot backup center in the NBA, also played backup to actor Peter Mayhew ("Chewbacca") in the filming of *Return of the Jedi*. His impressions of the experience? "There were so many incredibly intelligent people out there. New ideas just popped into their heads, and all these people worked together. It was the best team concept I ever saw."

Certain basketball-organizations represent a *team-based* approach to service. An example that overlaps composite production is the creative advertising agency. One of the "fathers" of creative advertising, William Bernbach, co-founder of Doyle Dane Bernbach (DDB), devised the "DDB creative team," an intensive example of a back-and-forth exchange between copywriter and artist, who until that time had been serially linked—with the writer coming first, both in sequence and in status. Historian Stephen Fox quotes copywriter Bernbach and his counterpart artist Bob Gage in the following account of DDB dynamics:

> At every level, ads were produced by an artist and [*sic*] writer working together as equals. "Two people who respect each other sit in the same room for a length of time," Bob Gage explained, "and arrive at a state of sort of free association, where the mention of one idea will

lead to another idea, and then to another." The artist might suggest a headline, the writer a visual device: the entire ad was conceived as a whole in this exchange between disciplines.

At its best, the process upgraded the art director to a full-blown advertising person, as concerned with the selling message as the copywriter was. It gave the creative team a sense of responsibility for their own work. "That's their property," said Bernbach. "They own it. And they walk with their heads up, and they walk with pride." The point of it all, the ad itself, thus integrated art and copy in a novel way—"the combination of the visual and the words," said Gage, "coming together and forming a third bigger thing."

Many basketball-organizations deal with complex problems not contained by any one discipline or functional skill area. Take the Wharton Applied Research Center (ARC), with which I have been affiliated for the past five years. The center was created in 1977 so that professionals from many different parts of the school could collaborate on projects that crossed disciplinary boundaries. Wharton faculty and ARC staff work together closely to develop novel solutions to nonroutine client problems.

In a long-term project with a consumer products company, for example, the center first helped the client to plan strategically. Before long that firm had begun to grow rapidly—whereupon the center was called on to aid the client in mounting a transition from a single-product domestic firm to a multinational conglomerate. Then, when it became clear that the major barrier to further growth was executive skills, the center developed a customized management development program.

It was not possible to "plan" the latter phases at the outset; their need became apparent only in the course of the project. Although many members of the ARC team—and key client contacts—were replaced over the course of this engagement (which really was a set of smaller overlapping projects), the reciprocal relation among team members remained constant. And just as each basketball player does a variety of things— passing, dribbling, shooting, and rebounding—so did almost every team member routinely carry out several related tasks— practical research, consulting, and writing for professional journals.

Similar teamwork can be found in CRS SIRRINE, a large architecture and construction management firm based in Houston, Texas. CRS SIRRINE differs from many of its competitors because of its belief in group interaction. Co-founder Bill Caudill does not mince his words: "The prima donnas have had their day. Now the architect is a team." Architects at CRS SIRRINE work in small groups. Typically, a group will be involved in three to six projects and be responsible for completing all phases of each project. As a result, architects are exposed to different aspects of the firm's business, including client relations and construction management. Says Michael Shirley, a senior design architect, "Each group forms almost a fraternal brotherhood. People cover for each other."

The same kind of commitment to teamwork can be found even in the world of stockbroking—an industry loaded with baseball-organizations. A.G. Edwards & Sons, Inc., the largest brokerage firm not based on Wall Street (it's headquartered in St. Louis), takes pains to reinforce cooperation among all employees—brokers and nonbrokers. A.G. Edwards is not for home-run kings. Al Goldman, a twenty-five-year company veteran, contrasts the organizational climate there with that at other brokerage houses: "There's less politicking here. You don't make people look bad. And so we tend to lose the superstar types. They wouldn't be good at A.G. Edwards."

One of the most common varieties of basketball-organization is an internal arrangement within a conventional (football-like) organization that brings together people from different operations—and often different levels—to attack complex problems. Such groups go by a plethora of names: task forces, task teams, objectives teams, project teams, product teams, business teams, and the like.

A prototypical basketball-organization that I worked with over a five-month period was formed in Hope's Architectural Products, a manufacturer of steel and aluminum windows for the nonresidential construction industry. Hope's president, Frank Farrell, suggested that a task force be created to consolidate the layout for a new product line (an energy-conserving window) that Hope's had just started to produce. This product was being worked on in two separate plants, and much excess handling was required. A composite task force included workers/local union officials and supervisors from the two affected buildings, along with technical representatives (notably, the chief manufacturing engineer and, later, a member of the product engineering department). The president effectively gave this group decision-making authority by committing himself in advance to whatever design they would recommend.

The task force developed a consolidated layout (in one of the two plants) within schedule, and at a lower cost than had been projected earlier by management alone. A number of economies were realized, which, although mostly small, were significant in combination. One interesting example of this process occurred when the task force encountered a nonstructural brick wall running across the middle of the building that they had selected. Independently, management then asked an outside contractor to estimate the cost of dismantling the wall. The contractor came up with a figure of $2,500. When this became known at a later task force meeting, one of the group members urged an alternative: Let the workers tear the wall down on their own time, in exchange for the bricks. The following Saturday the wall disappeared, at no cost, with the workers coordinating the entire operation—still another example of basketball.

If baseball is a player's sport and football a coach's, basketball is a combination—but with the apostrophe in "players" coming after the *s*, not before. Strategy in basketball is integration. It is developing the players' ability to coordinate themselves, because spontaneous teamwork is so critical to success. Tactics is "flow management"—intervening on an exception basis to change the process or tempo of a game. Player-management in basketball means creating and maintaining personal chemistry among the players and between the team as a whole and the coach.

Basketball-organizations range in size from "five persons in a garage" to billion-dollar corporations. But regardless of size, all depend on flexibility and reciprocal relations— player-to-player and players-to-coach. Hence, all basketball-organizations minimize their reliance on hierarchy, sometimes so much so that casual observers interpret their structure as free-form.

5

Sports Hybrids

WE HAVE DESCRIBED organizational models derived from base-ball, football, and basketball—the sports Michael Novak calls "the holy trinity." Of course, all corporations do not "match up" precisely with one of the three sports. Many companies appear to be blends of the sports models—just as the seasons of each sport overlap. The models themselves are much like primary colors, which can be combined to produce all the other colors. As Peter Drucker has written, "organization structures can either be pure or effective, but they are unlikely to be both."

Every large complex organization is an amalgam of all the sports, with its different units—departments, facilities, divisions, and so on—resembling different sports. The more fine-grained the analysis, the more likely it is that a host of team likenesses can be identified. Moreover, whether the corporation be a conglomerate (baseball-organization), vertically integrated (football-organization), or horizontally integrated (basketball-organization), various parts of it doubtless will resemble another sport, or sports.

But many firms' inherent resemblance to a particular sport is unmistakable. Many other companies appear to be nearly symmetrical combinations of two sports; they are "hybrids" that strike a balance between the following forces: (1) local autonomy versus global perspective (baseball/football); (2) central coordination versus flexibility (football/basketball); and (3) individualism versus group process (baseball/basketball).

Baseball/Football Hybrids

The most prominent type of baseball/football hybrid in evidence today is also the most prominent form of large-scale organization: the multidivisional corporation. Such a firm tries to obtain the advantages of decentralization with those of centralization. It strives for operating unit autonomy within a global framework.

Emerson Electric Company, a multibillion-dollar manufacturer, is such a baseball/football hybrid. In one sense a baseball-organization, the company has forty-four highly autonomous divisions, which, in turn, are divided into 116 small plants (average size, 150 employees) spread across the mid-South. Each division (and division head) historically has had the free-standing quality of a baseball player. According to *Business Week*, "Superachievers are rewarded handsomely. Division managers can increase their annual compensation up to 81% by exceeding preset goals." In the opinion of a former Emerson employee, the successful Emerson manager is "a numbers cruncher with an unusually strong ego [who can] stand up to [CEO Charles] Knight, is very aggressive, and is willing to go where angels fear to tread." This milieu conjures up baseball. After all, football players are not known for taking on the coach. And Charles Knight's one-on-ones are consistent with the fact that he played varsity tennis—an even more individualistic sport than baseball—at Cornell.

Knight was also a varsity football player, however, and there is a lot about his company that smacks of this sport. If, as *Business Week* has put it, Emerson's divisional managers "are princes . . . the domineering, ever-probing Knight is king." One of Knight's management tenets is "You need an ability to grab hold of tough problems and not delegate them. It's not fair to let the guy below you take the brunt of making the hard decisions. The leader has to get deeply, personally involved in challenging issues and set the policy."

Knight is known for personally overseeing major expenditures in this highly cost-conscious company. In fact, some believe that Emerson's elaborate planning and control systems are too risk-averse. As one of the division managers suggests, "Knight is a tremendously conservative guy, and risk-taking seems foreign to his background." One can almost picture the

CEO with game plan in one hand and lineup card in the other. Charles Knight seems to embody aspects of both the football head coach and the baseball manager, so it is not surprising that his team is a mix of these sports.

A somewhat different baseball/football hybrid is represented by the geographically dispersed, but technologically unified firm. There is perhaps no better example of this hybrid than McDonald's. Mcdonald's, as we have seen, has effectively designed individual discretion out of the production/service-delivery process. In fact, the corporation has assembled a 700-page operations manual that spells out each step of the process. Everything is engineered.

> Before McDonald's puts an item on its menu, for instance, it runs simulations in a test kitchen using register tapes from a busy period at one of its restaurants. As the tester reads from the tapes, he adds in orders for the new food. The results help McDonald's judge the effect a new product might have on the restaurant's overall efficiency, officials say.

The same attention to detail is required by logistics. *The Wall Street Journal* reports that "McDonald's had to line up enough supplies of chicken to sell five million pounds of its McNuggets a week. And with more than 6,200 of its restaurants in the U.S., the company can't afford to risk selling items whose ingredients can be affected by droughts or sharp swings in price." With this kind of central planning and coordination, it is small wonder that McDonald's founder, Ray Kroc, chose a football expression for the title of his autobiography: *Grinding It Out: The Making of McDonald's*.

But McDonald's also has several baseball characteristics—which is interesting, as Kroc was the owner of the San Diego Padres baseball team until his death in 1984. To begin with, corporate management effectively "fills out the lineup card" by authorizing franchises. Each franchise makes a discrete contribution to the corporation, and there is very little interaction among franchises. Geographically, McDonald's stores are spread all over the country (and abroad). Each franchise has its own territory and considerable autonomy, not unlike a baseball player in the field; in fact, 75 percent of the restaurants are owned by independent operators. Franchise owners have a voice at the corporate level; several new product ideas—including the Big Mac, the Fillet-o-Fish, and the Egg McMuffin—were first suggested by franchise owners. On the whole, then, McDonald's can be considered a baseball/football hybrid. But the worker who is a programmed cog in the food-delivery process clearly is playing football.

A-P-A Transport, a New Jersey–based firm that many believe to be the most productive in the trucking industry, is another baseball/football hybrid. The very character of trucking immediately evokes baseball: individual drivers tracing their own routes in myriad directions. The task brings with it a sense of competing against nature, because so many contingencies crop up, many of which—traffic congestion, accidents, bad weather, and so on—cannot be foreseen. Driving a truck is a completely different kind of activity from working a programmed assembly line.

A-P-A's philosophy, as expounded by chairman Arthur E. Imperatore, "is that we build men. Incidentally, we move freight." A-P-A is very selective about its roster: only 2 percent of all applicants wind up with a job there. Says Imperatore: "Every man chosen right can have the most singularly dramatic and forceful effect on impacting productivity favorably. The successful candidate becomes quite proud that he's been selected in preference to many others. This helps to underpin a strong spirit within the company that we aim to be the very best."

But A-P-A is as concerned about *how* the work is done— the game plan—as it is with *who* does it—the lineup card. In fact, the entire process of moving freight has been analyzed by Imperatore himself. He broke down the process into 225 individual steps, which he depicted in a fifteen-foot flowchart identifying what tasks must be carried out, when, how, and by whom.

The company has also developed a massive data base from time-and-motion studies of driver and dockworker functions. Historic "standard times" have been calculated. Every time a driver travels a particular route, his actual time is compared with the standard. A daily computer printout measures each driver's performance. According to chief engineer August Pagnozzi, the numbers effectively re-create the events in each driver's day. It is just like a box score in baseball, from which, as Thomas Boswell has noted, one can fairly reconstruct the game by analyzing the numbers in print.

This printout captures the dual baseball/football nature of A-P-A—and its leader, Imperatore.

"It's not that I don't trust them," he explains, "but I know human nature. I know that good and evil are constantly in the balance. What I've done is to pit each man against himself so he can tip the scales one way or the other by himself. Every man craves direction, a sense of purpose, a sense of dignity. I've planned out the problems. I've planned out the frustration and waste. I've freed him to enrich his life, to achieve greater self-awareness. That's why I fought the men in the early days, because they wanted to be human hulks and I wouldn't let them."

And the system, because it's impartial, because the numbers don't lie, and because every man writes his own record, also did something almost unheard of. It neutralized the traditional antagonism between the union and management. "There's nothing left to argue about," Arthur says. "I've given the men more security, and a better kind of security, than the union ever could. After all, every man protects his own job every day by his own performance."

Football/Basketball Hybrids

A number of companies today consist of two "collateral" or "parallel" organizations, one devoted to normal operations and the other devoted to change. The differences between these two types of organization, which form a football/basketball hybrid, are summarized in the following chart.

The basketball structure in this chart is essentially a supplement to the mainstream production design—the football-organization; it coexists with it. This dual system describes the majority of quality of work life (QWL) programs in established U.S. companies over the last fifteen years. These programs go under a variety of labels, for example, participative management, employee involvement, work improvement, and labor-management cooperation. In most cases, however, the QWL initiatives do not penetrate the normal work structure.

The most popular form of QWL is the *quality circle* (or quality control circle), a small group of employees and their supervisor who meet regularly to identify production and quality problems and to generate solutions. A common problem that quality circles address is the flow of work: What can be

COLLATERAL (PARALLEL) ORGANIZATIONS

	FOOTBALL-ORGANIZATION	BASKETBALL-ORGANIZATION
Focus	Routine production	Problem solving
Hierarchical levels	Many	Few
Locus of leadership	At top of hierarchy	Distributed throughout
Division of labor	High	Low
Use of rules and procedures	High	Low
Job assignments	Fixed	Flexible
Core competence	Efficiency	Innovation

Source: Compiled from Dale E. Zand, *Information, Organization, and Power* (New York: McGraw-Hill, 1981), p. 63; and Rosabeth Moss Kanter, *The Change Masters* (New York: Simon & Schuster, 1983), p. 407.

done to eliminate bottlenecks and reduce the time it takes to process an order? Often the answer to such a question is to do away with obsolete practices that inhibit communication—for instance, the tendency of individual departments to "mind their own business" and forget about the rest of the company. Other common problems that circles take on are how to improve yield, how to reduce customer complaints, and how to lower absenteeism.

Boeing Company illustrates another important football/basketball variety in its use of a liaison group between product and process engineering, as described by organizational theorist Jay Galbraith. *Product design* is concerned with the creation of new products, *process design* with their manufacture. Since a product must be conceived before it can be manufactured, these functions have to occur in sequence. But during times of high product-design activity, the complexity of the tasks requires much more back-and-forth communication between these functions than normal organizational channels can handle. In designing its 737 (and 727 derivatives), Boeing responded to this problem by creating a liaison group of process engineers who were physically located in the product design area.

The liaison engineers carried out two sets of activities. First, they worked closely with the product designers to come up with design ideas that would lend themselves to economical manufacture. Second, they helped to coordinate the two groups. When, for instance, they knew that product engineering was running behind schedule, they would communicate rough product specifications to process engineering so that the manufacturing system could develop in parallel. In effect, the liaison engineers made the relations between the two groups less sequential and more simultaneous; they complemented a football system with a basketball one.

Still another type of collateral-organization uses a group executive office as a top management forum for exchanging ideas. S.C. Johnson & Son, makers of Johnson Wax and other household products, has a ten-member office of the chairman. Explains CEO Samuel Johnson: "It is an enabling and facilitating and communicating mechanism. It doesn't replace other standing committees. We meet more as a collegial group with no agenda. We meet at least once a month and we bounce ideas off of each other and inform each other of things that may impact more than one segment of the company."

Delta Airlines is a different kind of football/basketball hybrid—one that blends the different pulls, rather than operating football-like and basketball-like systems side by side. For safety reasons, Delta (and all other airline companies) must comply with rigid step-by-step protocols; it must follow sequential checklists similar to the steps in long-linked production. According to management theorist Henry Mintzberg, airline companies are "safety bureaucracies" for good reason: "Few people would fly with an airline that had an organic structure, where the maintenance men did whatever struck them as interesting instead of following precise checklists, and the pilots worked out their procedures for landing in foggy weather when the need arose."

Checklists here are functional substitutes for hierarchy and mirror football's top-down character. Delta also resembles this sport in its devotion to long-range planning. The company has a fifteen-year planning horizon for flight equipment and support facilities, and, like an excellent football team, sticks with its game plan. Says *Business Week:* "Unlike many other airlines, Delta has never backed off on a fleet improvement program because of financial limitations. Year after year, it stays on course with its long-term plans, regardless of external conditions."

Finally, Delta is widely acknowledged to be the most effective scheduler of all U.S. airlines. Its *hub-and-spoke* system, based in Atlanta, has been widely studied and copied by such competitors as Eastern Airlines. This is a highly sophisticated, football-like centralized system that allows passengers to travel to any Delta destination by connecting at Atlanta.

Delta displays the flexibility of a basketball team in a host of ways, starting at the top. Since the death of founder C. E. Woolman in 1966, the airline has been managed consensually by a team of nine top managers. The teamwork at this level reinforces Delta's central tenet that employees will be treated like members of a family. Toward this end, Delta has adhered faithfully to a no-layoff policy, even in the face of such adversity as the 1973 oil embargo. During this crisis, flying cutbacks rendered 200 pilots and 400 flight attendants surplus. Rather than lay off these people, Delta found other work for them: loading cargo, selling tickets, handling reservations, and cleaning aircraft. On their part, the 600 "redundant" employees thus demonstrated the same kind of flexibility the senior management team demonstrated.

Delta's combination of football and basketball styles shows in its communication patterns. There is both an open-door policy on the part of top management and a respect for hierarchy. This dualism is captured in the following statement by Ronald W. Allen, now president and chief operating officer: "We do, of course, encourage people to go through the chain of command, but they know they don't have to."

Perhaps the most dramatic evidence that those who work at Delta truly feel part of a family came in 1983, after a financially trying year for the airline. All 37,000 employees chipped in to buy their company a brand-new Boeing 767, dressed up with a red ribbon around its fuselage.

Baseball/Basketball Hybrids

Baseball/basketball hybrids are potentially the most humanistic of the hybrid pairs because they operate with a minimum of external (football-like) controls. Their design is both person- and people-oriented. Put another way, this combination seeks a nearly equal balance of individual initiative and group process.

The most compelling large-scale example of a baseball/basketball hybrid is the Minnesota Mining and Manufacturing Corporation, known by everyone as 3M, which produces Scotch tape, Scotchgard, Scotchkote, and some 50,000 other products for ten major markets in ninety-one plants, scattered across rural and semirural areas of thirty-five states. Thus, 3M, like a baseball team, is spread out. In 1982, 3M's average plant had only 270 employees, and its median plant, only 115. If the plants as a set resemble a team of baseball players, so do 3M's thirty-nine quasi-autonomous divisions into which they are clustered.

Each division underwrites new projects out of its own earnings, constructs or rents facilities, and structures its own marketing and distribution plans. Divisions are evaluated not only on the basis of profitability, but also on new-product development: thus, 25 percent of sales is expected to come from products that did not exist five years earlier. In other words, a division has to bat .250—which is about the minimum a ballplayer (other than a pitcher) can hit and still remain in the big leagues.

In a recent product brochure, 3M reveals its concern for individual development:

> When you put too many fences around people, they can easily become like sheep in a pasture, and sheep don't produce new ideas. It takes a receptive environment, without boundaries, to advance any technology to a useful end product. So, no matter which technology an individual may be working with at 3M, we do everything we can to encourage creativity.
>
> We have an informal practice which allows our scientists and engineers to devote 15% of their work time to unassigned, personal research projects in their area of expertise . . . using company facilities to take them wherever their instincts lead.

And 3M scientists can earn performance bonuses of up to 40 percent. But they collect no royalties for their breakthroughs because of a firm corporate conviction that new products are the result of a team effort, not the labors of a single individual.

It is the pervasive emphasis on teamwork and sharing that binds 3M's multitudinous parts. This emphasis—3M's basketball side—is the psychological equivalent of the company's core technology: bonding and coating. Both the common technology and the common culture of cooperation temper 3M's celebration of the individual. To quote again from the recent brochure: "At 3M, listening is an important part of the communication that goes on between people in each of our specialized technologies. We exchange information through organizations like our Technical Forum. Often, that is what inspires new products. . . ." For example, 3M's precision coating technology has resulted in such products as wrapping tapes, recording tapes, and reflective highway signs.

Ironically, 3M's heterogeneity is a source of much of its unity: There is a prevailing belief among scientists "that somewhere in 3M someone will be able to use almost anything." The flow of listening and idea-sharing across units suggests the ball-movement of a crack basketball team. That extra pass is always made. At the same time, a person—or a division—can still hit one out of the park.

A very different company from 3M, but no less a baseball/basketball hybrid, is Herman Miller, Inc., the office furniture maker. Herman Miller is explicitly committed to individual excellence and to teamwork. Since the 1930s, under founder D. J. De Pree, the company has made it a practice to invite a succession of famous designers to its headquarters in remote Zeeland, Michigan. Sportswriter Jim Murray's characterization of baseball as a concert series by artists surely applies to Herman Miller; its lineup of visiting designers has included Gilbert Rhode, George Nelson, Charles Eames, and Robert Propst.

Why would a star designer trek to Zeeland, Michigan? Herman Miller chairman Max De Pree, son of D. J., explains how his father was able to lure such talent:

> He did it by inviting designers to come to a place where they could have a free hand—a company in which design is as important as sales or production. D. J. promised that no design would be changed without the designer's participation and approval. There would be no reliance on market research; the company would not be concerned with what was already popular. If designers and top management thought something was good, it would be put into production. D. J. and the early designers made one very important decision, one that it took a lot of courage to make, and they stuck with it: They decided that there was a market for good design.

As committed as the company is to innovative designs—the product of individual designers—"there is one more commitment that Herman Miller has made—in some ways the most important one. It is the commitment to all the people who work with us to turn a designer's vision into a real chair." This is the basketball side of Herman Miller.

Herman Miller has institutionalized its basketball nature through the initiation of the Scanlon Plan. The Scanlon Plan, begun in 1950, is a productivity gain-sharing mechanism in which everyone in the company, from factory worker to salesperson to president, benefits financially from operational improvements. Employee suggestions from throughout the organization are pooled so that all have a shared stake in improving productivity (in contrast to the case with conventional suggestion systems, which encourage employees to compete with each other for suggestion ownership—and rewards).

Another "basketball" institution at Herman Miller, the firm's employee stock ownership plan, was initiated more than twenty years ago. This plan is distinctive because it covers 100 percent of the full-time, regular Herman Miller employees who have been with the company for at least a year. In De Pree's words, "Nothing is being *given*. Ownership is *earned* and *paid for*. The heart of it is profit sharing, and there is no sharing if there are no profits. There is no soft-headed paternalism at play here. Rather, there is a certain morality in connecting shared accountability with shared ownership."

W. L. Gore & Associates, a 4,000-person manufacturer of a synthetic fiber called Gore-Tex®, operates without a hierarchy; everyone is an "associate." And the company, another baseball/basketball hybrid, clearly is not for everyone. Those who apply for work at Gore may receive a letter telling them what is in store: "If you are a person who needs to be told what to do and how to do it, Dr. Gore says, you will have trouble adjusting. . . . An associate has to find his own place to a high degree. There's no job description, no slot to fit yourself into. You have to learn what you can do."

Gore describes its structure as *lattice organization*, a term meant to convey the fact that "every individual within it deals directly with every other, one on one, in relationships best described as a cross-hatching of horizontal and vertical lines." At the crux of the organization is individual responsibility. Says company founder Bill Gore: "We don't manage people here. People manage themselves. We organize ourselves around voluntary commitments. There is a fundamental difference in philosophy between a commitment and a command."

Gore's approach to plant design shows the balance the firm strikes between baseball and basketball modes. Its twenty-eight plants are scattered worldwide, like players on a baseball field; but the plants also are kept small (200 or fewer persons) so that associates can interact with each other, as in basketball. Gore estimates that his firm's productivity is twice that of a typical manufacturing work force, and that creativity is three times as great.

Gore's decision-making system shows another balance between baseball and basketball. Most of the time associates decide things on their own, so the baseball mode prevails. They may or may not ask others' advice—it's up to them. But when what Bill Gore calls a *waterline decision* comes up, then they must consult with other associates. A waterline decision involves a problem that "could twist toward the company's waterline," that is, could threaten to sink the company. At these times, the relevant associates get together and arrive at a joint decision—a basketball approach.

Baseball/Football/Basketball Hybrids

In the United States, baseball was originally played in the spring and summer; football in the fall; and basketball, bridging the other two sports, in the winter. Over the years, sports in adjoining seasons have increasingly overlapped. Now we are at a point when, during one month—October—professional teams in all three sports are playing.

An example of a three-way sports hybrid in business—like the three-way "season" of October—is an organization with different *levels* that correspond to different sports. Consider General Motors' Inland Division, which produces a wide range of automotive products—including steering wheels, engine mounts, brake linings, and air-conditioning hose. Until the late 1960s, Inland's structure had been that of a classic football-organization: a functional design made up of engineering, finance, manufacturing, personnel, sales, and some additional departments. But as Inland's range of products expanded, the division experienced more delivery and cost problems. Coordination requirements began to strain the hierarchy. Inland also faced competitors that because they were smaller could react more quickly to customer demands—especially as these competing firms tended to specialize in a single product line. These companies also had lower wage scales and therefore enjoyed cost advantages. Given this competition, Inland's general manager decided in 1967 to reorganize by forming eleven separate "minicompanies" or product teams—each a baseball player—to supplement the organization's functional structure.

The idea behind the teams was to drive decision making downward and to encourage greater lateral communication among team members in order to gain some of the advantages of Inland's smaller competitors. Thus, although the overall structure of separate teams resembled baseball, the interaction within teams was much like basketball. The history of the product teams has been one of gradual development, in which the teams have come to exercise more and more authority. They started out by focusing on such operating decisions as the selection of materials and vendors and the improvement of the manufacturing process. Over time, the teams assumed greater financial responsibilities and became involved in joint goal-setting with Inland's executive committee—the general manager and his staff of functional heads—to which each team reported. In the last few years, the teams' orientation has become increasingly strategic, that is, concerned with long-term issues from a division-wide perspective.

Inland's product teams have proved effective in achieving flexibility and focus without abandoning economies of scale. Inland demonstrates that it is indeed possible to play basketball within a baseball framework that supplements a larger football design.

But apart from cases like Inland, in which each "team" represents a distinct organizational level, three-way hybrids are not easy to identify. This is understandable, because managing a hybrid of two sports is difficult enough. One form of the hybrid-management problem is becoming increasingly familiar: how to balance a high-volume, low-cost production game (football) with high-tech innovation (basketball). It is a problem that has confronted such computer manufacturers as Texas Instruments and Data General, as well as firms in old-line industries (including automobile manufacturing) that are trying to shift from electromechanical to electronic technologies.

The challenge is even greater when it involves moving from a two-sport to a three-sport hybrid. By assigning relatively equal priority to three criteria, an organization risks severe confusion. Thus, Emerson Electric—a baseball/football hybrid, as we have seen—is being seriously tested as it seeks to become more high-tech–oriented. High technology requires the voluntary sharing of resources (basketball)—no easy task in an organization steeped in efficiency (football) and divisional autonomy (baseball). According to a 1983 report in *Business Week*, "Several Emerson insiders suggest that the battle to change Emerson's old culture is far from won. Some division presidents openly acknowledge that they are wary about compromising their autonomy by cooperating with their peers."

Possibly the closest approximation to a three-way hybrid is Lincoln Electric, a Cleveland-based manufacturer of arc-welding equipment that in 1984 employed more than 2,600 people. Lincoln Electric resembles baseball in terms of its entrepreneurial approach to employees. To begin with, the company is very selective about filling its roster. Since 1958, Lincoln Electric has had a policy of guaranteeing employment for all its regular employees; hence, the firm has to be especially careful about its hiring practices.

Once hired, an employee is encouraged to compete with other employees because the best performers get the first opportunity to advance to higher rated jobs. In 1981, a good year, the average worker earned $44,000, roughly half of which was in the form of a bonus; in 1983, a bad year, the average was about $20,000, again half coming as a bonus. Some workers do especially well. Lincoln Electric has a group of skilled machine operators it refers to as "Million-Dollar Men," whose ability to operate as many as five different machines at the same time saves the company millions of dollars that otherwise would have to be spent on state-of-the-art equipment. As *Fortune* writer Gene Bylinsky has observed, "Encircled by the machines, these virtuosos look like so many Victor Borges playing five pianos simultaneously." A Million-Dollar Man can earn $80,000 in a good year.

On the whole, employees work under relatively little supervision (about one supervisor per 100 employees). They are responsible for their own inspection and must fix defects on their own time. Defects discovered by customers are traced back to the worker and lower his merit rating, bonus, and pay. A worker who misses a day because of sickness is not paid for that day.

All of this shows the baseball side of Lincoln Electric. The company, however, is also very football-like. In fact, James Lincoln, former general manager and brother of company founder John Lincoln, was a former football player. Lincoln Electric places enormous emphasis on planning, which is understandable, given the no-layoff commitment. To meet this commitment, management must continually solve two related planning problems: "(1) how to stabilize and optimize the overall size of the work force; and (2) how to move workers about in order to cope with inevitable fluctuations in production volume." In other words, management must do a superb job of line-balancing.

Lincoln Electric management has the authority of a football head coach. Management can unilaterally transfer workers among jobs, vary the length of the workweek, and assign overtime without restriction. But the worker-manager relation at Lincoln appears to be more one of interdependence (basketball) than of either independence (baseball) or dependence (football).

The origin of this interdependence is the commitment, first articulated by James Lincoln, that the interests of employees come before those of shareholders—hence, guaranteed employment, and a situation in which 50 percent of the employees own about 40 percent of the company's stock. The company has an advisory board, made up of representatives chosen by workers, which meets with top management twice a month to share suggestions. Status differences separating managers and workers are minimal. Both groups have identical perquisites and fringe benefits, and they share the parking lot, building entrances, and the cafeteria.

Workers exhibit the flexibility of basketball players. According to Robert Zager of the Work in America Institute, who studied the Lincoln case, workers are willing to learn new jobs; to train on a different machine when their own is being repaired; to work half a day on one machine and the other half on a second; to shift between overtime and short time to meet varying production schedules; and to cover for one another when a gap results from tardiness or absenteeism. Zager concludes that "Lincoln Electric places a high premium on freedom from rigidities of any kind." To this end, workers' bonuses depend as much on demonstrated teamwork as on individual achievement.

The pace of work resembles a fast-breaking basketball game without the time-outs: There are no break periods. The same level of activity applies to Lincoln Electric's suppliers. William Baldwin of *Forbes* compares Lincoln's materials procurement system to that of Japanese firms:

You have perhaps heard of *kanban*, the on-time delivery that allows Japanese automakers to run with a few hours' inventory. Lincoln has been practicing a version of this technique for years. It has no central stockroom; supplies are delivered directly to a work area through one of the many loading docks in the oblong factory in which work flows crosswise.

The system works only if Lincoln's suppliers are reliable. They are, because they want the predictable, steady business that comes from a company that is deliberately shaving the peaks and valleys in the demand for its products.

In its entirety, Lincoln Electric represents an uncommonly even balance of baseball, football, and basketball. There may be no other U.S. firm that comes close to paralleling it. According to William Serrin in *The New York Times*, "While some scattered companies elsewhere are trying out some of the worker management features in evidence at Lincoln, no other sizable company appears to have used so many of them—nor for so long." It is not an easy balancing act.

What Lincoln Electric really shows us is just how much choice we have about how to run our organizations. On the surface, Lincoln is your archetypal football factory: high-volume, low-cost, no-frills manufacturing in a marketplace that it dominates the way Vince Lombardi's Green Bay Packers once dominated the NFL. Bone-crunching execution. This kind of firm usually conjures up images of dictatorial top management and an absolute split between those who give the orders and those who take them. We have a mental picture of supervisors barking at alienated workers who have precious little sense of individual competence or team membership. But it just ain't so; Lincoln Electric belies the stereotype. And fortunately, as distinctive as Lincoln is, it is not the only example of organizational choice out there from which we can learn.

6

The Right Team

TO GET THE kind of performance you want from your corporate team, you need a clear strategy for managing your players—one that both matches your game and is internally consistent. People-management strategies that are effective in one game often will not work in another. Indeed, each game has its own distinctive set of requirements.

Interpersonal "fit" is generally less important in baseball than in the other two sports because of the relative independence of each player on the team. With few exceptions, a player must *fit* his particular role, but need not *fit in* so closely with other roles. Baseball accommodates wider personality differences than either football or basketball. Author and former pro football player Peter Gent, no conformist by any stretch, observes that "Baseball players are the weirdest of all. I think it's all that organ music." Music or no, the game does reward an individual's desire and ability to function autonomously. In fact, many believe that baseball rewards individual arrogance. Future Hall-of-Famer Joe Morgan claims: "I've never seen a good player who wasn't cocky and a little arrogant."

By contrast, football requires a tighter meshing of individuals with each other. A player must submit to a team's "system," which is a function of its organizational philosophy. This is especially true for offense. Former New York Jets offensive captain Sam DeLuca puts it this way: "The pro coach does not often have the problem of adapting his offense to his personnel.

More often he will draft people that fit into his scheme of things rather than change his offense to capitalize on the strengths of his people." A football player must also be able to coordinate his efforts within the context of both a small group (line, backfield, and so on) and a large group (platoon). He is anything but freestanding.

The issue of fit is most complex in basketball. Many factors combine to render this dimension critical: the game's interactive character, its intensity and close quarters, the small size of a team, and the discretionary nature of teamwork in basketball. Because a basketball team is so small, one player can make more of a difference than he can in football. But because teamwork is more a matter of discretion in basketball, team performance depends significantly on the player's willingness to make sacrifices. A basketball player, then, must be *predisposed* to cooperate with his teammates. At the same time, his style must complement that of the other players and the team as a whole. And unlike football or (especially) baseball, style in basketball has as much to do with interpersonal relations as it has to do with technical (athletic) proficiency.

In football, intergroup conflict can be functional. Rivalry, for example, between the offensive and defensive platoons can physically and psychologically prepare players for the conflict of the next game. Reports that fights are breaking out as offense and defense "bang on each other" during practice may be a positive sign. And player:coach tensions can also be used to advantage. Football coaches have long known that player anger at them can be bottled up and productively displaced onto the next opponent. Vince Lombardi once admitted, after physically attacking one of his linemen he considered too mild-mannered: "In a game they beat on him. Everybody whacks him, and he laughs. I guess I was trying to get him to hate me enough to take it out on the opposition, because to play this game you must have that fire in you."

Baseball is filled with examples of successful teams in which players could not stand one another and/or the manager and/or the owner. The Oakland A's won three straight World Series (1972/73/74) under the cantankerous Charlie Finley; the New York Yankees won it in 1977 and 1978 under the volatile George Steinbrenner. In fact, the 1977 Yankees featured not only Steinbrenner, but also the superheated manager Billy Martin and the candy-bar man Reggie Jackson. Maybe there have been baseball teams with a mix of self-propelled egos to match the 1977

Yankees. But have they won it all? Probably not.

What is the practical relevance of all this to corporations? If your game is baseball, be more concerned with the technical qualifications and autonomous desires of potential "players" than with their ability to be "team players." As baseball author Charles Einstein has observed, baseball teams do not have chaplains (some football teams do) and they do not hold hands before the game (as many basketball teams do). If baseball is your organization's game, look for signs of independence. But this does not mean that a player need not "fit" the corporation's norms or culture. It is just that the culture tends to reinforce individual autonomy. Consultant Stanley Davis relates a story about Ned Johnson, CEO of Fidelity Management and Research Corporation and son of the firm's founder. Johnson had initially believed that Fidelity lacked a corporate culture "because every one of our managers does his own thing and is measured by the growth of his own [mutual] fund." But as Davis notes, one of the guiding precepts of Johnson's father had been to focus on the individual performance of each fund manager. The firm clearly had a powerful *baseball* culture.

If your game is football, look for signs of "dependence" in employees, for people willing to play a bounded role in a tightly managed setting. In football, fit has more to do with matching up internally—with the team's systems and with adjacent team members—than it does with matching up externally with a customer, client, community, or technical discipline (as in baseball).

The role of a corporate "football player" is subordinate to organizational purposes, structure, and technology. This is abundantly clear in traditional production settings in which the physical layout of machines and work centers reinforces the sense that the player is defined chiefly in terms of an over-arching design. He or she is not nearly so freestanding as a corporate baseball player. Neither is the football player so long-ball-oriented. In December 1983, *Fortune* ran a feature story on management. One of its conclusions was that

> Operations . . . is the new buzzword among MBAs.
> These jobs at the divisional or plant level have become
> more important as companies recognize the need to get
> back to the basics of business. "What we're talking about
> here is Vince Lombardi football—an off-tackle play with
> five yards every time, rather than some guy throwing the

long bomb all afternoon," says [Michael] Brose of the Technology Consulting Group.

The contrast here is between operations and the more glamorous jobs, such as investment banking and management consulting; it really has less to do with different versions of football than with different sports: football versus baseball.

Finally, if your game is basketball, concentrate on chemistry—among players and between the players as a group and the coach. Technical fit and social "fitting in" are equally important. Coach and players have to work together too closely and intensely, in real time, to allow an adversarial relation to develop. And there is no other "platoon" onto which players can project anger.

Whether your company will do best by hiring from the outside or promoting from within depends in part on the game it is playing. As a rule, baseball teams have more leeway than either football or basketball teams. Excepting pitchers and catchers, any major league baseball player can move to any other team in his league and have to make only minor adjustments. He will find differences in the new home park (weather, turf, lighting, outfield distances, and so forth), but not in much else. Baseball players are "modular"; they can be added or deleted with a minimum of disruption.

This portability has reinforced "free agency," a league arrangement that allows a player to bargain with other teams after that player has spent six years with the team that originally signed him. Free agency seems to complement the ownership culture of baseball, which has a long tradition of wheeling and dealing, no doubt lubricated by such rules of thumb as Branch Rickey's maxim: "Trade a player a year too early rather than a year too late." But more than that, there is the matter of enjoyment. In the words of Chicago White Sox general manager Roland Hemond, "It's a lot more fun trading a player than signing him."

It is the fun and workability of "dealing" that have given rise to the popularity of "Rotisserie League" (RL) baseball, which is something in between bubble-gum cards and the real thing. It is vicarious baseball, in which a group of people form a league and then competitively "bid" for actual players. League standings are calculated weekly by adding player statistics, both offensive (batting average, runs batted in, stolen bases, and home runs) and defensive (pitching staff wins, cumulative earned-run average, total saves, and the ratio of hits and walks per inning pitched).

But RL football or basketball would make no sense at all because interdependencies among players in each of these sports are too complicated. The Cowboys' Tom Landry once said that defensive players have to play together for at least four or five years to be able to execute successfully against a multiple offense. There are, moreover, significant differences among teams. According to Irv Cross, a CBS sports commentator who had begun his NFL playing career with the Philadelphia Eagles, "an Eagles player could never make an easy transition to the Dallas Cowboys; the systems and philosophies are just too different."

The close teamwork that football and basketball require favors internal development. Development from within has been a hallmark of most of the consistently successful pro football teams—for example (in addition to the Cowboys under Landry), the Green Bay Packers under Vince Lombardi, the Minnesota Vikings under Bud Grant, the Miami Dolphins under Don Shula, and the Pittsburgh Steelers under Chuck Noll. These coaches (have) worked with what they inherited (or first assembled) and primarily from the college draft, rather than from trades.

The major exception to this pattern is the Oakland/Los Angeles Raiders. The Raiders have been highly successful while trading liberally. This is true in part because their owner, Al Davis, a brilliant football thinker, has an uncanny ability to match a player with the Raider system, and also because the Raiders have perpetuated a strong internal culture over the years. Despite their penchant for acquiring experienced players from other teams, the Raiders have reinforced the organization's values in large part by developing from within. According to former head coach John Madden, "For all their talent, you learn as a coach not to rely on new older players as *your* players. The ones you rely on must be those who grew up with your organization. The more of those players you have, the better your team is." Madden continues: "It's easy to look at a player on another team and think *I'd love to have that guy, he'd be great with us*, but it doesn't always work out. You can never be sure of that guy being as good or better than he was on another team."

Although the record in pro basketball is mixed, the sport's coaching legend, Red Auerbach of the Boston Celtics, also did it chiefly from within—often with draft choices that other teams had passed over. Says Auerbach, "To me, the best trade is no trade. Even if you can get a player who's better than your guy, it's not always a good deal. The new guy might rub your players the wrong way—and that's a killer in basketball."

If your organization resembles baseball, you have considerable flexibility in acquiring "players" from the outside—as well as developing them from within. But if yours is a football- or basketball-organization, your flexibility in hiring from the outside will be limited—for reasons of both task-completion and psychological climate. Consultant Arch Patton indirectly reveals why:

> The greatest single advantage of a promotion-from-within environment is that when an outstanding performer is promoted, the whole organization knows about it. But when the best performers leave to join another company, the negative message to the rest of the organization is all too clear. The legendary Vince Lombardi once explained the effectiveness of his Green Bay Packers in these terms: "Every man on the team trusts every other player to do what he is trained to do, win football games." The key words in this sentence are "trust" and "trained." As corporate executives increasingly accept job-hopping as the way to succeed, the trust essential to teamwork almost certainly suffers. As more and more companies come to rely on executives trained by others, often with different work standards and internal corporate cultures, the common will to attain company objectives must lose something.

Because a baseball-organization's individuals or units are spread out—often both functionally and geographically—these "teams" can tolerate less promotion from within than football- or basketball-organizations. Similarly, conglomerate baseball-organizations can acquire whole companies with a minimum of disruption to other organizational units. Whether a football-organization can succeed with a similar strategy is problematic. The recent tendency of a number of vertically integrated football-organizations to diversify through this route—for example, U.S. Steel's acquisition of Marathon Oil—will provide interesting tests. The top management of well-run conglomerates are accustomed to letting the operating parts—units, divisions, and so on—function relatively autonomously. Top managers of football-organizations may have a harder time leaving acquisitions alone because these individuals are so used to getting involved in the nitty-gritty. And the bigger the purchase, the stronger the temptation to interfere. As market analyst Scott Smith said of General Motors' 1984 acquisition of Electronic Data Systems (EDS), "It's tough to ignore a $2.5 billion investment."

To the extent that they are truly flexible, basketball-organizations may be more able to go the acquisition path than football-organizations. That is, their cultures may be more hospitable to change—and to difference—than those of football-organizations. The limiting factor for basketball-organizations, however, is size. The difficulty of maintaining back-and-forth interaction—everybody in touch with everybody else—would probably rule out large acquisitions, or a rapid succession of acquisitions, by this kind of firm.

A company can hire or acquire from the outside and then hold on to those persons/units for a long time; alternatively, a firm can develop from within and then divest itself of people or units relatively early on. In any case, as evidenced by Arch Patton's comments in the above quotation, the popular management literature is biased in favor of organizational continuity. This bias is understandable. It is in reaction to a fickleness on the part of many employees and employers that has resulted in an increasing rate of gratuitous turnover.

Organizational continuity is least important in baseball, in which managerial turnover is as common as player turnover. Going into the 1983 season, only two managers—the Dodgers' Tom Lasorda and the Pirates' Chuck Tanner—had been with their clubs for as long as seven years. Some managerial continuity can, of course, be advantageous—from the Giants' John McGraw at the turn of the century through the Dodgers' Walter Alston to the Orioles' Earl Weaver—but there is abundant evidence that continuity is not necessary for success. The most compelling such example is George Steinbrenner's Yankees. Since Steinbrenner bought the club in 1973, the Yankees have averaged one manager a year: Yogi Berra, who started the season in 1984, represents Steinbrenner's eleventh managerial change. During this period (1973 through 1984), however, the Yankees have had the third highest winning percentage (.561) of all twenty-six clubs in the major leagues.

A 1983 study of the performance of National Football League teams over a thirteen-year period (1970—the year the National and American Football leagues were merged—through 1982) found a stark contrast to the above pattern. The top five teams were those that demonstrated continuity in ownership, management, and coaching staffs. In fact, in every case but one, these teams were guided by the same head coach for (at least) the entire thirteen years. At the same time, the worst teams were characterized by chronic organizational instability. Three of these—the New York Jets, the Baltimore (now Indianapolis) Colts, and the New Orleans Saints—averaged seven coaches and nine losing seasons.

Pro basketball again presents a mixed picture, not unlike baseball. Going into the 1983/84 season, only three of the NBA's twenty-three coaches had been with their club for seven years or more. In fact, no fewer than nine of this number were beginning their first year with a team. There are teams that have done well under different coaches, and coaches (including current ones like Jack Ramsay, Dick Motta, and Doug Moe) who have done well with several different teams.

On the other side of the ledger, by far the strongest argument for coaching-managerial continuity is the Boston Celtics under Red Auerbach. As coach and/or general manager, Auerbach led the Celtics to a remarkable fifteen NBA championships over twenty-eight years. In five of the six championship years when he was general manager but not coach, the Celtics were coached by a former Auerbach player: Bill Russell (two titles), Tom Heinsohn (two titles), and K. C. Jones (a title his first season with the Celtics, 1983/84).

If yours is a baseball-organization, continuity is not essential. In the view of Ralph Saul, former CEO of INA Corporation, continuity may even be dysfunctional. Saul, who came to INA in 1974, found that property and casualty insurer to be staid and bureaucratic. He promptly set out to make the company more free-swinging by hiring bright, ambitious managers who liked to take risks. When many of these self-starters left the firm after only a short stay, INA was criticized for its "high turnover." But for Saul, such turnover was a plus because it signified "a constant infusion of new fresh talent." It meant a dynamism, an entrepreneurial spirit, that far exceeded the cost of discontinuity. Despite—or because of—its turnover rate, INA under Saul became a more aggressive, more successful competitor, a winning baseball-organization. Paradoxically, this new style would lead to problems (as we shall see in Chapter 7) when INA later merged with Connecticut General Corporation, a football-organization.

The phase of baseball in which continuity can probably make the most difference is scouting—talent identification and evaluation. It is significant that of the three sports, only in professional baseball do we find major-league teams with elaborate scouting-and-farm-system complexes. Scouting in baseball is especially difficult because of the long lead-times involved in assessing talent. Baseball scouts must be able to look at a kid and project him several years out. Football and basketball scouts have it easier in this respect: what they see is closer to what they get.

The real name of the baseball game is stars. As Tom Boswell suggests, "It isn't the quantity of good minor leaguers that matters, but the occasional superstar—the Mike Schmidt or Robin Yount—who defines a franchise's fortunes. Teams are built on a foundation of stars; supporting-role players are a dime a dozen (if you know what you're looking for)." An obvious baseball-organization is Phibro-Salomon, an investment banking and commodities trading company that features a roster of highly paid stars. In 1983, some twenty-five to thirty officials of that company each earned over $1 million. In the same compensation league is Dallas-based real estate developer Trammell Crow, which may sport more millionaires per capita than any other U.S. company—better than 5 percent of its payroll.

Although these two examples may be extreme, all baseball-organizations are willing to pay top dollar for high achievers. Consider Advanced Technology Inc., a professional services firm with headquarters in Virginia. Advanced Technology not only pays 10 to 15 percent above the industry average, it also gives achievement-related bonuses to 60 to 70 percent of its professionals, and it recognizes superstar performers by rewarding them *before* they ask for salary reviews."

Individual statistics are especially meaningful in baseball-organizations. As Intel cofounder Robert Noyce told a *Harvard Business Review* interviewer, when asked how it is that employees stay challenged there: "I think it's because people have the control of their own destiny, and they get measured on it. They get their M&M candies for every job. . . ."

Football is a far cry from baseball in this regard. Continuity is critical throughout—from scouting players to team development to game preparation. Because football requires the ability to coordinate a large number of highly specialized roles, continuity is most essential at the top—that is, with the head coach. In pro football this is where true stardom resides. As basketball's Bill Russell has opined: "The first real superstar in modern professional football was not Jim Brown or Joe Namath, but a coach—Vince Lombardi. He was much more of a celebrity across the country than any of his players. . . ."

It is critical for football-organizations to "guess right" when they do have to replace their head coach because of the control the top position carries with it. But there is another reason why it is important to guess right: the profound organizational disruption that each top management change provokes. If a replacement fails in a football-organization, the ripple effects are likely to be far more severe than would be the case in a baseball-organization.

A notable recent example is Kaiser Steel, which between 1972 and 1982 had no fewer than six chief executive officers. Kaiser's financial performance during this period clearly suffered from turnover at the top. *Fortune*'s Andrew C. Brown wrote in 1982 that "Investors in Kaiser Steel may well feel they've been kicked around like a pigskin in some endless scrimmage. . . . Successive managements expanded or contracted the business, put it up for sale or resisted selling it. A huge 1981 write-down made Kaiser the third-biggest loser on this year's *Fortune* 500, with a deficit of $438 million on sales of $1 billion."

On a smaller scale, a $20 million industrial products fabricator that I observed endured five top managers in the space of two years. Not only was this operation losing money, its constant state of flux had eroded its capacity ever to become profitable. Much of the work force had simply given up hope. As one worker put it, "Nothing's going right here. How can it? It all flows from the top guy, but before you get to know him, he's gone. And every one of them wants to do things different."

• • •

Basketball-organizations call for a mix of continuity and change. Effective teamwork depends on the players' learning each other's moves and moods, inside and out—their tendencies, strengths, and weaknesses—so that five men can, in Jack Ramsay's words, play as one. Bill Bradley once remarked that "players who jell together often age together." The converse is also true: Players who age together often jell together—like the old Celtics teams with Bill Russell, K. C. and Sam Jones, Tommy Heinsohn, John Havlicek.

The paradox in basketball is that although continuity is important, it occurs only when individuals and teams—players and coach—are able to change. If Red Auerbach was right when he defined a basketball generation as six years, then the sport requires as much malleability as continuity. Whereas in baseball we tend to see a change *of* individuals, in basketball we see change *by* individuals. So it is with basketball-organizations, especially those in fast-moving, high-tech environments. As product life cycles continue to shrink, basketball-organizations must quickly rearrange themselves into new sets of teams concerned with the next novel product or concept. The pace of change in this milieu increasingly resembles a fast-breaking NBA game. Consider Hewlett-Packard Company, the state-of-the-art electronics firm that introduced twenty-three varieties of calculator between 1972 (its first offering) and 1980. Hewlett-Packard's divisions have been expected to devote 40 percent of their time to short-term projects. But whereas "short-term" used to mean three years or less, now it means one year or less.

Because baseball is so individualistic, we would expect to find more highly paid players in that sport than in either of the others. Because football is so hierarchical, we would look for a pay structure more sharply graduated by the importance of player position than in baseball or basketball. And because basketball calls for a lot of teamwork, but only a little hierarchy, we should find the smallest percentage salary spread between stars and nonstars. Certain publicly available data do support these tendencies. (For details, see Appendix 2.)

If your organization is playing baseball, do not be afraid to pay a premium in order to attract or retain real stars—regardless of what position they play or what level they occupy in the hierarchy. An internally consistent salary structure is probably less important in baseball than in either of the other sports. Thus stockbrokerage firms—most of which are classic baseball-organizations—can afford to pay their top producers lavishly, and at the same time pare marginal producers from their ranks. (Most brokers receive no salary; their income is strictly a function of commissions.) Merrill Lynch is a case in point. In 1983, superbroker Richard F. Greene brought the firm $4.2 million in commissions and earned a cut of about 40 percent. That same year, Merrill Lynch informed its "experienced" brokers (those with at least six years' service) at the lower end of the scale that "they should bring in gross commissions of [at least] $250,000 or look for work elsewhere."

In football-organizations, it is important that salary structure match the internal power/status structure because people and/or units are so tightly and hierarchically linked; therefore, quarterback-equivalents—those who lead the action—probably should, on the whole, receive higher salaries than lineman-equivalents—who follow the quarterbacks' directions. Certain football-organization units within Canadian Pacific Ltd.—a firm with major positions in rail and air transportation—are instructive. Management experts Raymond Miles and Charles Snow have described these units' pay systems as appropriately "oriented toward position in organization hierarchy" and have noted that "total compensation . . . [is] driven by superior/subordinate differentials." But a football-organization is courting danger if it allows the spread between highest-paid and lowest-paid to become too great—a tendency many such organizations have.

If yours is a basketball-organization, you have less flexibility in designing a pay schedule than has a baseball-organization because of the close cooperation required on the part of your players; they have to work and live together too intensely to be able to accommodate the low-high salary extremes a baseball-organization can. On the other hand, basketball-organizations do have more salary flexibility than football-organizations because basketball lacks the hierarchical gradations of football. Indeed, all basketball players must be ready to play the role of "quarterback" when the need arises.

As a rule, basketball-organizations are "flatter" than their football counterparts. Take Tandem Computer. A software programmer who had previously worked at other computer firms, including Four-Phase, observed that "There are only three levels between me and the president of Tandem. At Four-Phase there were seven levels." Fewer levels usually means less income difference between top and bottom.

The following chart summarizes the key personnel matchups

in baseball, football, and basketball.

Combining the four dimensions of this chart reveals just how different the task of player-management is in the three games. Player-management in baseball is, without question, the management of independence. The baseball-organization's challenge is to fill out the roster and the lineup card with the right players—and then to evaluate and reward each player's performance, chiefly on individual statistics. Whether the players be Mary Kay's beauty consultants, Schlumberger's field engineers, or General Signal's component businesses, each thrives on autonomy. For its part, the baseball-organization has considerable flexibility in acquiring, developing, assigning and compensating its players.

Player-management in football is the management of dependence. Football-organizations have to be concerned not only with who is on the team, but also with how the team is to be organized; and not just with what players are in the game, but also with how they will be coordinated. In a football-organization, everything has to fit the plan. Players are linked together in train, often over a long distance (as in the traditional automobile assembly line) or over a long time horizon (as in Caterpillar's long-range planning process in which "product plans, which are mapped out far in advance . . . [issue in] facilities

PERSONNEL MATCHUPS

	BASEBALL-ORGANIZATIONS	FOOTBALL-ORGANIZATIONS	BASKETBALL-ORGANIZATIONS
Importance of Interpersonal Fit	Low	Moderate to high	High
Developmental Flexibility (from outside versus from within)	High	Low to moderate	Moderate
Importance of Organizational Continuity	Low	High	Moderate
Reward System Flexibility	High	Low	Moderate

planning, financial plans, and human resources plans"). If player roles are circumscribed, so is the football-organization's flexibility with respect to player development and compensation. The bywords for player-management in this game are *continuity, consistency,* and *constraint.*

Player-management in basketball is the management of interdependence. The major task of a basketball-organization is to develop team chemistry—to get the best possible mix of individuals—on the team and in the game. Because of the intensity of their work and the close quarters in which it is often performed, basketball-organizations emphasize human relations skills, in addition to task skills. It is the *process* through which work is carried out that is crucial in basketball— whether the team be high-tech (like Tandem Computer), low-tech (like Donnelly Mirrors), or essentially no-tech (like advertiser Doyle Dane Bernbach's "creative team" of copywriter and artist).

7

The Right Game

IF THE BASIC model for your organization is the wrong one, internal consistency may do more harm than good. To help you identify which sport or mix of sports is most appropriate to your own organization, you should systematically consider the strengths and weaknesses of each.

Strengths of a Baseball-Organization

A baseball model diminishes the need to coordinate centrally, which can be essential if an organization is too difficult to manage from the top down. A company may become so large that no one individual or executive group can stay in touch with operational matters. Similarly, a corporation may become so diversified (whether large or small) that those at the top are unable to understand the product, market, and production system requirements of each unit. As the president of one such company admitted, "When you're as diversified as we are, you must have substantial decentralization. With our dissimilar product lines, trying to *quarterback* decisions at the corporate level would be extremely hazardous" [emphasis added].

Or a firm may become so geographically dispersed that regardless of size or complexity, coordination from a single point is unrealistic. The logical thing to do in each case—and many multibillion-dollar conglomerates display all three of these characteristics—is to create relatively freestanding units and allow each unit considerable scope in managing day-to-day activities. In short, the manager of such a company should create a baseball-organization.

A baseball design also makes sense when the nature of the work is so highly individualistic that it cannot be coordinated from the top, and need not be coordinated laterally, through mutual adjustment. This is the case in a research-based organization, like a university. In such a structure, many an administrator tends to be treated like a second-class citizen because he is like a football coach on a baseball team.

The members of a baseball-organization are—individually (as persons or units)—where the action is and can thus respond to local conditions in a way no remote manager can. But responsiveness also implies the authority and ability to act. Corporate baseball players have both. For example, an effective corporate "field" sales staff—just like fielders in baseball—are intimately attuned to local developments and are able to respond instantly. When the need for such a response appears, they no more have to wait for orders from headquarters than a centerfielder has to get the go-ahead from his manager before he chases a fly ball.

A problem experienced by one member of a baseball-organization need not spill over and affect all other members. The problem can be isolated or compartmentalized. This property is analogous to the construction of watertight compartments in a ship. A rupture leading to a leak can and must be contained (until repaired) in whatever part of the ship it has occurred, so that the rest of the ship is not in danger of being flooded. A rightfielder's problem, then, is localized to right field; it does not affect everyone else on the field.

Because the parts of a baseball-organization are self-contained, adding or subtracting parts is less difficult than would be the case if the parts were intertwined. Each part may be regarded as a building block or module that may be readily attached to, or detached from, the rest. Either growth or retrenchment can be pursued without great concern about part-to-part relations.

Similarly, a baseball design aids organizational change within a unit because it avoids the political difficulties that develop when the unit is embedded in a rigid hierarchy. Each unit, because of its relative independence, can take its own tack without worrying too much about how its actions will affect others around and above it.

The baseball approach helps settle problems involving conflicting parties when removing one or more of them is not an easy option. When people or units in an organization cannot get along, one possible response is to reduce their *need* to get along—that is, reduce their need to interact—by physically separating them. Under certain circumstances, a baseball design can do this by dividing the organization into relatively self-contained parts. Richard B. Madden, CEO of Potlatch Corporation, once used this solution when he was a manager with Mobil Oil Corporation in the 1960s. Madden believed that the production problems at a particular plant stemmed from a lack of focus. He responded by building a wall that separated the building into two discrete operations.

This kind of solution is not unfamiliar in many family businesses, in which relatives at odds with one another cannot be fired. Instead, the firm may give the sparring individuals separate pieces of the enterprise—based on geography or customers or some other dimension.

No other organizational design favors individual entrepreneurial instincts or inventiveness so much as a baseball organization, which can approximate the workings of a free market. A baseball design encourages a "long-ball" approach —high stakes, often long-term ventures, research and development—in which batting average is sacrificed for the tape-measure home run, what Reggie Jackson calls the "tater."

Entrepreneurs and inventors are notoriously individualistic. A baseball design frees them to follow their own imagination and gut feelings by keeping the rest of the organization off their backs. At the same time, it keeps them from interfering with the normal operation of the rest of the organization.

Allied Corporation, a company with more than 110,000 employees, set up a new-ventures unit that, in 1984, numbered only thirty-six people. This unit has been patterned after a small business: It is largely free of the bureaucratic and financial reporting systems that obtain elsewhere in the corporation. The new-ventures unit is also able to see far into the future. According to L. James Colby, Allied's director of research and technology, whereas heads of operating divisions "don't look ahead much beyond three years, new ventures can take the long view; that's the secret of the program."

Tektronix Inc. established a new-venture unit, Tektronix

Development Company, in November 1983. Part of the corporation's reason for forming this unit was the desire to continue its association with employees who might otherwise leave to start their own firms. In the opinion of Tom Long, president of Tektronix Development (and a vice-president of Tektronix): "We'll never be completely able to stem the tide of people who want to leave. But we are creating options that can help us prevent some of the losses."

Responsibility in a baseball-organization can be pinpointed; "players" do not become lost in the confusion, as often happens in companies resembling other team sports. In baseball, much more than in football or basketball, the box score reveals each player's contributions; it is a miniature, after-the-fact analysis of the game. Such accountability exists in business even when the task is complex and feedback is slow, as with basic R & D. Even if the *process* may be difficult to untangle in retrospect, the "who" is never in doubt.

Weaknesses of a Baseball-Organization

Perhaps the greatest liability of a baseball design is that it does not work in cases in which the activities of several different individuals or units must be carefully orchestrated—as with vertical integration and long-linked production (as detailed in Chapter 3).

Reduction of the need to coordinate and the advantage of local responsiveness come at a price. The price is the absence of economies of scale—and sometimes even the presence of *dis*economies of scale. If team members are to coordinate themselves and be able to respond to local conditions, then all must possess the requisite skills. Hence, duplication of skills (and functions) throughout the organization is unavoidable.

Consider the case of a centralized firm that makes three different products. Such a firm may need only one industrial engineer to respond to the manufacturing process needs of all three products. But if the company were to reorganize into a baseball-organization made up of three separate organizations—one for each product—then each new organization would need an industrial engineer for its own operations (assuming that part-time engineers are not available). This would result in an excess of two engineers for the company as a whole: three for the work of one.

The flip side to isolating problems is isolated solutions. Because members of a baseball-organization are freestanding, a problem experienced by one of them cannot readily be covered by other members. In baseball terms, the centerfielder cannot very well compensate for the lapses of a shaky right-fielder without leaving his own area vulnerable. Each individual (role or unit) acts on his own; it is not, therefore, easy to bring to bear the resources of peer individuals or units. Neither is it easy to obtain top-down leverage on a localized problem, especially if the problem is technical, as the level of required expertise probably does not exist at the top. Thus, although a baseball approach favors within-unit problem-solving and change, it inhibits efforts *between* units.

Those aspects of a baseball-organization that make it easy to shuffle and separate personnel also work to pull the organization apart. The more discrete and self-contained the parts of an organization are, the more likely it is that the parts will go their own ways. Some parts—individuals or whole units—may simply become isolated. Others may shift their loyalties from the corporation to a particular operating facility, to a local community, to a certain customer, or—especially in the case of technically trained individuals—to a discipline or profession.

Xerox Corporation, for instance, has lost many prominent scientists from its Palo Alto Research Center (PARC); they have left to join other firms or to create their own companies—in good part because that center was designed to be a star system. According to Charles Simonyi, a former researcher at PARC, "Xerox brought together very high-powered people, very much the stars in their fields. But how do you expect them to work together? Stars of a certain brightness tend to explode." In general, baseball-organizations are vulnerable to the centrifugal force that stars exert. Individuals who are most attracted to a baseball-organization in the first place are often those least willing to make a long-term organizational commitment. There is a fine line between self-starting and selfish, between independent and opportunistic.

Many baseball-organizations are also prone to undue internal competition—to a point when team members compete more against each other than against the firm's competitors. *Business Week* had this to say about PepsiCo Inc. in 1980:

Managers are pitted against each other to grab more market share, to work harder, and to wring more profits out of their businesses. Because winning is the key value at Pepsi, losing has its penalties. Consistent runners-up find their jobs gone. Employees know they must win merely to stay in place—and must devastate the competition to get ahead.

This kind of extra-hardball philosophy may make a difference in the marketplace, but it can also have an unintended side effect: defections of key managers to other companies, as Pepsi learned when several of its executives left to go to work for arch rival Coca-Cola. A more recent assessment by former PepsiCo manager Chris Armstrong: "People say there are a lot of great jobs at Pepsi, but very few careers."

From my own experience, both as a consultant and as a corporate project manager responsible for multiplant tasks, the centrifugal tendency of manufacturing plants varies directly with their distance from corporate headquarters and their inaccessibility. The farther away and more isolated the location, the greater the pull—no doubt partly because remote facilities receive fewer visits from corporate officials than nearby facilities.

Strengths of a Football-Organization

Global coordination can be critical in attaining many corporate goals. Situations requiring such coordination tend to be *strategic* in the most common senses of the word. That is, they involve some or all of the following: long lead times, substantial commitment of resources, relatively irreversible decisions, and intensive front-end effort. A football design is applicable under such conditions irrespective of whether the tasks are large scale or "macroscopic" (macro) or small scale or "microscopic" (micro).

Prominent examples of macro tasks that are well suited to a football design are provided by Frank Davidson in his appropriately titled book, *Macro*. Davidson defines macroengineering as "the study, preparation, and management of the largest technological undertakings of which human society is capable at any given time." Some historical examples are the

St. Lawrence Seaway and Power Project, the Grand Coulee Dam, the Interstate Highway System, and the Trans-Alaska Pipeline. Possible future examples, according to Davidson, include melting the polar ice cap, supersonic underground transit, and industrializing space. All are strategic and require strategic planning:

> Mature individuals have learned to expect the unexpected, and to the extent that circumstances permit, a good plan will be good "for all seasons"; nowhere is this stricture more necessary than in the planning of macroengineering developments. Such enterprises take a long time to prepare, to build, and their outcomes may be with us for scores or hundreds or even thousands of years. The decision to enter upon such an undertaking is *necessarily* a *strategic* decision: It asserts priority interest and must accept the fact that it is preclusive in nature and will preempt other options. No major investment is made without some sort of effort to discern its likely implications and impacts.

All macro projects have long-term consequences that reflect interconnected problems; many of these interdependencies can and should be anticipated. The importance of central coordination on a micro scale is brought out by Frederick P. Brooks, Jr., in a provocative book titled *The Mythical Man-Month*. For computer programming to succeed, in Brooks's view, "the entire system . . . must have conceptual integrity, and that requires a system architect to design it all, from the top down. To make that job manageable, a sharp distinction must be made between architecture and implementation. . . ." Preparing the game plan is central.

Brooks forcefully shows that in certain domains—like software engineering—a long-linked sequence cannot be shortened, regardless of how much effort is applied: "The bearing of a child takes nine months, no matter how many women are assigned. Many software tasks have this characteristic because of the sequential nature of debugging."

Although certain long-linked tasks can be completed without central coordination, the price usually paid is reduced efficiency. Unless scheduling is globally coordinated, some work stations (units or individuals) will have too much to do, and others too little. Lines will be out of balance. But even when coordination is not strictly a matter of sequencing, a nonfootball design may be costly—especially where it results in redundant resources. Apropos efficiency, Henry Mintzberg has written the following about *machine bureaucracies*, a prominent type of football-organization: "As long as we demand standardized, inexpensive goods and services, and as long as people remain more efficient than automated machines at providing them—and remain willing to do so—the Machine Bureaucracy will remain with us."

One of the favorite metaphors of pro football coaches is golf. Coaches liken football to golf because the trick in golf is to make one's swing as machinelike as possible. A machine is grooved and predictable; it performs the same way every time. In a word, it is efficient. So too is a football-organization, even on a massive scale. A representative example—at least in principle—is LTV Steel, an amalgam of LTV's Jones & Laughlin Steel and Republic Steel. In a full-page ad in *The Wall Street Journal* announcing the 1984 union of these two companies, LTV Corporation claims "By combining some facilities and updating others, LTV Steel will be able to generate savings of millions each year. Savings will also result from the realignment of raw materials and the reduction of transportation cost by the rerouting of materials."

In general, football is a useful model for streamlining operations, especially since this can free people to do more creative work—in effect, to play baseball. Thus does McGraw-Hill advance its services in a 1984 brochure titled "What Marketing Should Learn from Robotics." The idea here is to leverage salespersons' time by unburdening them of such preliminary sales tasks as creating recognition, gaining acceptance, and building preference for a company and its products/services. These activities lend themselves to more cost-efficient (robotics- or football-like) approaches—in particular, advertising, which the brochure defines as "the robotics of marketing."

In some instances, the cost of failure to an organization is tolerable; in others, it is not. In the latter case, a football design is essential: A firm cannot afford the luxury of experimentation without attention to consequences by its individual members or units. For instance, if a substance is toxic and/or carcinogenic, its use must be tightly monitored. Thus, until recently, the federal government severely limited corporations' scientific experimentation with recombinant DNA because of fears that "incremental errors in local laboratories could result in wide-spread cancer epidemics." Similar regulations govern the generation of nuclear power. Local experimentation may accelerate learning, but at a price that no one would ever be willing to pay. Hence, "safety equipment and procedures are centrally specified and enforced for nuclear power plants."

In sum, a prohibitively high cost of failure calls for taut, football-like control. Such conditions often require the use of a checklist, which is conceptually similar to a head coach's game plan.

Because a football-organization is so closely joined, resources from higher levels and other parts of the company can be quickly brought to bear in solving problems. Top managers of football-organizations, unlike their counterparts in baseball-organizations, usually have technical skills that are relevant to problem solving at lower levels in the company. And other nearby organizational units or members can also contribute— just as one lineman can help cover for another by double-teaming an especially troublesome opponent.

A football-organization's top-down, one-way flow of authority allows it to respond quickly to crisis—as long as the crisis falls within a predetermined repertoire. The military is replete with examples. Thus, on a naval ship hit by enemy fire and beginning to sink, there is little time for building consensus or taking a vote as to who should vacate in what order. Everybody must follow the plan formulated and practiced well in advance.

A common corporate situation requiring crisis response is the turnaround—the company foundering and in danger of bankruptcy. Often the only salvation for such a firm is an authoritarian top manager who can unilaterally set a new course and make a series of unpopular decisions. This kind of manager is scarcely different from the typical head coach in pro football who unilaterally prepares the game plan and calls the plays. A case in point is Robert Smith, head of General Refractories Company, a Pennsylvania-based manufacturer of furnace linings. After several consecutive quarters of red ink, Smith was able to turn the company around. "The cure: Slash costs, close sluggish plants, liquidate poor or marginally performing subsidiaries, and cut total debt by liquidating inventories."

A football design can provide a high level of product/service consistency and a correspondingly high level of organizational coherence. Each part has a clear place. As a result, those outside

the organization can look in and get a sense of which units/
individuals perform what tasks; they can easily figure out whom
they must deal with. Few things are more frustrating than having to puzzle over which of several organizational parts is the
most relevant one to contact for a particular purpose—a state
of affairs painfully experienced by so many of us after the
breakup of AT&T. A variation of this problem is the dilemma
of a buyer inundated by four different salespersons from four
different parts of the organization—all pushing similar or overlapping products. Confusion of this sort rarely happens with
football-organizations, which are coherent partly because they
are stable and predictable. Football-organizations bring profound meaning to the slogan popularized by Harold Geneen at
ITT, and later by Holiday Inns: "No surprises!"

Weaknesses of a Football-Organization

Just as machines historically have been special-purpose devices, so are football-organizations special-purpose organizations. They can do only certain things. In general, the greater
the variety a football-organization confronts, the less able it is
to cope. If you are making only one product—or two or three
related products—it is easy to operate as a football-organization. But if you have fifteen products, most of which are truly
different, then a football design will not work. There will be
simply too much complex information to process hierarchically.
It is one thing to remain in touch with the state of the technological art for a couple of strongly related products, but quite
another to stay on top of several unrelated products/processes.

The product/market narrowness of a football-organization
is often mirrored in the restricted orientation of many of its
managers. Football-organizations tend to be structured by functional departments—engineering, manufacturing, marketing,
and so on (or their equivalents). Too often, functional managers
"suboptimize": They put departmental interests ahead of what
is good for the organization as a whole. A football-organization
encourages this behavior because it reserves the task of integration for the very top of the hierarchy. In a functional (football-like) design, according to Richard Vancil, "The president
is the only executive who can look dispassionately at the interrelationships among the functional activities; the only one
who can view the business as a whole and worry about how

to make the whole greater than the sum of its functional parts; and the only one who can resolve the inevitable conflicts that arise among his functional subordinates."

Because of their limited compass and limiting structure, football-organizations afford only modest opportunities for employee innovation. As Henry Mintzberg has written with reference to machine bureaucracies, "[Such organizations] work best in stable environments because they have been designed for specific, predetermined missions. Efficiency is their forte, not innovation. An organization cannot put blinders on its personnel and then expect peripheral vision."

Because football-organizations are set up to carry out a tightly circumscribed "mission"—a plan or program—they tend to be insensitive to local conditions. Their dominant communication flow is top-down; consequently, football-organizations often fail to appreciate tendencies or developments visible only at their lowest levels. Not surprisingly, then, football-organizations frequently fail to be "close to the customer." They may even be perceived as arrogant to the extent that they require the customer to accept a standardized product—or process— no modifications permitted. For example, Timken Company adheres so tightly to its standard procedures that it reportedly once rejected a $40,000 order because the part numbers requested were improperly sequenced. Some examples of "nonresponsive" products: Henry Ford's monochrome car ("any color as long as it's black"); the hamburger that comes with a fixed set of condiments (ketchup, mustard, and pickle—like it or not); and the "one size fits all" garment (which probably means that it fits none).

Of course, simplifications like these often reflect sophisticated market research, and they may lead to huge commercial success—at least for a while. But after a football-organization has locked in on its product or service "package," it has only a limited ability to alter this package in response to changing customer preferences. In other words, football-organizations lack flexibility. A football design implies relatively irrevocable commitments to a particular direction, so that changing direction is not easy.

As I indicated earlier, an advantage of a football-organization is its ability to deal with problems that fall within its repertoire. But once problems are encountered that are outside this range of responses, a football-organization is highly vulnerable. In the language of organizational ecology, a football-organization exhibits a high degree of *adaptation* to a particular environment, but because of this, a low degree of *adaptability* to new environments.

A problem in one part of a football-organization will affect other parts and, quite possibly, the entire organization. It cannot be sealed off or localized as it can with a baseball-organization. This "problem contagion" is especially serious when it has an impact on line balance (in long-linked production and vertical integration) or critical path (in construction and project management).

An unlikely example of possible problem contagion comes from the retail sector—Sears, which has diversified into financial and other services in a way that suggests vertical integration. According to a 1981 *Business Week* article,

> Sears will be able to provide the infant's crib, the child's bicycle, a savings instrument for college, a home, business suit, and insurance benefit on death. "It's almost back to the old company store concept," notes one consultant. Because the Sears name will be attached to most of its offerings, its quality control must cover an incredible lineup of products and services. Otherwise, one bad experience could turn off a customer to other Sears products.

Strengths of a Basketball-Organization

Synergy, as noted earlier, describes a condition in which the whole is greater than the sum of its parts. Basketball-organizations create synergy by using the power of groups to generate ideas and solutions that would be unobtainable by the same individuals working singly. Basketball-organizations do not simply add the contributions of different skills; they meld them.

Members of an effective basketball-organization are excited, challenged, motivated, and reinforced in the process of working on the tasks before them. Organizational and individual needs are met simultaneously, through the mainstream organization. No parallel organization need be erected—for reasons of either quality of work life or problem-solving efficacy. Task accomplishment and human development, in an effective basketball-organization, are integrated.

Stanford's Everett Rogers draws an important distinction

between invention and innovation: "*Invention* is the process by which a new idea is created or developed, while *innovation* is the process of adopting an existing idea." For our purposes, invention is equivalent to basic research (a baseball model), whereas innovation is equivalent to applied research (basketball). Innovation is not necessarily less inventive. As Wharton's Russell Ackoff affirms, "Progress comes as much from creative reorganization of what we already know as from discovery of new things."

Basketball-organizations are innovative because, metaphorically, they pass the ball around a lot. They bring a lot of people, ideas, and organizational capabilities together. Yale's Rosabeth Moss Kanter has observed that "to produce innovation, more complexity is essential; more relationships, more sources of information, more angles on the problem, more ways to pull in human and material resources, more freedom to walk around and across the organization." Basketball-organizations have all these qualities—and must have them—to perform in the first place.

Basketball-organizations are made to respond to change. A basketball design has to be as dynamic as the environment in which it will operate. In architectural terms, this design is closer to a tent than to a palace or a fortress. Because a basketball-organization does not pigeonhole people by hierarchical level or department or discipline, it can—and will—allocate them in virtually any combination for a variety of purposes. Thus, in Hewlett-Packard, "Human resources units at both the division and the corporate level have the constant task of starting new groups, and finding and deploying managerial and technical resources."

Traditional organizational separations are absent in a basketball design. There is no meaningful distinction between "line" work (concerned with accomplishing the organization's main mission) and "staff" work (providing supporting expertise to those in line positions). Members of a basketball-organization do work that encompasses both simultaneously. Neither is there a clear boundary between formulating and implementing plans. A basketball-organization's environment changes so rapidly that the team has to be adept at planning on the run—that is, planning while doing. It must be able to respond flexibly to changing demands—just as a basketball team in the NBA can shift almost automatically between offense and defense.

Finally, the conventional relation between leader and follower is absent in a basketball-organization. Leadership is distributed across all team members. Different individuals will come to the fore as new situations arise. This is especially true in project-based basketball-organizations. Consider the Wharton Applied Research Center with a core staff of specialists from several academic disciplines. Some of these individuals have decades of experience; others are rather recent Ph.D.s. But just who will lead a given project depends entirely on the mix of skills required. It is not uncommon for a senior staff member to be involved simultaneously in two or more projects, each led by a junior person from a different discipline.

Weaknesses of a Basketball-Organization

The intensive interaction that a basketball design calls for limits its application to relatively small groups and organizations. As I argued in Chapter 4 there are, to be sure, basketball-organizations among the ranks of our major corporations, especially in high-tech areas. In just about every case, however, the range of products is either limited or highly integrated by a common technology (and/or other dimensions). Otherwise, back-and-forth exchanges between organizational units could not occur because no common frame of reference would exist. Limits to growth in basketball-organizations are inevitable. As consultant Roger von Oech observed in 1984 with respect to Apple Computer, famous for its counterculture ambience: "A billion-dollar corporation trying to act like a $30 million company is just plain contradictory." Companies like Apple—and People Express, in which rapid growth has brought with it some morale problems and the need for organizational restructuring—are daily testing these limits.

To mix metaphors, it is often difficult to tell "who's on first" in a basketball-organization—a problem for members of the firm as well as for outsiders. This is especially the case when the company is changing rapidly. Many basketball-organizations are perpetually in such a state of flux that their structures defy definition. They resemble the obverse of bureaucracy— what Henry Mintzberg, among others, calls "adhocracy." One prominent example from the 1960s is the Manned Spacecraft Center of the National Aeronautics and Space Administration

(NASA), which reorganized seventeen times during its first eight years.

Such organizational ambiguity can lead to confusion about the company's direction and can reduce individual accountability. Thus, the group executive office, a basketball variety that we considered in Chapter 5, may be used in a way that clouds responsibility—as when various divisions report to the "office" as an undifferentiated whole. Charles F. Allison, senior vice-president of Booz, Allen & Hamilton, the consulting firm, describes what happens then: "The company looks to an amorphous grouping of people, any one of whom is empowered to make decisions and give direction. That model has been tried fairly often with not much success, because of confusion from the line people over who's running this place."

STRENGTHS AND WEAKNESSES OF EACH SPORTS MODEL

	BASEBALL	FOOTBALL	BASKETBALL
Strengths:	Minimal need for coordination	Ability to coordinate globally	Synergy
	Local responsiveness	Efficiency	Innovation
	Compartmentalization of problems	Protection against high-cost failure	Flexibility
	Ease of within-unit change	Leverage in solving organizational problems	
	Risk-taking behavior	Crisis-response capability	
	Individual accountability	Consistency/coherence	
Weaknesses:	Inefficiency	Narrowness	Size limitations
	Restricted correction capability	Nonresponsiveness	Organizational ambiguity
	Centrifugal tendencies	Inflexibility	
		Problem contagion	

The sports models' respective strengths and weaknesses are summarized in the chart on page 118.

We have seen how some very disparate companies are aligned with a particular sport or combination of sports. But the practical value of the sports models is even more apparent in terms of misalignment. By using the sports framework as an analytical tool, we can understand many organizational problems as the equivalent of playing the wrong sport. The solution is to move in the direction of the right sport. A company needing to become more like a baseball team should give its players more *autonomy*. The need to become more like a football team is a requirement for more *control*. And the need to move toward basketball is a call for more *cooperation*.

As we saw in Chapter 2, Amoco CEO John Swearingen gave his subordinates the authority to make decisions on their own. Amoco's game was baseball; Swearingen knew this and let his players play. In vivid contrast is the recent behavior of Superior Oil CEO Fred Ackman, who seemed to be trying to play football. Ackman, described by others as "imperious" and "unwilling to entertain ideas that don't fit in with his," reportedly humiliated one senior manager by assigning him the task of ensuring that the company's executive urinals smell better. Within a year of Ackman's coming to Superior, nine of the top thirteen managers had left the company.

But perhaps the greatest potential damage from Ackman's style lay in his effect on decision making. When Ackman joined Superior, the company's batting average on wildcat wells had risen to about three times the industry average. According to one former executive, however, "Ackman didn't recognize how that had been achieved—by delegating, by giving responsibility and freedom. His concept of management was to get presentations, with no discussion, and then he would make a decision, even in areas where he wasn't qualified. It was a one-way street."

Another instructive case of playing the wrong game is the experience of Genesco, Inc., during the 1970s. Genesco was an apparel and retailing conglomerate in a dynamic market environment. But under Franklin Jarman, who had become CEO in 1973, the company became increasingly centralized and bureaucratized. Jarman exerted football-like control over baseball-like units—to the point that many in the firm came to feel paralyzed. In one instance, Jarman insisted on a seventy-five-page report before approving the opening of a $44,000 shoe store. What was in the report? Such trivia as whether the store should have a water cooler and hot running water.

Jarman appeared to espouse management-by-exception, the practice of focusing on things that go wrong—the exceptions— rather than wasting time on what is going well:

> Jarman's style was to work from computer printouts, checking them for aberrations. He reportedly used to say that managing a corporation was like flying an airplane— his avocation. "You watched the dials to see if the plane deviated off course and when it did you nudged it back with the controls."

According to insiders, however, this just was not so. Jarman would sometimes disbelieve the printouts and bring in consultants to verify a division's numbers or policies. Jarman's controlling behavior, many believed, had contributed to the fact that Genesco lost money during two of his four years as CEO. In January 1977, the company's board of directors stripped Jarman of his title and authority.

A head football coach in charge of a retail conglomerate may seem like an obvious mismatch. And it is. Less obvious but no less significant is the example of Jerry Dempsey, former president of Borg-Warner, a manufacturer of auto parts, air conditioners, and industrial equipment. Dempsey's background and style apparently clashed with the direction Borg-Warner had set for itself in 1983.

Dempsey had spent much of his Borg-Warner career in traditional manufacturing businesses. The company, however, was increasingly emphasizing services, including consulting and inventory financing. And Dempsey's authoritarian style did not sit well with divisional managers, who historically had enjoyed considerable independence. As a recently retired senior manager commented at the time (December 1983), "Jerry is a nuts-and-bolts guy who was inclined to get into excruciating detail on issues that the division heads should have been left alone to deal with. Some managers felt like he was putting them in a schoolboy role."

This behavior ran contrary to the management philosophy of Chairman James F. Bere, whose perspective evokes baseball: "The job of [the top] executive is not to make decisions. It is to put good people in place and judge if they are making good decisions. You give them the power. When they come in and say, 'How should I do something?' I say: 'That's your problem.'"

Moving from a regulated-monopoly environment to one of open competition is a classic call for baseball, as AT&T demonstrates. Soon after its breakup, AT&T changed its functional structure—in which units lacked a market-responsiveness—to a product-oriented design. Concomitantly, the company flattened its hierarchy and took actions to increase individual independence and accountability. In the process, AT&T abolished its corporate "general departments," which "used to issue tomes of detailed instructions on how every task should be performed."

Sometimes it is not the company as a whole that must move toward a baseball design, just a part of it. Familiar recent examples are the "intrapreneurial" units of several major firms. Such units abound in high-tech companies. They are usually attempts to stimulate entrepreneurial R & D under the umbrella of a large corporation. A chronic problem confronting "intrapreneurialism" is the tendency of corporate management to impose its own game plan on unit operations.

Exxon is a well-known example. In the late 1970s, Exxon attempted to diversify into office systems by starting up or acquiring several ventures, including Vydec, Qwip, and Qyz. The entrepreneurs behind each of these ventures received Exxon's assurance that they would continue to enjoy autonomy under the parent corporation. But things did not exactly work out that way.

Whereas the entrepreneurs thought they would be playing baseball, Exxon chose football. After the risk-takers found out, they pulled out. As *The New York Times* reported, "when the giant oil company began to merge these ventures into one operation, it found itself caught between its own corporate grand scheme and the goals of the individual entrepreneurs. The entrepreneurs fled and the whole endeavor ultimately rolled up tens of millions in losses."

A common instance of mismatching "part" with "whole" is the ill-conceived corporate acquisition. Consider the case of Dallas-headquartered Diamond Shamrock, a chemical and energy company. In fall 1983, Diamond Shamrock acquired San Francisco-based Natomas, an energy company. Although the deal appeared to make sense from a business standpoint, sig-

nificant social barriers existed. Diamond Shamrock's football
culture collided with Natomas's baseball culture:

> Diamond Shamrock boasted loyal, long-term employees,
> respectful of authority and convinced that hard work and
> long hours were sure ways to get ahead. Natomas man-
> agers tended to be outspoken, talented young profes-
> sionals recently enticed to the company by high salaries
> and often more loyal to their personal careers than to
> Natomas. "They felt," says ex-Natomas human resources
> V.P. Barry D. Leskin, "more like independent contrac-
> tors."

Fortune reports that even this difference could have been ac-
commodated had Diamond Shamrock operated Natomas as a
self-contained entity—a baseball player—as it had said it would.
Instead, Diamond Shamrock reaffirmed that everyone had to
play football by announcing that it would fold Natomas into
its Dallas base. This turned out to be an expensive decision.
Natomas had negotiated a hefty severance provision that granted
six months' pay to any employee who quit because he or she
had been hurt by the acquisition. No fewer than 75 percent of
Natomas's employees took the money and ran.

The same kind of mismatch has been known to take place
on a smaller scale. One compelling instance occurred in the
maintenance department of a large manufacturing plant with
which I am familiar. Plant management was interested in developing a quality of work life (QWL) program both to increase
productivity and to improve labor relations. They decided to
start with the maintenance mechanics.

The choice of the maintenance department posed no problem. But what did lead to difficulties was the QWL model
management tried to apply. Management's guiding concept of
QWL was the self-managing team, a structure in which employees learn each other's jobs and take turns doing them.
Historically, self-managing teams had been organized to "enrich" dull, repetitive work—such as assembly operations. The
maintenance mechanics' work, however, was anything but rote
and paced. Mechanics, who worked independently and at their
own rhythm, had to contend with a wide range of variables in
the course of a normal shift. The nature of this work, and the
depth of knowledge required within each craft, ruled out "multi-

skilling" of the type envisioned by plant management. Attempts to cross-train mechanics failed miserably. Management later came to see its error. It had attempted to get baseball players to play basketball.

Mismatches like those just described are found outside of business as well. Consider the behavior of the dean of a major university's business school. In the face of increasing competition for students by neighboring universities, this administrator set out to reduce costs however possible. He clamped down on faculty pay hikes, disapproved requests for sabbaticals, and worked hard to increase teaching "efficiency," that is, the number of students each professor taught.

At one point, the dean was approached by a faculty member who had, on his own, found an outside funding source for an innovative research project. The professor requested an unpaid year's leave of absence to carry out the project—which would probably have led to valuable publicity for the university. The dean responded negatively: "We just can't have people around here doing their own thing. They've got to start putting the university's interest ahead of self-interest." The professor resigned shortly thereafter.

This vignette was repeated in one form or another several times over a four-year period. Some of the most promising young professors left the business school. Things got so bad that a formal personnel committee was chartered to investigate the situation. What it found was the dean's concept of a university was decidedly industrial. He was trying to impose top-down control on a research-oriented faculty accustomed to pursuing their own academic interests with minimal interference. As one professor remarked, "He doesn't know the difference between faculty and factory."

The dean, in other words, failed to appreciate that professors are baseball players who joined the university precisely to "do their own thing." In attempting to convert the business school into a football team, he not only lost many stars, he also lost the historical attraction that had brought bright students to the school: faculty reputation. The business school continued to lose ground to its competition because it came to be regarded as an ordinary, low-cost institution instead of a special, high-quality one.

• • •

Any sports model can be overapplied. When this happens, alternative sports models, representing different pulls, must be considered. Conglomerates, a prominent category of baseball organization, are a case in point. Many conglomerates have become agglomerates; they have become so disparate and diffuse as to cease to cohere. Financial performance typically suffers as a result. In response to this centrifugal tendency, some well-known conglomerate companies have recently begun to tighten up. They have moved in the direction of football.

Textron, the original conglomerate, is a good example. Textron's divisions had enjoyed enormous independence over the years. Divisions typically met financial growth targets, which had been set without regard for inflation, so there was no need for close corporate monitoring. But when inflation accelerated during the 1970s, meeting these targets was no longer sufficient. In fact, by the end of that decade, Textron's senior management had rethought its entire operating philosophy.

Corporate management decided that a key practice required changing. Until that time, when Textron acquired another company, the top manager of that company was retained. But this practice seemed to be effective only when Textron was made up of a set of small companies, each with annual sales under $100 million. By 1980, eight of Textron's units had sales exceeding $150 million. A dose of football was in order. Said CEO Robert P. Straetz: "We want new managers to be professionals who see a need for corporate direction. We plan to coach the team a little closer than in the past."

Toward this end, Textron appointed its first formal strategic planner, whose task was to oversee a corporation-wide review of operations. The company also indicated its intention to dovetail new acquisitions with current product lines—a departure from the typical conglomerate pattern of accreting unrelated businesses.

Textron is a company that had gone too far in its baseball-organization; it then accurately saw the need to introduce some football-style control. A manufacturing plant that I worked with in the early 1970s represents a football-organization that had not gone far enough in that direction. But instead of being understood for what it was, this plant became inappropriately seen through a baseball lens.

The plant was a high-volume, highly integrated producer of small durable goods. The operations vice-president in charge of this and several other facilities believed that the key to effective manufacturing was an overachieving plant manager. When this particular plant ran into trouble, the vice-president quickly hired a new, more ambitious plant manager. Six months later, with the plant still foundering, the vice-president declared: "I've had it with singles hitters; I need someone who can turn it around with one swing." Thereupon he brought in still another manager, even more aggressive than his predecessor. The decline continued.

As the plant's production control staff later recounted, the problem was never the plant manager; it was an incomprehensible production/inventory control system that no one—at the plant or at corporate headquarters—had ever really understood. Unfortunately, the vice-president's long-ball model, in which the crucial individual carries the day, prevented him from seeing this. The vice-president had gone through a lineup of baseball players when what the plant needed was a single football coach who would take the time—indeed, be granted the time—to understand the system.

A poignant case of the need for a football approach is Arp Instruments, Inc., a manufacturer of musical synthesizers: instruments that produce electronic music. The Arp experience is particularly compelling because in 1981 the company failed. Arp was run by three individuals: CEO Alan Pearlman, president David Friend, and legal counsel Lewis Pollock. The problem was that each of the three went in a different direction; each functioned just like a baseball player. In fact, management consultant and former Arp board member Joseph Mancuso suggests that the three "took turns" managing—as though batting: "It was difficult to tell who was running the company. They were doing what I would call management by turns—'Pollock is away a week, I'll run it'; 'Friend is away a week, I'll run it.' And Pearlman would run it by default when the two of them were away."

Arp's "management-by-rotation" no doubt contributed to a series of financial pinches. These pinches led the company to try to bail itself out by hitting a home run with a new product: first a new guitar synthesizer called Avatar; next a sixteen-voice electric piano; and finally a microcomputer-operated polyphonic synthesizer named Chroma. Arp's go-for-the-fences mentality only exacerbated its financial plight. The end came when the company could not raise enough cash to produce

Chroma—which, like the other products before it, might have been good enough to keep Arp afloat.

Mancuso attributes Arp's failure to the lack of direction and coordination at the top, specifically the trio of Pearlman, Friend, and Pollock. "Among the three of them, I couldn't get one full-time chief executive officer. Alone, they're each worth about 0.4 on a scale of 1 to 10; together, they add up to about a 2." Another case of Where's the head coach?

A recent demonstration of the need to play football is Convergent Technologies' abortive effort to produce a "lap model" portable computer, called Workslate. Before trouble surfaced, Karen Tolland, Workslate's marketing manager, publicly praised the informal, basketball-like group process used to launch the new computer: "I don't have to go through two department heads and write six memos if something needs to be changed. I just walk across the hall and say, 'Hey, Charlie, this space bar feels like . . . and then he fixes it.'"

But less than a year later, in 1984, Convergent gave up on Workslate and discontinued the product. What went wrong? According to *Business Week*, Convergent had disregarded basic management control principles. In the view of Tolland, who had since left Convergent, a necessary step had been deleted from the project's sequence: "We were under tremendous pressure to ship the product and simply didn't have enough time . . . [to go] through the usual intermediate stage in which products are fully tested, refined, and streamlined." Even high-tech electronics firms in dynamic environments need some measure of football-like control—and coherence.

Consider Digital Equipment Corporation (DEC), a baseball/basketball hybrid that is frequently cited as an example of corporate excellence. In spring 1984, Harold Seneker of *Forbes* had this to say about DEC:

> In the old days DEC . . . didn't even need a coherent product line. Entrepreneurial product groups developed and sold their own machines and negotiated internally for corporate manufacturing space and the like. If they left big holes in the product line, it didn't matter: Everybody was concentrating on the best opportunities. . . .
>
> But now the holes do matter. When you are supplying a system, you need even the low-demand pieces on hand. With systems it also matters if a dozen separate salesmen

from six or eight different product groups swarm over a company; if billing comes from six or eight addresses; if service has six or eight phone numbers. . . . A unified . . . system needs unified service.

An isolated example? Five months later, *Fortune*'s Bro Uttal wrote the following about Hewlett-Packard, another excellent, high-tech baseball/basketball hybrid: "Under the old organization, Hewlett-Packard operated as a loose agglomeration of small, autonomous businesses, each focused tightly on its own product line. The structure worked wonderfully as long as H-P pursued hundreds of niche markets. But as customers began demanding systems of H-P products that could work together, the structure turned into a liability."

Acme-Cleveland, an old-line machine-tool manufacturer, is representative of much of industrial America. Its strength lay in fighting prior wars with mechanical skills, not future wars requiring electronic and software skills. In the words of chairman and CEO B. Charles Ames, "This company was *geared* to a business world that no longer exists" [emphasis added].

In order to adapt to change, Acme-Cleveland has had to change its organization. The firm has replaced key managers, won work rule concessions from its unions, and driven decision making downward. Whereas Acme-Cleveland had manufactured machines that efficiently produced thousands of a single part, now the company is concentrating on flexible machining systems that can make several different parts without costly setup changes. In other words, the firm has shifted from the production of machines that function like a football team to those that function like a basketball team.

Acme-Cleveland's relationship with outside concerns has mirrored this shift. Instead of relying solely on internal resources, the firm is collaborating with other companies. For example, Acme-Cleveland has jointly developed a machine with Japan's Mitsubishi Heavy Industries; Mitsubishi is to make the machine and Acme-Cleveland is to distribute it in North America. Similarly, Acme-Cleveland is becoming involved in computer-aided design (CAD), computer-aided manufacturing (CAM), and robotics through investing in several small entrepreneurial companies.

The costs of inflexibility—of placing all of one's eggs in

a highly "dedicated" manufacturing systems basket—can be enormous. In a 1982 *Harvard Business Review* article, Bela Gold describes the predicament Ford Motor Company faced after going this route in its most automated factory. Every machine in the factory had been designed and tooled to carry out a very limited range of operations connected with the manufacture of eight-cylinder engines. "When market conditions led Ford to opt for . . . smaller [six-cylinder] engines, the company reluctantly closed the plant because it could not convert its specialized equipment to a different set of tasks."

Acme-Cleveland and Ford Motor Company are industrial examples of the need to move away from football and toward basketball. Johnson and Johnson (J & J) is a health-care example of the need to move from baseball to a baseball/basketball hybrid. Johnson and Johnson has for years been a classic study in decentralization. Its 170 "companies" are highly autonomous, and most of its divisions have their own board of directors. But CEO James E. Burke is convinced that the firm must increasingly move into high-tech areas. "Otherwise," he fears, "we would be headed toward being just another company."

Burke believes that sharing R & D and marketing resources across J & J units is vital to accelerating new product development. Toward this end, he has worked to stimulate cooperation among managers from different divisions. He has, for instance, encouraged information exchanges and personnel movement among divisions. But Burke admits that making the transition will not be easy, and he knows full well that J & J's proud history of decentralization rules out top-down mandating. Under such conditions, convincing divisions to cooperate with each other has required, in his words, "a sea change in attitude."

Xerox Corporation is an information-industry example of the need to move from baseball toward basketball. Until the year 1983–84, Xerox maintained two different sales organizations: one for photocopiers and another for computer systems. The company had resisted marketing computer-related products through its photocopier sales force for fear that this would dilute Xerox's response to Japanese competition in copiers.

The price that Xerox paid for this separation, however, was steep. Not only were duplicate offices—and sometimes buildings—required, Xerox's customers also had to deal with different salespersons for different products. And as there were no incentives for cooperating with other salespersons on the same account, referrals between copier groups and computer groups were few.

Xerox responded to this state of affairs by creating *Team Xerox*, an organizational concept designed to foster a cooperative process in sales and marketing. Under Team Xerox, the copier sales force is learning about computers and office systems; the copier and computer sales forces are sharing offices and forming account teams; and each team member's performance is being appraised in terms of overall team performance.

Another aspect of Team Xerox is its attempt to integrate the wide variety of office machines that Xerox produces. A two-page advertisement in *The Wall Street Journal* claims that "Getting machines . . . to work as a team has proved the answer to getting the right information to the right place at the right time. But to apply this concept to your business requires people with the expertise to analyze your needs and the commitment to help you meet them."

How well is Team Xerox doing? Although the approach has drawn some criticism ("too limited" and/or "too late"), there are indications that it is working—just like a basketball team. After Xerox won a multimillion-dollar account with the University of Pittsburgh, Paul Stieman, director of the university's computer center, paid this compliment: "They understand how to fit their products to our needs as well as a shoe. They know each other and know what one another's business is—they appear to be a team."

If it had been developed sooner, Team Xerox might have served as a model for a consulting firm that I observed in the 1970s. One of this firm's largest projects was a multidisciplinary engagement at a client's site. About a year after the engagement had started, the leader of the consulting team abruptly resigned. In the interest of continuity, he was replaced by the most senior consultant. The new leader brought together all project staff to explain his approach to management: "When you have a team of Mike Schmidts, Dave Parkers, Johnny Benches . . . you don't manage them. You just let them play. Well, that's what you guys are. You're all-stars. You can manage yourselves." Several consultants took this literally. They began to work more and more on their own, just as the project demanded greater collaboration across disciplines. The client organization soon became dissatisfied with the overall consulting performance and terminated the engagement. This base-ball/basketball hybrid had begun to emphasize baseball when it should have moved toward basketball.

As these examples show, it is no easy matter to change from one game to another. Neither is it easy to get an acquired company to play your own game—if it is a different game—as Diamond Shamrock learned when it purchased Natomas. But it is even tougher to *merge* two companies that represent fundamentally different sports models. There may be no better evidence of this than the 1982 union of INA Corporation and Connecticut General Corporation (CG) into Cigna Corporation. Shortly after this merger, a cartoon made the rounds at INA's Philadelphia headquarters. It depicted the confrontation of two armies: "a disciplined phalanx of Roman legionnaires, with 'CG' . . . on their shields" and "a ragtag band of barbarians waving clubs and axes and led by a figure clearly resembling INA's chairman. . . ." What was attempted was the merger of a football-organization and a baseball-organization.

The following chart shows the difference by quoting the impressions of two business writers along five dimensions:

MERGING CONTRASTING GAMES:
INA and Connecticut General

	INA (A BASEBALL-ORGANIZATION	CG (A FOOTBALL-ORGANIZATION)
Business environment	"Unpredictable events and boom-and-bust cycles prevail" (characteristic of property & casualty insurance)*	"Things move . . . slowly" (characteristic of life insurance)*
Management style	"Free-wheeling, entrepreneurial"**	"Disciplined, deliberate"*
Approach to planning	"Oral rather than written**; smart risk-taking, not management skills"*	"Written goals . . . everyone can identify with their part of the plan. . . . Once you got the plan, the plan is what you achieve.

	INA (A BASEBALL- ORGANIZATION)	CG (A FOOTBALL- ORGANIZATION)
		You don't see other opportunities"*
Personnel	"Individualists, eager to be rewarded more for their own performance than for the group's success"**	"Loyal organization men"**
Hiring/turnover patterns	"Key . . . officials . . . came from outside the insurance business. . . . INA people are recent comers, and therefore goers"*	"Hired right out of school"** "CG people are stayers"*

Sources: *Daniel Hertzberg, "Merger of Two Insurers into Cigna Corp. Brings Discord, Layoffs, and Profit Drop," *The Wall Street Journal*, July 29, 1983, p. 36.
**Myron Magnet, "Help! My Company Has Just Been Taken Over," *Fortune* (July 9, 1984), pp. 47–48.

From hindsight, former INA president John R. Cox contended that "the companies had two very distinct cultures that just couldn't be blended. One of them had to come out the winner." Most observers believe this to be Connecticut General. But questions remain. Why could not the cultural difficulties have been more seriously understood beforehand? And can there really be a "winner" in the future, given the differences in business environment as well as internal cultural patterns? Or is the only viable strategy to operate both pieces as a baseball-organization, that is, with each (the old INA and the old CG) as a relatively freestanding player within the corporate team?

Judging by the operating difficulties Cigna has experienced since its formation, much more could have been done early on to confront the cultural differences. *Fortune* reported in mid-1984 that "only last year did the company begin what human resources V.P. David W. Lacey calls an 'emotional integration' program, figuring out and communicating what Cigna stands for so it can address such employee questions as 'Do I want to invest my energy and talent in this new organization?' The results: 'We won't know for ten years,' Lacey says."

I believe that the sports models could have been helpful in systematically showing just how different these companies were—as the chart suggests. Such an analysis might have driven home the magnitude of the cultural divide in a way that would have led to concerted action.

8

Taking Stock of Your Company

IS YOUR COMPANY a baseball-, football-, or basketball-organization—or some hybrid? By answering the following questions you will be able to tell.

What Game Are We Playing?

This basic question should be the first you ask. And to determine the "name of your game," you need to analyze your competitive edge—your distinctive competence. Try to respond to this question in terms of the sports models. If your competitive edge is the ability to add value through star performers—whether individuals or units—then you are playing baseball. Value can be added in a lot of ways. You may produce a product or deliver a service of top-level quality—a fine piece of furniture, a gourmet meal, a first-class hotel room, expert social service counseling, and so on. Even an automobile. At Porsche's Stuttgart plant, according to *Fortune,* "all work is done by hand—painstakingly, expensively, slowly.... Only about six hours are required to assemble a mass-production auto, but a Porsche ... spends ten days or so abuilding."

Or perhaps your service or product has special features that separate it from all others—for example, the technical sophistication of Schlumberger's field engineers' logs (as we have seen) or the distinctiveness of E.T. Wright & Company's Arch

Preserver shoes. At Wright's Rockland, Massachusetts, plant, the shoes (which sell for over $100 a pair) are carefully built by skilled artisans, who initial their work. "The lesson: if hand labor is the only way to turn out a unique product of high quality, and if the market will pay the cost, then that's the way to go."

Another example comes from academe: Frederick Terman's concept of "steeples of excellence" for building Stanford into a first-rate research university. According to Terman, "Academic prestige depends upon high but narrow steeples of academic excellence, rather than upon coverage of more modest height extending solidly over a broad discipline." A steeple is "a small faculty group of experts in a narrow area of knowledge"—in other words, academic stars.

In baseball, increasing the advantages—value—takes precedence over decreasing the disadvantages—cost. This is not to say that cost is irrelevant, only that it is not the most important criterion. Thus, General Electric ran a full-page ad in *The Wall Street Journal* titled, appropriately enough, "The Name of the Game"; the message (in part) ran as follows:

> It's commendable to cut your cost of production.
> But there is another side to the coin.
> Adding value to your brand name.
> In a real sense, that's what General Electric's technologies can do for you. As you'll discover when you call the GE Business Information Center.
> Ask about the qualitative difference technology can make. And be prepared to hear some impressive stories.

And in baseball-organizations it is the individual—or individual unit—that has primacy. This is just as true of a conglomerate as it is of a university or a studio of craftsmen to the extent that each part of the conglomerate—facility, division, group, whatever—enjoys autonomy.

If your distinctive competence is the ability to reduce costs and/or complexity through global coordination, then you are playing football. Your concern is almost the reverse of that of a baseball-organization: You want to reduce the negatives—inconsistencies, redundancies, bottlenecks, errors, rejects. John Bryan, Jr., CEO of Consolidated Foods Corporation, is comfortable with metaphor. "Listening to Bryan plot his strategy is a bit like hearing [former Ohio State head coach] Woody

Hayes talk football. 'Keep the ball on the ground,' Bryan says. 'There's no question, but the fundamental thing you're trying to do is not make many mistakes.'"

Another classic example of a football strategy is that of Harnischfeger, a manufacturer of cranes for rough terrain. Harnischfeger planned both its product and its production process for simplicity of operation and maintenance by minimizing material content, using modular components, mechanizing assembly, and ordering parts in bulk.

Whereas in baseball-organizations the challenge is to open up the system so that the players can display their talents, in football-organizations the imperative is to close off the system so that there are few or no surprises. Holiday Inns is so confident that its accommodations are surprise-proof that at the time of this writing it was providing a "no-excuses" room guarantee. As the brochure on the bureau promised, "Your room will be right. Or we will make it right. Or that night, you stay free."

Just as a head coach in the NFL strives for a foolproof game plan, so does the top manager of a football-organization strive for machinelike perfection. The top manager, or planner, or system designer is the star. As Frederick Brooks has argued with respect to large-scale software engineering, "the conceptual integrity of a system determines its ease of use. . . . If a system is to have conceptual integrity, someone must control the concepts. That is an aristocracy that needs no apology."

If your major competitive strength is the ability to innovate by combining resources in novel ways, then you are playing basketball. Your strength may be either value-addition or cost-reduction—or a blend of these, and other competencies. In any case, your organization is flexible and your players are able to apply their skills in new ways to unfamiliar situations. They may have to be multiskilled. Thus, in an ad for customer service managers, People Express tells the prospective employee that he or she will be "working in all areas from In-Flight Service, Ground Operations, and Reservations to staff support functions such as Marketing, Scheduling, Training, Recruiting, Accounting, and more."

Basketball-organizations excel at synthesizing—imaginatively linking what had been different worlds. In advertising, for instance, playing basketball means the involvement of creative, marketing, and media departments together from the start of a campaign; not separately and in sequence. "Getting involved from the beginning does a lot to get rid of the 'us and them,'" affirms Michal Lawrence, a vice-president at the Dallas-based Bloom Agency.

New product development, a different variety of basketball, requires integrating basic research and practical use, whether in an established firm or in a new start-up. According to *Business Week,* start-ups often do not really produce basic technology—"invention"—so much as they devise commercial applications of basic technology. Thus Cetus Corporation and Genentech rely on gene-splitting technologies developed through university research.

Basketball's stars are the players-and-coach as a unit. The performance of a basketball-organization depends more on player:player and player:coach interaction than on the independent actions of either the individual players or the coach. It's chemistry—the right chemistry—that wins in this game.

What Game Are We Organized to Play?

The crux of sound organization is the effective management of *task interdependence:* how the different parts of an organization are related to each other and to the whole. There are three forms of interdependence: pooled, sequential, and reciprocal. In *pooled* interdependence, the simplest kind, the parts are relatively independent of each other and make discrete contributions to the organization as a whole—like a sales force of individuals, each with his or her own products, territory, and accounts, or like a pure conglomerate, in which the various operating units have nothing to do with each other and interact only minimally with the parent corporation. In pooled interdependence, the parts are soloists—independent players—like the players on a baseball team.

In *sequential* interdependence, the parts interact in serial fashion and each part makes a cumulative contribution to the organization as a whole. The archetype of sequential interdependence is the classic factory that first fabricates parts (by cutting, bending, drilling, and so on), then assembles the parts into a whole product, tests the product, and finally packages and ships it. Each activity occurs in a specified order—like a football being snapped by the center to the quarterback and then handed off to the running back or like a string of first downs in a typical football scoring drive.

THREE FORMS OF TASK INTERDEPENDENCE

1. POOLED

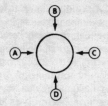

2. SEQUENTIAL

3. RECIPROCAL

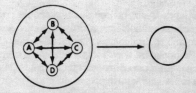

The third type of interdependence is *reciprocal*, in which virtually every part of an organization interacts with every other part. Interaction is frequent and initiated by each part—as in the case of a think-tank consulting firm in which experts from several specialties work together feverishly to solve an interdisciplinary problem. The pattern here is just like that of a basketball team that whips the ball continuously around the court. The three forms of interdependence are illustrated in the diagram above.

The typical organization, of course, offers examples of every kind of interdependence. In fact, sequential interdependence implies pooled, and reciprocal implies both the other kinds. But one or two forms is/are almost always dominant. If it is not intuitively obvious which is/are dominant in your company, then look at the flow of work and information between units— the path that transforms inputs (materials, technology, skills, and so on) into outputs, whether products or services. If there is virtually no flow of work or information from one unit to another, your dominant form of interdependence is pooled, as in baseball. If the work/information flow is unidirectional between units, your interdependence is sequential, as in football. And if the flow is back and forth between units, your interdependence is reciprocal, as in basketball.

Verify how the parts of your organization are coordinated. There are three ways to coordinate an organization's activities. The first way is to design freestanding, self-contained units that effectively coordinate themselves; in such cases, the very design of the organization achieves coordination because it eliminates the need for the various parts to interact. This is a baseball design: The nature of the sport provides built-in coordination. The second method relies on central planning and hierarchical direction. Senior management plans and calls the shots—clearly a football design. The third option is for the organization's parts to coordinate themselves spontaneously through mutual adjustment and responsibility-sharing—a basketball design.

Interdependence and coordination should go together. Pooled interdependence calls for coordination by design; sequential, by plan; and reciprocal, by mutual adjustment. But it does not always happen that way. I know of several companies that have used the wrong coordinating mechanism. One of the best examples is a manufacturing firm composed of two large facilities located in different states but within the same metropolitan area. A new senior management team believed that significant economies could be realized by consolidating production operations that were being carried out at the two plants. So it called in a consulting firm to work with both facilities to produce an overall plan.

From the very start, managers from both plants rejected the premise imposed on them by senior management and the consultants: that the two plants could be merged and then centrally coordinated by sequential decision making from the top down. In fact, each plant was self-contained. Each made distinctive products for separate market niches and had very different production processes. In addition, the two work forces were not at all alike: One was unionized and dominated by a particular ethnic group; the other, nonunion, was composed primarily of workers from a different ethnic group. In all, each plant was a highly idiosyncratic culture as well as a discrete product/process center. There was little basis for integrating them and, in fact, the plants historically had had little to do with one another. Each was a baseball player unsuited to football-like coordination and control. After a series of meetings involving senior management, plant management, and the consultants, the two facilities' inherently pooled interdependence was acknowledged, and the consolidation project was abandoned.

If you can establish your organization's dominant form of interdependence, and you find that it does match the appropriate kind of coordinating mechanism, then it may be clear what game your organization is structured to play. But ask yourself a further question: Do organizational information and reward systems correspond to this game?

Consider your information system. A locally controlled information system—perhaps rooted in a plethora of micro or personal computers—is rather like baseball. Each individual has his or her own data base, with considerable autonomy in deciding how to use it. A good example of such a system is found in Travelers Corporation, a large insurance company. As of fall 1984, Travelers had more than 6,000 personal computers, with another 19,000 on order. According to Travelers' senior vice-president Joseph T. Brophy, "the name of the game is . . . putting power where the people are"—in the form of work stations that combine electronic mail, word processing, spreadsheet analysis, and file-storage capabilities.

A centrally controlled, global information system—possibly rooted in a mainframe computer—is very much a football model, especially when those who operate the computer make the decisions about which programs will be run, who will receive what information, and when they will receive it. Prudential Insurance Company of America, the largest insurance company in the world, is a case in point. Prudential was one of the first companies to install a mainframe computer, some thirty years ago. Currently the company has twenty-five mainframes at the heart of its information system. Information-system managers make the decisions about equipment and applications: "Employees have access to data bases through terminals, but they are limited to applications programmed into the central computer."

A distributed information system—combining global perspective with local initiative—is analogous to basketball. Hercules Inc., a chemicals manufacturer, appears to have such a system. Hercules' headquarters building in Wilmington, Delaware, includes a satellite disk on the roof, five video-conferencing rooms, and a "network of more than 400 word processing terminals and 205 personal computers." Headquarters is linked by satellite to operating facilities throughout the world. Communication among units in the firm takes place routinely through video conferences—as many as one hundred a month.

As was pointed out in Chapter 6, the different sports have somewhat different rewards structures. A baseball-like rewards system is individualistic, based on the performance of the single player and designed to reward star soloists—whatever rung of the organizational ladder they are on. A good example of such an organization is Simon & Schuster, a truly hardball publisher known for paying big bucks to star editors, as well as to star authors. As Steven Flax of *Fortune* observes, "Employees are paid some of the highest salaries in publishing, then they're expected to get a hit every time at bat."

A football-like system, in contrast, is hierarchic; it is closely aligned to the organization's status and power systems so that the higher one goes, the more money one makes. A basketball system may best be described as mutualistic. The spread of salaries is essentially flat; it is based more on competence and contribution than on hierarchical position. And there is less percentage spread between the highest and the lowest paid in a basketball-organization than in either a baseball- or a football-organization.

People Express exemplifies the basketball model. In 1982, founder and chairman Donald Burr was making only $48,000; the company's pilots were earning $30,000—only half the amount then earned by members of the Air Line Pilots Association; and customer service managers began at $17,500—*more* than their counterparts at other airlines. According to Burr: "This is a very democratic company. We've leveled the compensation scales and we intend to keep it that way. We want people motivated by feelings of ownership and peer pressure."

Like salary structures, incentive systems also parallel the different sports. Individual-based schemes, such as sales commissions, obviously resemble baseball. So do arrangements that divide a company into several "profit centers," each responsible for its own performance. An enthusiastic advocate of the profit center concept is Tandy Corporation, whose Radio Shack stores sell consumer electronics products. Currently each of Tandy's 10,000 Radio Shack units prepares a monthly profit-and-loss statement. Because of this bonus structure, "except for some hourly manufacturing, distribution, and clerical people, no two people can expect to have the same paycheck at Tandy."

Companies that have group incentive systems as part of their rewards structure are likely to resemble either football or basketball teams. If the payoff is on a significantly different basis for different levels of the organization—that is, a higher formula for higher-ups—then the system is more like football. This seems to be true of many—but not all—profit-sharing programs. Publix Super Markets Inc., for example, puts 15 percent of annual profits into a fund that is allocated among all employees who have worked at least 1,000 hours during the year; bonuses have averaged 6 to 8 percent of salary, irrespective of an employee's level in the company. This is a basketball variety, as are most gain-sharing programs that use a single formula to split productivity savings between employees and the firm.

As we saw in Chapter 1, the players in baseball are widely dispersed; those in football are somewhat clustered; and those in basketball are highly concentrated. A company made up of "computer commuters," each working out of his or her own home, is geographically analogous to a baseball team. At the other extreme, five persons in a garage resemble a basketball team. Or consider office layouts. I've worked with some senior management teams whose players were on separate floors or even in separate buildings—clearly a baseball-model. Other teams are arranged in a typical "executive row"—a football model in which office sequence may mirror both the hierarchy and the production process. Still other top-management teams are concentrated in or around a commons area—and therefore resemble basketball.

And of course, the "players" may be operating units, not just individuals. Your judgment as to which geographical description applies to your own organization will necessarily be subjective. Use whatever points of reference you believe are most appropriate—for example, the way things are now versus how they used to be or your organization's physical layout compared with those of peer organizations or competitors.

What Game Does Our Style Suggest?

An organization's style is its characteristic way of doing things. Style embodies organizational values, whether or not they are written down. If the dominant value of your company—or unit, department, or work group—is self-reliance, then its style is baseball. Baseball-organizations cherish individual initiative and self-determination on the part of their players. Often this amounts to competitiveness. In the opinion of one editor who worked briefly at Simon & Schuster, "It takes a certain type of very competitive person to thrive there, but when they do, they thrive beautifully—like weeds. It's no place for violets." Especially when many of an organization's players are physically spread out—as with authors, computer commuters, maintenance mechanics, or field sales/service personnel— self-reliance may be absolutely critical.

If, however, your organization's dominant value is loyalty, then its style resembles football. Employees are expected to be dedicated to the organization in the same way that the manufacturing or conversion process of a football-organization is often "dedicated"—that is, confined—to producing/delivering a particular product/service. The individual accepts a limited, highly specialized role for the sake of the larger organizational plan—in contrast to a baseball style, in which it often seems that the organization exists to support individual players. Seniority and tenure are part and parcel of dedication; they provide the glue that maintains continuity.

A test of the strength of this value is the anger and disillusionment that follow when the organization violates it. Talk to any laid-off steelworker: "I went to work at the mill the day I got out of the service. I gave 'em thirteen years, and now they're gonna take my *truck* away because I got too far behind in the payments. My *wife* is working, and now *you* tell me. ... *What the hell did I do wrong?*"

If the dominant value in your organization is cooperation, then your style is basketball. There is a more even balance between individual and organizational primacy than in either baseball- or football-organizations. Interaction with others is more important than either doing one's own thing or following marching orders. A big reason why innovation flourishes at 3M is that people look beyond their own particular roles and organizational units. With respect to new-product development, for instance, there is a prevailing belief among scientists that almost any idea will be useful somewhere in 3M.

How would you describe to others outside your organization the kind of teamwork that occurs within it? If teamwork is situational—that is, if it takes place only occasionally and typically involves just a few individuals or units—then your organization resembles baseball. If, however, teamwork is systematic—meticulously planned and involving just about everyone—then the parallel is with football. But if much teamwork occurs without being carefully orchestrated in advance—if much of it is spontaneous—then your organization is playing basketball.

Consider also the way communication takes place. There are three alternative patterns: one-way, two-way, and three-way. One-way communication is top-down; hierarchical "superiors" give instructions/directives/orders to subordinates, who are then expected to carry out whatever the superior wants, no questions asked. This is football-like communication: from the head coach to the team—or from the head coach to the quarterback to the team. Such a pattern may exist within top management as well as between top management and the rest of the organization. Thus, Richard J. Censits, financial vice-president of Campbell Soup Company, describes staff meetings under former CEO Harold A. Shaub: "Shaub always did a lot of work ahead of you so that the meetings were held not to figure out what to do but to tell you what to do."

Two-way communication is vertical, as is one-way. The difference is that it goes up as well as down. Players initiate communication with their bosses as well as vice versa. Two-way communication is characteristic of baseball. Just compare the confrontations you see on television between player and manager in baseball with those between player and head coach in football. There is not a whole lot of challenging of or talking back to the head coach, but many baseball players seem to delight in having it out with their skipper in plain view of 40,000 fans and a national TV audience.

In basketball we find three-way communication: upward, downward, and laterally. In fact, the lateral direction—player to player—is probably the most important of all. Because of the speed of their game, basketball players need to be able to communicate with each other in subtle, nonverbal ways; they

have to be able to communicate almost instinctively. A
basketball-organization works the same way. Its players must
develop the capacity to exchange information rapidly and with
minimal distortion. The real challenge is to break down barriers
of function, status, and history that have worked against these
all-important lateral information flows.

Try to determine the leadership style that predominates in
your organization. A laissez-faire, hands-off style is characteristic of baseball. An authoritarian, highly controlling style—
like that of Harold Geneen, former chairman of ITT—typifies
football. In his autobiography, *Managing*, Geneen describes
the concept of a CEO that he brought to ITT: "I had long
believed that the primary role of a chief executive was to serve
as a management team's quarterback and show his team where
the goalposts were *and how best to get there, and finally to
lead the way down the field*" [emphasis added].

Leadership in basketball is viewed as a group task, to be
shared among all the players; it is facilitative. The manager
(coach)'s responsibility is to help the group exercise this capability. You may recall the vignette about Celtics coach Red
Auerbach's purposely getting himself thrown out of a game to
force his team to exhibit more leadership out on the court. This
is exactly the kind of behavior one expects to see when a
basketball leadership style is being practiced.

Look at the way your organization has filled openings over
the years. If slots at all levels are open to people outside the
organization—and often go to such individuals—then your
recruitment/promotion pattern is like baseball. If, alternatively,
the only outsiders recruited are those to fill entry level positions—so that promotion is strictly an internal affair—then
your pattern resembles football. Organizational continuity is a
familiar feature of football-organizations; discontinuity of
baseball-organizations. Basketball-organizations have recruit-
ment/promotion patterns that are a mix of inside and outside.
This is not surprising, because such organizations have to do
a better job of balancing continuity and change than either
baseball- or football-organizations.

The patterns just described apply to organizational units as
well as to individuals. As we have seen in business, baseball-
organizations often grow by acquiring other companies. In contrast, football-organizations tend to develop from within. Again,
basketball-organizations are likely to do both.

Consider the developmental pattern of American Express

Company. This corporation's rapid diversification has raised questions about its ability to control all its parts. Walter B. Wriston, former CEO of Citicorp, commented in 1984 that "Their management team has been assembled mostly by purchase. I don't think there's any question that if a team has played together for 10 years, you have a better chance on Saturday afternoon than the all-star team that was assembled that morning." Wriston's implicit model is football ("Saturday afternoon"), and his concern would be more appropriate if American Express were a football-organization. But it's not; it's more like a baseball-organization, with considerable flexibility in developing from the outside.

How does your organization feel about differences among employees? Organizations that have a baseball culture are more likely than not to value diversity highly. Ed Carlson, former CEO of United Airlines, made it a point to surround himself with managers representing many different styles and backgrounds—some with airline experience and others without, some young and others old. John G. McCoy, chairman of the executive committee at BancOne in Columbus, Ohio, has long been a pioneer in cultivating diversity. When he took the reins in 1959, McCoy resolved to convert BancOne into a high-quality "Tiffany" bank, instead of a high-quantity "Woolworth" bank. His methods? "Hire people who are exceptional at something and give them some rope." Mr. McCoy says he would hire the world's best plumber for some position or other if he stumbled across him. He says that if he owned a baseball team, he would have hired Ted Williams "but I wouldn't tell him how to hold his bat."

A football culture is much more conformance-oriented. Typical of this pattern is ITT Corporation under Rand V. Araskog, who became chairman in 1979. Araskog, a West Point graduate, has put together "a management team fashioned, to an unusual degree, in his own image." Among the mechanisms he has employed are a sixteen-page "code of corporate conduct" and a requirement that his subordinates turn in written reports to him every two weeks, and also submit their monthly calendars to him for review. Says senior vice-president Robert J. Braverman, "If I were concerned about being by myself and not having someone watch what I do, I would have left ITT long ago."

A basketball culture is more concerned with interpersonal compatibility than with either individual diversity or conformance. Because a high degree of teamwork is both necessary (unlike baseball) and largely discretionary (unlike football, where it is programmed), a basketball style requires voluntary co-operation throughout the organization. Thus John Sculley, president of Apple Computer, Inc., asserts that "Failure for us doesn't mean going out of business"; rather, it means discovering that Apple is not "a great place to work any more."

One can often get a good fix on cultural bias by examining an organization's training methods and facilities. A baseball style is exemplified by Citicorp's Rye, New York, center, called "Arrowwood of Westchester." Arrowwood comes with golf course, tennis courts, masseurs, and executive suites containing fireplaces and Jacuzzis; "it looks more like a Club Med than a school, and Citicorp rents it out to other companies and vacationers." In stark contrast is the football-style training center of Arthur Andersen, the large accounting firm. Managing partner Claude Rodgers has compared this training operation to a Marine Corps boot camp. As *The Wall Street Journal* reported, "Arthur Andersen places a premium on consistency and says the huge, busy center turns out 800 new accountants per class, all able to do everything exactly the same way—'the Arthur Andersen way.'"

A basketball style is suggested by Xerox's futuristic facility in the woods of Virginia. The guiding concept of this center seems to be forcing people to interact with each other. Bedrooms have neither easy chairs nor televisions so that in order to relax, students must come together in lounges. Even the hallways promote interaction: They follow a zigzag pattern that makes it highly likely that people will bump into one another en route to their destinations.

Another important aspect of style is the organization's posture with respect to taking risks. A baseball style is risk-embracing. Salomon Brothers, Inc., the investment banker, is a familiar baseball example from the financial community. Salomon Brothers is known for "its willingness to risk millions for the sake of winning another trade or client." Internal competition at Salomon is the norm, and individual rewards can be substantial—if one survives. In the words of a partner at rival Goldman-Sachs, "They're very tough, very aggressive, and brash. It's like a boiling cauldron over there, but it works."

Perhaps the strongest penchant for risk is demonstrated by those in the entertainment industry. Whether it be shows or motion pictures or records, success depends on "hits." I once heard a claim that only one recording in fifty was successful. When I mentioned this statistic to Alan Livingston, former CEO of Capitol Records, he responded that the ratio sounded "in the ball park." He then casually added: "But it only takes one big one to cover a lot of mistakes."

But a risk-embracing style is also found in certain more conventional corporations. Take General Electric (GE) under CEO Jack Welch. Welch expects every GE division to be(come) a leader in its league. To make this happen, he believes that "We have to get people to trust that they can take a swing and [for the right reasons] not succeed." Welch's competitive philosophy is definitely long-ball. As he has said about the idea of America, "For me, that idea is: Shun the incremental and go for the leap."

A football style is risk-avoiding; the whole point of centralized planning and coordinating mechanisms—and checklists—is to minimize individual and organizational risk. Surprises are to be minimized because they are regarded as harmful. In the words of Harold Geneen, "Ninety-nine percent of all surprises in business are negative." It's no wonder that Fran Tarkenton prefers the sustained scoring drive to the "bomb."

A football style is found not only in heavy industrial and classical manufacturing settings; it is also exemplified by the following sales training approach outlined by Shelby Carter of Xerox:

> we lay the cards right on the table when sales representatives first start their careers with Xerox. We tell them how difficult the job may be. We also tell them that if they run with the team—and we'll teach them the plays— they'll learn to execute what they've been trained to do like a pro football player.

A basketball style is risk-accepting—that is, it is a style that falls between the individual risk-embracing of baseball and the organizational risk-avoiding of football. Whereas a baseball style strives to open up the environment and a football style tries to close it off or control it, a basketball style tries to engage the environment by sharing risks among players.

Look at the physical status symbols in your organization. Which, if any, groups of organizational members receive preferential treatment with respect to parking privileges? Are there separate building entrances for, say, white collar and blue collar employees? Different cafeterias or restaurants? In general, when status symbols separate people horizontally they have a baseball-like character. Thus, the leading salesperson, stockbroker, or researcher may occupy the corner office, but the competition for it is mainly horizontal—salesperson versus salesperson, broker versus broker, and so on. In contrast, when status symbols separate people vertically—by hierarchical level—one finds a football ambience. Some of the most obvious examples are tall buildings in which one's floor denotes one's standing in the pecking order. There may be no more graphic example of this effect than the Transamerica Building in San Francisco—a steep pyramid that reinforces hierarchy. When status symbols are minimal, a basketball-like atmosphere is encouraged; if anything, physical symbols and objects work not to separate but rather to integrate—both horizontally (player-to-player) and vertically (player-to-coach). Thus, at Nucor Corporation, a minimill steel company, every plant employee wears a hard hat of the same color—a dramatic contrast to the hierarchy of colors one finds at conventional steel works.

What's in It for the Player?

What is it that people really get out of playing your organization's game? And what sacrifices do they make? A baseball-organization will permit the individual player maximum autonomy—elbowroom—and, at the same time, showcase his or her personal contributions. Bernard Malamud chose the correct title for his first novel: Baseball is truly a game for *The Natural*. The 1984 movie adaptation also got it right: Both the character and the actor, Robert Redford, rise above the context. Of the three sports, only in baseball is physical size (weight and/or height) largely irrelevant. It is talent—as epitomized by the ability to hit a pitched ball with a rounded bat—that really matters. All-star Fred Lynn of the Baltimore Orioles claims: "I never saw anybody with mediocre ability become a star through more batting practice. Either you have natural ability or you don't." A *Forbes* analysis of the sport concludes that "hitting a baseball . . . is the hardest single act in all of sports. Nothing else—not sinking a basket, hitting a tennis ball, throwing a touchdown pass—makes so many otherwise gifted athletes look so futile so often." But even for those with the ability, a baseball-organization often brings with it a sense of isolation, of disconnectedness from others. And the price of visibility is self-exposure; players are truly on their own in this game.

Raychem Corporation, which bombards plastics with high-energy electrons, clearly fits the baseball mold. The California-based firm hires the most qualified people it can find and then expects them to craft their own careers within the company. According to the authors of *The 100 Best Companies to Work for in America*, Raychem is "a great place for self-starters," but "if you get lost here, you have to find your own way around."

A football-organization provides both a sense of stability and a feeling of reflected power—like belonging to the U.S. Marines. In terms of style, at least, the player at Anheuser-Busch can take vicarious pleasure in being part of a gestalt that includes Clydesdale horses and the slogan "King of Beers." In the same vein, as a long-time Exxon employee put it, "There's instant prestige when you say you work for Exxon." But the price for being in a football-organization is apt to be regimentation. Thus, even executives at Timken Company, the bearings manufacturer, have to punch time cards.

Regimentation may lead to alienation—especially if one is deep down in the hierarchy. Even in such a respected company at Caterpillar, there has been, as in so many other old-line, football-like manufacturers, "a split at the bottom of the executive chain." According to one plant manager who was interviewed in 1981, management's relations with workers "have been going downhill for 30 years, and it's going to take at least 10 years to turn them around." But whether or not corporate football "players" become alienated, they run the risk of depersonalization. Reflected power is an organizational property that often comes at the expense of individual identity.

A basketball-organization provides two mutually reinforcing pluses: stimulation and a true sense of group belongingness. Both of these qualities are captured in the enthusiasm of technical engineer Nick Larsen:

> There's an intensity to it that makes Silicon Valley exciting to work in. I was part of a team that went from watching a water buffalo in a rice field in Penang, to building a producing semiconductor plant in less than eight months. You get kind of cocky. Hell yes, this is the way to do it. You go around with your bony chest

sticking out and say, "If you were from General Motors, you couldn't make it in this Valley." We're the best there is.

But the negative side is all too familiar: physical and emotional exhaustion. Everett Rogers and Judith Larsen find that in Silicon Valley, which teems with basketball-organizations,

> working conditions—competition, the importance of being first to market a new product, peer pressure— encourage marathon "pushes." . . . Employees can get wrapped up in this team spirit, allow nothing in their lives but work, turned on to being part of a team that makes a supreme effort. They can do it once, maybe twice, but not more than that. Especially if a marathon effort doesn't succeed. Then they burn out, like the circuits with which they work.

Thus, although players on Apple Computer's Macintosh development team wore T-shirts that proclaimed, "Working 90 hours a week and loving every minute of it," sources inside the company revealed that fatigue and poor health were taking their toll.

Moreover, because of a basketball-organization's interdisciplinary character, members may experience role confusion. They may be called upon to perform a changing variety of functions that do not add up to a neatly defined role. At the extreme, role confusion may lead to career confusion as players become distanced from the state of the art in their respective disciplines—and uncertain whether their future lies within one discipline or across several.

We have touched a lot of bases. It is time to pull things together and see how all this material can be applied to your own situation. The accompanying chart summarizes the dimensions we have discussed.

This chart can be used as a checklist to analyze or "diagnose" your organization. It can be especially helpful in determining how consistent different individuals' perceptions are. I recommend a three-step process:

1. Define the current organization;

2. Define the desired organization; and

3. Decide on changes to move toward the desired organization.

A DIAGNOSTIC PROFILE

	BASEBALL	FOOTBALL	BASKETBALL
What Game Are We Playing?			
• Distinctive competence	Adding value through star performers	Reducing costs and/or complexity through global coordination	Innovating by combining resources in novel ways
What Game Are We Organized to Play?			
• Task Interdependence	Pooled	Sequential	Reciprocal
• Coordinating mechanism	Design of free-standing roles/units	Central planning and administration	Mutual adjustment
• Information system	Locally controlled	Centrally controlled	Distributed
• Reward system	Individualistic	Hierarchical	Mutualistic
• Geographical distribution	Widely dispersed	Somewhat clustered	Highly concentrated
What Game Does Our Style Suggest?			
• Dominant value	Self-reliance	Loyalty	Cooperation
• Teamwork	Situational	Systematic	Spontaneous
• Communications patterns	Two-way	One-way	Three-way
• Leadership style	Laissez-faire	Authoritarian	Facilitative
• Recruitment/ promotion/ development	From the outside	From within	Mixed
• Cultural bias	Diversity	Conformity	Compatibility
• Risk-taking posture	Risk-embracing	Risk-avoiding	Risk-accepting
• Effect of status symbols	Horizontal separation	Vertical separation	Integration

What Are the Advantages & Disadvantages of Our Game to the Individual Player?

• Advantages	Autonomy; visibility	Stability; reflected power	Stimulation; group belong-ingness
• Disadvantages	Isolation; self-exposure	Regimentation; depersonal-ization	Exhaustion; role confusion

If there is a significant difference of opinion about what game you are in, this will become immediately apparent. One of the strengths of the diagnostic profile is that it provides a lot of probes into the complex issue of organizational competence/design/behavior. The various categories and subcategories form a coherent whole so that it becomes impossible to achieve a consensus on organizational competence, for instance, without also agreeing on design and behavior. In other words, the profile shows just how interconnected organizational dimensions really are. It shows that you cannot seriously define what game you are playing without examining many facets of the organization.

Realistically, no organization is ever perfectly consistent across all the dimensions. But meaningful patterns should emerge from your analysis. If not, then the organization may be vacillating unknowingly between two games (or more), and succeeding in neither direction. At a minimum, you should be able to establish organizational priorities in terms of the three sports: Which model does the organization most resemble (first priority), and which does it least resemble (third priority)?

Once your organization has agreed on what its game is, the next step is to decide whether this is the appropriate game for the future. To make this assessment, respond to the diagnostic profile chart (page 151) a second time, substituting "should (be)" for "are" or "does." You might also want to review the strengths and weaknesses of the different sports models, as laid out in Chapter 7. After working through this process, you should be able to agree on a desired rank-ordering of the three sports models. If your desired priorities differ from those describing the current organization, then changes are needed. In fact, even if your desired priorities match actual priorities, change may still be necessary, given environmental uncertainty. That is, you may have to do some new things just to keep organizational priorities as they are, much as a ship in heavy seas must make repeated steering adjustments to keep on course.

As a way of graphically communicating the direction and

rough magnitude of change required, I have found it useful to array the sports models as points of an equilateral triangle, as shown in the following diagram.

SPORT TRIANGLE

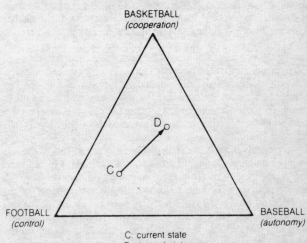

C: current state
D: desired state

The Sport Triangle is a variation of the diagram in Chapter 1 (page 15), which depicts the three sports as competing "pulls." The need to become more like a baseball team reflects the need for more *autonomy* ("Get the players right"); a football team, more *control* ("Get the plan right"); and a basketball team, more *cooperation* ("Get the process right"). Any blend of the three sports can be represented by a point inside the triangle. In the Sport Triangle, for example, point C indicates a hypothetical current state (in which an organization conforms to a football model), and point D a hypothetical desired state (a baseball/basketball hybrid). This visual display reinforces the need for change that has emerged from organizational diagnosis; it is a powerful way to condense an abundance of information.

It is now up to the organization to specify measures that will move it toward the preferred sports model(s). As a general guideline, any organization should strike a balance between (1) responding adequately and appropriately to the need for change and (2) its own capacity for change. Thus, the correct response

may range anywhere from gradual fine-tuning of a current
model to radical transformation into a new model—involving
significant changes for just about every dimension.

Whether the required change be large or small, there are
usually several actions an organization can take early on to
promote movement in the desired direction. One common change
is to alter the physical location of persons/units—for instance,
to bring closer together several scattered people who need to
play basketball. Communications patterns and, sometimes, information systems, also may lend themselves to ready change.
Of course, the matter of what is relatively easy and what is
difficult to change usually depends a lot on the situation. In
some cases status systems can be altered overnight; in other
cases, they may be almost impossible to change—as when the
entire physical facility is itself a status symbol (like the Transamerica Building).

The sports models can be applied at any organizational level,
to large units, and to small groups of individuals. I have found
the models particularly useful in patterning the behavior of
senior management teams. To wit: the plant manager of an
engineered products firm, an ardent believer in delegating decision making, had effectively filled out the lineup card for his
staff and then walked away. His managers—the players on his
team—frequently feuded over organizational priorities. Because some of these individuals had to share manufacturing
resources, scheduling problems continually arose. In all, the
players clamored for more control—that is, for more of the
qualities of a football coach in their boss.

Or consider the general manager of an old-line industrial
supplies firm, who insisted on dealing with his staff members
one-on-one—a baseball style. This pattern by itself was problematic because it meant that many important interdepartmental
issues were ignored. The style's negative effect was com-
pounded by the fact that the general manager communicated
in a one-way fashion—like a football coach. His staff felt a
compelling need for both more cooperation and more autonomy. The sports models helped this top management group
conceptualize—and thereby understand—the origin of their
frustrations. They were then able to begin to change their behavior as a team.

Still another example involved the top three levels of a
multidivisional high-technology company. The team was made

up of divisional heads, functional heads, and product-group managers. As complex as this team's dynamics were, many of its difficulties clearly stemmed from the behavior and expectations of its leader, the president. As one of the team members expressed it to this individual, with the rest of the team present: "You view us like star baseball players, try to control us like football players, and expect us to behave like a basketball team." The president accepted this characterization and resolved to do his part to change. It is doubtful that any abstract analysis could have had the impact that this concrete description did.

The use of sports models to describe and prescribe corporate behavior, of course, has limitations. I would never recommend trying to use this methodology as a comprehensive change program. Indeed, although the models do provide parallels for many organizational aspects, they say nothing about the most important dimension of all—purpose. And unless an organization is unequivocal about its purpose—its reason for existence—no amount of change is likely to be very effective.

Another caveat: Every organization must have some proficiency in each of the games—just as it must pay attention simultaneously to quality, cost, and innovation/flexibility, no matter which is number one. As important as it is to have your game priorities straight, a second or third priority is still a priority. Consider the case of Battelle Memorial Institute, the largest independent (fee-based) research laboratory in the United States. Battelle has long been a baseball-organization—an appropriate model for the task of research. But the institute has recently had to tighten management controls in order to make the transition from smokestack technologies to high-tech. Despite the irony—football-like controls to move beyond football-like industries—the Battelle example demonstrates the importance of balancing the pulls represented by the different sports. The baseball pull of antonomy had to be tempered with the football pull of control.

Although each sports model is a consistent configuration, nonsports organizations do have considerable choice with respect to their style regardless of what game they are playing. With this in mind, is one pattern more or less desirable than another? A glance at some of the language used to describe a football style suggests as much. Although a value like loyalty may be admirable in America today, many other aspects of a football style—authoritarianism, conformity, and vertical separation, for instance—are not.

Father truly knows best in football, as the litany of successful head coaches shows—from Chicago's legendary George "Papa Bear" Halas, the winningest coach in NFL history, to future legends like Don Shula. But how do players interact with such figures? The experience of Miami Dolphins running back Tony Nathan may be representative: "You sit in front of Coach Shula and it seems like your chair gets shorter. It was like that [at Alabama] with Coach [Bear] Bryant, too. You'd sit in that couch and sink lower and lower, and pretty soon you were looking up at him."

Although there are corporate situations that do call for a football style, so many others do not. Yet all too many contemporary organizations that are not playing football—literally or metaphorically—are being run as if they were. This is management of the past, not the future. We need new models.

9

It's a Whole New Ballgame

JACK TRAMIEL, OF Commodore International and Atari fame, lives by the credo, "Business is war." When Tramiel took over Atari, says vice-president Bruce Entin, "The guy was in command. He was kind of like a general." Among *Fortune*'s 1984 list of "the toughest bosses in America" is Robert Malott, chairman of FMC Corporation, who has declared, "Leadership is demonstrated when the ability to inflict pain is confirmed."

Is such behavior justified on economic grounds? Not according to *Fortune*, which found the financial performance of its toughest-boss firms to range "from superb to pathetic." Is such behavior commonplace? Absolutely. In fact it seems to be admired by many in management. Thus, one of the "toughest" managers that *Fortune* identified, Simon & Schuster's Richard Snyder, reportedly expressed "glee and delight" when he found out. In the same vein, we find books with titles like *Life and Death on the Corporate Battlefield* and *Corporate Combat* and advertisements like that of Signal Technology Inc., which features a computer forming the body of a tank, under the heading "How to run all over the competition for fun and profit."

The military metaphor is a hangover from industrial society—an era that peaked in significance forty years ago. In fact, it was the production bonanza of World War II that saw both the culmination of this era and the beginning of its decline. William S. ("Big Bill") Knudsen, who left the presidency of

General Motors to lead the war production program, was on
target when he claimed that the United States "smothered the
enemy in an avalanche of production." Yet the radar and sonar
technologies developed to fight the war—and Japan's need to
reconstruct its economy as a consequence of the war—signaled
the coming of postindustrial society. Clearly, we have by now
arrived at the postindustrial age, even if our dominant management philosophy has not.

We reached the postindustrial era in the mid-1950s, when,
for the first time, more people were in white-collar work than
in blue-collar production work. Most of the white-collar jobs
involve information processing—by managers, professionals,
technicians, and clerical workers. According to MIT's David
Birch, by 1984 only 10 percent of our population was actually
making things. And even in a high-tech growth area like
microelectronics, experts believe that future American jobs will
increasingly lie in design and development, not production.

John Naisbitt, in his best-seller, *Megatrends*, calls ours the
"information society," contrasting it with the industrial and
agricultural societies that preceded it. Naisbitt sums up our
progression in terms of the dominant occupations of each society; we have gone from farmer to laborer to clerk. Our "game,"
in his words, has changed from competing against nature, to
competing against fabricated nature, to needing to interact with
each other.

If the military metaphor ever had general applicability to
business—which is doubtful—it would have been during the
industrial era. To persist with this metaphor today may be
comfortable for some, but it is dangerous for all. In the view
of organizational theorist Karl Weick, "military images restrict
flexibility, encourage narrow solutions, assert nothing very interesting about organizations, and are self-perpetuating."

I believe that team sports represent a far richer and more
constructive management metaphor. This idiom provides the
breadth Weick advocates. And it does so by supplementing,
rather than scrapping, the military metaphor. The baseball-
football-basketball triad includes the military model in the form
of football; the triad simply reframes it in light of other, more
appropriate models.

A common criticism of team sports is that they encourage
and reward conflict, even to the point of being a kind of substitute for war. Many sports enthusiasts would say, "So what?
Better a substitute than the real thing!" But even if we ac-

knowledge the dangers and abuses in sports, there is no reason not to recognize their strengths as well—what team sports say about enthusiasm, hard work, perseverance, striving, cooperation. These positive qualities are present in all team sports. They can indeed be an inspiration. Bill Bradley summed it up as well as anyone: "Those who have ever played on a *team* never forget the excitement of their work or the fulfillment of a championship. Those who have watched on the night of a final game must sense that they have witnessed ultimate cooperation, that they have seen an unusual kind of sharing, that they have glimpsed a better world. . . ."

And despite such declarations as "Winning isn't everything; it's the only thing," the reality in team sports is quite different. Even for the best sports teams, losing is an inevitable part of the game. A successful pro season—usually guaranteeing a trip to the playoffs—is winning 95 of 162 games in major league baseball; 10 of 16 games in the National Football League; and 50 of 82 games in the National Basketball Association. In other words, a successful season means winning about 60 percent of the time and losing the other 40 percent. The better teams in all sports understand this and know how to take losing in their stride.

The lesson for business is not only that losses are a fact of life; it is also that some losing—or failure—is essential for long-term development. A corporation simply cannot improve if it does not attempt new things, and the more novel the try, the more likely it is to fail—but in the process, learning occurs. Sports at their best carry with them a spirit that has to do more with realizing one's own potential than defeating, much less "conquering," others. It is a spirit entirely consonant with that expressed by Edwin P. Land, the founder of Polaroid: "Our competition is our own sense of excellence."

True, certain sports have more to recommend them as models than others, and these are not necessarily the most influential. If we were to measure the relative influence of the major U.S. team sports on corporate America's thinking up until now, we would probably find the following rank-ordering: (1) football, (2) baseball, (3) basketball.

That football is number one stands to reason: If the dominant management metaphor is military, we would expect the most influential sport to be the most military in nature. Business language is laced with football allusions—running with the ball, goal-line stands, two-minute drills, Monday morning quarterbacking. Football is planning and control, coordination, consolidation, efficiency. It is also strong and macho. Decisive. Football is the world of the coach and the quarterback—and metaphorically, the world of business *managers*, those who call the shots. For this reason, football is also a model of conflict in business—between manager and managed—just like the real thing on the field.

If football is the archetypal industrial sport, baseball, America's number two sport, is preindustrial. Baseball still has wide appeal in business, for essentially two reasons. First it evokes a benign past—a time when things were not so complicated. People were craftsmen then; they knew how to do the whole job and took pride in their work. This is the quaintness that comic George Carlin has depicted in his well-known skit contrasting "pastoral" baseball and "technological" football.

The other appeal of baseball is the game's inherent individualism. Baseball is pluralistic; it permits a high degree of individual diversity and autonomy. Indeed, baseball is the John Wayne of team sports: free markets, pure competition, the unfettered individual taking on the world and making it on his own. This strain still runs deep in America; it has only been reinforced by recent governmental deregulation of such industries as transportation, financial services, and telecommunications.

Basketball is number three. Although it is the only one of the three sports that was invented in this country, basketball has yet to achieve the degree of general—or business—popularity that baseball and football have long enjoyed. I believe this is partly because we have not yet lived basketball the way we have lived the other sports. Basketball is postindustrial. In meaning as well as chronology, it is newer than football, just as football is newer than baseball. Basketball is *flow, process, spontaneity, chemistry*. Although some of these nouns are current business buzzwords, their deeper meaning has only begun to penetrate the corporate psyche. Basketball signifies a different kind of teamwork from the other sports—and eras: dynamic cooperation that transcends traditional boundaries. It is a game that represents where we are going more than where we have been.

Despite its current third-place standing in the United States, basketball is by far the most international of the three sports. According to *The Wall Street Journal*'s Frederick C. Klein, basketball is becoming "the most-played game worldwide, outstripping even soccer." Interestingly, soccer's growing popularity in the United States parallels that of basketball in the rest of the world. The two games have much in common: Both are fluid and flexible and require the players to coordinate themselves as a unit. Coincidentally, the first basketball ever used—by the game's inventor James Naismith—was a soccer ball.

It is worth noting that a fifth sport, ice hockey, offers a basic choice between football and basketball. In his book, *The Game*, former Montreal Canadiens goalie Ken Dryden contrasts two disparate styles of hockey: "dump and chase" and international. The *dump-and-chase* style is a possession game, low on generalist skills and high on physical intimidation. It is siege warfare—very close to football. By contrast, the *international* style is a transition game; it emphasizes multiple skills, passing, and spontaneous teamwork—like basketball. As Dryden shows, dump-and-chase hockey cannot compete with the international style.

Football Futures

Is football an obsolete organizational model? As a style of people-management, I believe it is. Consider two of the most flexible *and* successful teams in recent years—the 49ers under Bill Walsh and the Raiders under Tom Flores and owner Al Davis. These teams have won four of the last five Super Bowls (two apiece). Each is known for permitting more elbowroom than the league norm. The 49ers feature humor. Quarterback Joe Montana tells of a characteristic Walsh stunt: "Once, when we were losing in his first season and players were in and out all the time, he showed up in a taxidriver's cap and leather jacket, saying, 'Anyone need a lift out of town?'" The Raiders have a history of acquiring controversial players from other teams who then seem to blossom with their new squad.

But even in these clubs, the elbowroom takes place within a very tight structure. Despite the surface manifestations of freedom for each team, both are tightly organized outfits. They have to be. The nature of the sport just will not allow a coach to "let go" and still win. Thus, according to Walsh, the 49ers "play as controlled as any team in the NFL." A football team is, after all, a "paramilitary organization," as Al Davis likes to remind us. Corporations, however, are not—or at least they should not be.

Jean Fugett, a former tight end with the Cowboys and Redskins, describes the "fear factor" in pro football, much of which has to do with being evaluated microscopically: "Few fans will understand the terror felt by players watching game films. Every player is graded a plus or minus for every play. Some players lose their jobs before the film ends." Is there any real difference between this sentiment and that expressed below about computerized control of telephone workers?

> "You've got to meet the bogey," said Ann Crump, a union official in Milwaukee, referring to the time limit, usually about 30 seconds, that telephone operators are allotted for each call. "You can be as little as two seconds off and be unsatisfactory."
>
> "They have a printout on every move an operator makes," said Jo Dentino, who works in a directory assistance office in Woodbury, N.J. "I think that is too much."

Of course, an actual football team's stress and conflict can be productively displaced onto next week's opponent. But members of a corporation cannot respond this way. And the more cost-conscious their football-like company is, the more stress employees must cope with. In general, according to researcher Robert Karasek, "The higher the emphasis on volume and price, and not on quality, the higher the stress factor."

It is football's cerebral side that is and will remain most relevant to corporate management—no small irony given the intensely physical and emotional nature of the sport. Football is a far more useful model for system conceptualization than for people-management. Behavioral scientist P. G. Herbst has argued that the central organizational design task is to define a system's "minimal critical specifications." In other words, do not overspecify the system or organization up-front; leave it with the flexibility to adapt over time. But Herbst's message has another implication, and its importance is often missed: Make sure the specifications that are adopted are truly critical.

Above all, the specifications chosen should define organizational purpose and direction. The corporate football coach—or coaching staff—can play the role of a conceptual architect whose general design provides the boundaries for subsequent organizational development. The clearer senior management is in articulating its vision, the better the chance that the organization as a whole will have to play the appropriate game. Clear direction shows people the limits of their discretion; it therefore minimizes the need for senior management—indeed, all management—continually to reinterpret boundaries or to pick up the pieces that fall outside boundaries.

Boundary clarity is especially important because the name of the game—the pivotal business game—is no longer football. Writing in 1982, Harvard's Wickham Skinner notes a frenzy of shop-floor activity throughout the United States to reverse productivity stagnation. But he finds this activity to be fundamentally misdirected:

> Industrial management has gone back to basics. It's blocking and tackling again—the old game plan which led to American industrial leadership has been pulled off the shelf, dusted off and vigorously reapplied.
>
> The only trouble is that this time the old game plan doesn't seem to be working as well as it used to. The focus in U.S. industry has always been "productivity," and for 75 years the basic management approach to achieving it has been to rationalize, streamline, simplify, cut, squeeze, and apply the pressure. Top management is now returning to these basics. But the paradox is that the harder we seek and press for more productivity, the more elusive becomes the objective of recovering competitive strength.

What matters today, and even more tomorrow, is non-efficiency-based performance: quality, service, responsiveness, agility, innovation. One of the central findings of Thomas Peters and Robert Waterman's best-seller, *In Search of Excellence*, is that "for most top-performing companies something besides cost usually comes first." The models that business should follow are baseball and, especially, basketball. Outlines of these models are becoming increasingly visible in business.

Baseball Futures

In 1974, Wickham Skinner wrote a landmark article in the
Harvard Business Review titled "The Focused Factory." His
message was that a manufacturing plant can do an outstanding
job against only one or two criteria (such as quality *or* cost *or*
delivery) at the same time. Skinner's point was the factory
equivalent of Texas Instrument's belief that more than two
objectives is no objectives. He was responding to the tendency
of many manufacturing facilities to take on, over time, diverse
products that often carry with them different demands. When
this happens, the variety of products can become so great that
the plant loses its ability to make anything competitively.

Skinner's observation is having a continuing effect on American manufacturing strategy. More and more corporations are
reassessing the way they organize production and are deciding
to split complex shared facilities into several focused factories.
This thrust is toward freestanding or self-contained units—in
other words, toward baseball.

The drive toward focus may also be fueled by the difficulty
of competing against a host of smaller, more maneuverable
companies. Earlier, we saw how General Motors' Inland Division reorganized itself into eleven minicompanies to compete
successfully against such Mom-and-Pop operations. Kollmorgen Corporation's printed circuit boards division faced a similar
competitive challenge and chose a similar strategic tack. "The
problem," according to current division vice-president John A.
Endee, "was that by the time our salesman in the field conferred
with his regional sales manager, who would then confer with
the division sales manager, who then went to manufacturing
to schedule the order, 'Pop' had the boards made and delivered
to the customer." Kollmorgen responded with a strategy it dubbed
productization: Five separate product groups were set up, each
with its own sales force and manufacturing capability. It worked.
Inside a year, the division went from monthly sales of $280,000
to a monthly *profit* of $280,000.

Still another impetus for greater focus may be new-product
development. A case in point is NCR. This $3.7 billion com-
pany (1983 sales) has gone from a highly centralized structure
that frustrated the creation and launch of new products to a set
of self-contained divisions that face minimal red tape. Among

the divisions' many freedoms is the opportunity to buy from outside vendors as well as from each other.

One division in particular—the Data Entry Systems Division—has really taken focus to heart. Under the leadership of vice-president Donald E. Coleman, this 3,000-person division was split into five independent units of 500 to 1,000 people, each responsible for its own planning and numbers. Later, Coleman took the further step of dividing these units into thirteen autonomous subunits with annual sales that range from $10 million to $100 million. Says *Inc.*, "One consequence of all this—and a measure of the reorganization's success—is that 50% of the division's revenues last year [1983] came from products it did not sell the year before."

NCR's subunits—like Kollmorgen's product groups—are baseball players that thrive on their own. They had better. A baseball-organization, like baseball itself, spotlights the individual player directly. In the words of sportscaster (and former catcher) Joe Garagiola: "Baseball gives you every chance to be great. Then it puts every pressure on you to prove that you haven't got what it takes. It never takes away the chance, and it never eases up on the pressure." Or more simply, according to pitcher Gaylord Perry, "Do for yourself or do without."

Basic research—invention—is the seed corn of applied research, which is the seed corn of application. Edward E. David, president of Exxon Research & Engineering Company, argues, "As modern technology becomes more complex, basic research has never been more important to ensuring that we can pull the right white rabbit out of the hat at the right time." Baseball is the ideal model for managing basic researchers because baseball permits autonomy to coexist with teamwork.

An excellent corporate example is du Pont, which has researchers active in a number of arcane areas the commercial relevance of which is as yet unknown. In the words of Howard E. Simmons, Jr., vice-president for central research and development, "If someone wanted to research moon rocks, I'd only want to know why." Success in basic research depends more on creativity than on energy. For Simmons, the contrast between basic and applied research is like that between "a great painter and a commercial artist."

We are seeing more and more examples of intercorporate collaboration, in R & D and other areas. In 1984, *Business Week* did a special report on "reshaping the computer industry," in which it observed, "To survive, once fiercely independent companies—even former competitors—are scrambling to form alliances and partnerships to broaden their range of products." In fact, interfirm cooperation is an aspect of a more general phenomenon—networking. *Networking* represents the limited cooperation of autonomous players—individuals or organizations. It is baseball. Thus, Microelectronics and Computer Technology Corporation, better known as MCC, has brought together an impressive array of companies—including Boeing, Harris, Honeywell, Lockheed, 3M, RCA, and Sperry—to meet foreign competition in high technology. MCC head Bobby Ray Inman foresees collaborative projects occurring within such industries as energy, chemicals, and perhaps even steel: "We'll see a substantial surge in these joint ventures as a way of accelerating research no individual company would be willing to take [*sic*]."

As the world approaches Marshall McLuhan's vision of a "global village," the strict separation of organizations and sectors—business, governmental, educational—becomes less and less tenable. Societal problems are too complex to be solved by single initiatives. The advantage of networking is that it does not threaten the independent status of those taking part in the network; hence, companies can collaborate, when it is in their collective self-interest, without compromising their autonomy.

Ironically, a stark example of the consequences of not networking is provided by the high-tech mecca of Silicon Valley. Despite the successes of individual firms, their shared geographical setting now suffers from "a severe housing shortage, a lengthy commute by workers, and creation of a bimodal North County/South County work force characterized by socioeconomic inequality." The reason? According to Rogers and Larsen: "the greedy, self-serving forces of the sixteen communities, the thousands of companies, and the legions of on-the-make high-tech entrepreneurs."

Until now, most companies in Silicon Valley have confined themselves to competing with each other; that is, they have dealt only with the business problems of succeeding within the private sector. They now need to play baseball with each other and their host community—to network—in order to resolve problems that affect their shared context.

Basketball Futures

The state of the art in services is flexible teams that resemble basketball far more than they do football. People Express exemplifies the new emphasis. According to CEO Donald Burr, "Most major airlines have bureaucratic support structures, which they credit as responsible for their competitive edge. At People Express we put our money on the flexibility that comes from operating as a nonbureaucratic, entrepreneurial organization." At Harvard Business School, People Express is put forward as a prototype of advanced management practices. According to transportation professor D. Daryl Wyckoff, "Anyone who isn't studying People Express and the way they're managing people is out of their minds [sic]."

The same kind of flexible designs characterize leading-edge manufacturing. Just-in-time (JIT) production techniques are a good example. The essence of JIT is to minimize inventory by making sure parts arrive exactly when needed (not hours or days or weeks before), and to minimize setup time—that is, the time it takes to prepare a machine to process a certain part. In a nutshell, JIT converts a rigid, long-linked, hierarchically controlled sequence into a nimble, flexible process that is controlled by those who are where the action is—the supervisors and workers.

Workers are not stuck in fixed positions, but rather are able to move about to respond to bottlenecks or other production problems. And work stations tend to be physically close together so that workers can support each other. Because of this proximity, conveyors are not needed; workers can pass the work among themselves—a process that supervisors encourage. In fact, the supervisory model that JIT evokes is vintage Red Auerbach. In the view of former player and current Celtics coach K. C. Jones: "The thing about Red is that he would listen to you. . . . Red always allowed players to use their creativity."

Another model of flexible manufacturing is continuous-process production, as exemplified by the chemical industry. A *continuous-process* system is a series of operations that transform a liquid or gas—or "slurry"—into an end product. A useful way to visualize a continuous process is as a giant gaggle of pipes and vessels through which materials are altered as they pass. A familiar example is a refinery that takes raw crude and converts it into gas, oil, and various by-products.

Continuous-process production is actually the ultimate JIT system, in which "discrete products will ideally flow like water through the system." This vision of continuity suggests the continuous play—and scoring—of an NBA basketball game. But more significantly, it gets at the inherent nature of continuous-process production and the importance this mode places on flexibility.

Larry Hirschhorn has shown that the more technically sophisticated a continuous process becomes, the more it is subject to new errors: "Each increase in self-regulating capacity is matched by a new context that stretches the newly developed capacity to new limits." Hirschhorn uses the example of Three Mile Island to show that increasingly complex control systems invariably bring with them new vulnerabilities. In other words, there is no such thing as a perfect or a "fail-safe" production system.

What are the practical implications of this? To run and troubleshoot such a system requires highly skilled and *flexible* workers—as in JIT systems. The paradox in each case is that the more finely honed the system, the greater the reliance on worker capabilities. Workers must be able to learn and go on learning as they work, and they need to understand how the different jobs all fit together—just as basketball players, to succeed, need "court awareness," the ability to integrate everything that is happening on the court. This is the opposite of classic assembly-line logic, which tries to design worker discretion and collaboration out of the job. The new need is to play basketball. If anything, the future will see this need increase.

When most people talk about the need for more "teamwork" within their organizations, their implicit model is basketball. One of the most rudimentary organization development exercises is a "best/worst analysis," in which people are asked to list the qualities of the best and the worst organizations they have ever been a part of. I have run this exercise at virtually every organizational level, in a wide variety of companies. The results are always the same. The best organizations are invariably characterized by

- A common sense of direction
- Common goals
- Close teamwork

- Good communication among members
- A family atmosphere
- Group pride
- Shared successes

But does corporate reality usually correspond to this ideal? Nope. Reality—among management teams as well as worker teams—is often a far cry from the "best organization." Twenty-five years ago Douglas McGregor claimed, "Many executives who talk about their 'teams' of subordinates would be appalled to discover how low is the actual level of collaboration among them, and how high is the mutual suspicion and antagonism. Yet these same executives generally create the very conditions which would appall them if recognized."

Although the pattern described by McGregor may still be prevalent, a growing number of senior management teams are playing basketball. A good example is Renn Zaphiropoulos's former team at Versatec. Said Zaphiropoulos: "We spend a lot of time making sure that we cover for each other. If I go out of the office for a month, any one of the guys can run the whole show. They may not do it quite the way I would, but they have all the same information at their disposal, so they know roughly where the whole thing is going."

An even better example may be James River Graphics (JRG), a manufacturer of specialty coated products. In 1984, JRG Group Vice-President Karl V. Kraske and his staff committed themselves to playing basketball by forming a ten-person "management operating committee" responsible for consensually determining company policy. From then on, issues of company-wide concern—for example, product/market strategy, environmental responsibility, and personnel development—were worked out mutually through a give-and-take process. This committee extended basketball further into the organization by developing a "decision matrix" that showed which players—business unit managers, functional managers, and others—needed to interact for each major decision area. The decision matrix effectively created operating basketball-organizations throughout JRG's management ranks.

There is increasing evidence of basketball at the work system level. Hirschhorn estimated that in 1984 some 500 U.S. factories operated with autonomous or partially autonomous work teams—compared with just one in 1970. The role of the supervisor (when it exists) in such a design becomes one of a facilitator—like a basketball coach—instead of a controller and enforcer—like a football coach. Most scholars of work design believe that autonomous groups will eventually become the rule, not the exception.

There is also reason to believe that such teamwork is critical to developing truly novel products capable of transforming economies. Tohru Moto-oka, a Tokyo University professor, acknowledges that breakthroughs within disciplines like physics and mathematics will remain the province of individual thinkers—baseball players. But where research is interdisciplinary, a basketball approach is called for: "Some new scientific fields have become very complex. To create new breakthroughs, the cooperation of a group is needed. One person alone cannot change these fields very much anymore."

Basketball-style teamwork breaks boundaries; it cuts across hierarchical levels, disciplines, functions, and often locations. It is fluid, even spontaneous. This kind of teamwork is rooted in the small group. Indeed, for Peters and Waterman, "small groups are, quite simply, the basic organizational building blocks of excellent companies." As our organizational environments become ever more complex and dynamic, the relevance of basketball-style teamwork will only increase.

British economist E. F. Schumacher heralded a wave with the 1973 publication of his book *Small Is Beautiful*. In the decade-plus since, American corporations have increasingly seen the value of thinking small. Perhaps the most powerful symbol of "downsizing" is the digital computer. Not only has this instrument itself shrunk almost unimaginably, and continuously, it has also played a critical role in organizational downsizing. Microcomputers have made it possible to eliminate excessive managerial layers previously needed to coordinate lower level activities. And computer-aided design (CAD) and manufacturing (CAM) have allowed companies to reduce the size of many machines, and their facilities as a whole.

These tendencies will no doubt continue. They may even accelerate, since we are on the verge of seeing a new generation of computers—computers that can execute calculations in parallel, rather than in serial fashion as is the case with the current generation. The advent of such a computer would thus mirror—as well as contribute to—what may be the dominant production thrust of the information era: the compression of long-linked sequences. Or in sports terms, the movement away from football's linear sequence of "forward" (that is, one-way) passing, to basketball's pattern of all-around passing.

A football-organization example shows the transition that is necessary today. A major company with which I'm familiar designed and built a 1 million-square-foot manufacturing/office facility in the late 1960s. This plant was an industrial engineer's dream. Everything was geared to full-bore volume and efficiency: two thousand people's tasks blueprinted to mesh—truly a world-class production machine (long before the expression *world-class* appeared). It bombed. The design could tolerate no surprises, which would have been fine if all the plant's products had been standard, off-the-shelf varieties. But few were. Although the major components of most products were standardized, customers typically requested custom features. In short order the new plant became overrun by expediters crisscrossing the floor trying to find jobs and get them completed. And labor relations were dreadful. Workers had absolutely no sense of human scale in the monolith; they responded predictably by repeatedly going out on strike.

This plant was eventually salvaged by dividing it into several *neighborhoods:* clusters of work that were relatively self-contained so that workers could have some feeling of belonging. But even this solution fell short of performance expectations. Management later admitted that the place was just too big.

This brief history illustrates, by exception, many of the reasons that small has become beautiful in terms of factory—and office—size. Thus minimills like Nucor Corporation and Chaparral Steel Company are thriving in the otherwise anemic domestic steel industry, in good part because they are designed to be fast on their feet. Both have minimal management staffs and feature profit/production-sharing plans that cover all employees—managers and workers alike. Explains Nucor maintenance technician Rod Zilles, "When something goes down, people ask me how they can help. Nobody sits around. Every minute you are down, it's like dollars out of your back pocket. So everybody really hustles."

Minimills are based on the concept of the small group. Raritan River Steel Company, for example, demonstrates the ability to mobilize multiple skills with the fluidity of a basketball team. Says George Mischenko, vice-president and general manager of steel production, "We're able to diversify people's jobs. An operator might pull maintenance. A welder might tap a furnace. An electrician might help a mechanic. This is a team effort. People are always moving here." The image is of crisp ball-movement, with each player constantly looking for the open man—the essence of basketball.

One of the most compelling examples of small size anywhere in corporate America is 3M. Although 3M employs over 50,000 people in the United States, its average plant size in 1982 was only 270 people. The company believes a unit loses vitality if it gets too big. But the "small" philosophy is applied not just to production facilities and workers. Managers and professionals typically work on product/market-based project teams of twelve or fewer people. According to Robert M. Adams, 3M's vice-president for research and development, "One consistent request we get from our people is that they be allowed to run a business of their own. Our project system gives a lot of them the chance to do just that."

The Baseball/Basketball Hybrid: America's New Winner

As we saw in Chapter 5, 3M is a prime example of a baseball/basketball hybrid. In fact, many of the companies that we have discussed in terms of either baseball or basketball—for example, NCR, Kollmorgen, American Express, and NEC—are actually a combination of these two models. I believe that the baseball/basketball design has general relevance for a wide range of organizations, and is especially appropriate as organizations grow to a size that tests the limits of a basketball design. As another airline CEO said of People Express's Donald Burr in early 1985: "He's passed a point of critical mass. There's a point where structure counts. It's great to be an entrepreneur and provide direction. But when you get big you've got to delegate. Believe me, I learned the hard way."

The core issue, in the words of Wharton's Russell Ackoff, "is one of designing corporations to simultaneously minimize the interdependence of their parts and maximize their inclination to interact cooperatively." A baseball design minimizes the interdependence of parts; a basketball design maximizes the likelihood of voluntary cooperation among them.

Baseball and basketball are malleable designs that complement each other. Baseball is essentially modular, so that parts can be added or subtracted without serious effects on the whole.

Basketball, although anything but modular, is a highly adaptive form that can mobilize its parts' capabilities rapidly in novel ways. Together, these two designs provide a powerful repertoire of responses for dealing with the dynamic, uncertain environment corporations increasingly face.

The most general baseball/basketball model involves playing baseball *between* groups and basketball *within* groups. An increasingly familiar form is the company made up of several small basketball-organizations (business units, product teams, focused factories, profit centers, autonomous work teams, whatever) that are tightly connected internally, but are only loosely connected externally, that is, to each other—like players on a baseball team. Conceptually similar is the automated office consisting of several multifunctional work stations that are flexibly linked together—perhaps through a local area network. In fact, the growing importance of "local networking" is revealed by the language of David M. Wood, IBM's director of office systems and marketing services (National Accounts Division): "It's a whole new ball game. We're selling connectivity."

The nature of the organization, though, is only part of the picture; What about people in the organization? Here, especially, both baseball and basketball designs offer something different from football. As we have seen, football reinforces player dependence on the wisdom and initiative of the coach; the player's job is to carry out his narrow piece of the coach's plan. Decision making is driven upward. The corporate football player is vulnerable, psychologically, in the same way the professional football player is. Each is instrumental to his team, not vice versa. The effect of such dependence is seen most vividly when the corporate player finds himself out of a job and forced, perhaps for the first time in his life, to take the initiative in finding another one.

Business Week, in a recent article about white-collar unemployment in smokestack football-organizations, claims that many individuals "lost not only their jobs but the assumptions that had defined their lives. A substantial number of the more than 1 million displaced white-collar workers had taken pride in working for such important, Rock-of-Gibraltar companies as U.S. Steel, John Deere, or Firestone Tire & Rubber." According to Ronald A. Graf, director of Bethlehem Steel's outplacement center in Lackawanna, New York, that firm's white-collar work force had become paralyzed by dependence:

"These people were so damn loyal they couldn't see what was happening. They couldn't take their lives into their own hands."

In contrast to football, baseball reinforces player independence—the autonomy to act on one's own. Decision making is driven downward. Although players in a baseball-organization may go overboard in using this freedom, at least their individualism is preserved. In a sense, the organization is instrumental to them; it is there to support their own initiatives.

For its part, basketball reinforces player interdependence—voluntary cooperation. Decision making is driven across the organization. Player and team are instrumental to each other, and individual needs are met through the process of meeting team goals. Both baseball and basketball designs are really about self-management—of individuals and of groups, respectively. Taken together, these two sports models constitute "networked teamwork." We need more of this in corporate America today.

The era of the grand game plan is over. In a world that moves faster and less predictably every day, top management no longer has the time or information to script all the plays. Neither can organizations continue to neglect the enormous resource offered by self-motivated groups and individuals. We are entering a future that will increasingly reward flexibility and responsiveness, spontaneous teamwork and invention. Perhaps, if all of us in business can better understand the game we need to play, we will have less need for game plans dictated from on high.

APPENDIX 1

THEORETICAL LINKAGES

My theoretical framework* for developing the sports models was Thompson's (1967) three forms of task interdependence: pooled, sequential, and reciprocal. As I progressed in my work, it became clear that the sports models overlap a significant portion of the organizational design and behavior literature. One of the most striking points of intersection is with Galbraith's (1973) generic organization design strategies—creation of self-contained tasks, investment in vertical information systems, and creation of lateral relations. (Galbraith's fourth "strategy," creation of slack resources, is a form of strategy by default, as it implicitly or explicitly accepts reduced performance; in my terms, this option represents a nonteam.) This likeness is not surprising, because Galbraith himself was strongly influenced by the work of Thompson.

Another close parallel is with Ouchi's (1979, 1980) three control mechanisms: markets, bureaucracies, and clans. The following chart, although oversimplified and far from exhaustive, conveys a sense of the commonality between the sports models and these and other theoretical constructs in the fields of organizational design, behavior, strategy, and planning.

Let me make the following qualifications with respect to this chart. Basketball is not the *average* of baseball and football;

*Author citations in Appendix 1 refer to the bibliographic references contained at the end.

175

Sports Models in Relation to Other Theoretical Constructs

THEORIST	CONCEPT	LIKENESS:		
		BASEBALL	FOOTBALL	BASKETBALL
Thompson (1967)	Task interdependence	Pooled	Sequential	Reciprocal
Galbraith (1973)	Organization design strategy	Creation of self-contained tasks	Investment in vertical information systems	Creation of lateral relations
Ouchi (1979, 1980)	Control mechanism	Market	Bureaucracy	Clan
Ouchi (1984)	Organizational type	H-form	U-form	M-form
Vancil (1978)	Organizational form	Decentralized divisional	Centralized functional	Matrix
Herbst (1976)	Group organization	Network	Bureaucratic hierarchical	Composite autonomous; matrix
Segal (1974)	Type of organization	Mediatively structured	Chain-structured	Adaptively structured
Scott (1981)	Organization as system	Natural	Rational	Open
Miles & Snow (1978, 1984)	Organizational adaptation type	Prospector	Defender	Analyzer
Lawrence & Dyer (1983)	Organizational readaptation outcome	Innovation	Efficiency	Member involvement
Porter (1980, 1985)	Generic strategy	Differentiation	Cost-leadership	Focus
Greiner (1972)	Organizational growth stage	Creativity; delegation	Direction; coordination	Collaboration

		Fluid pattern	Specific pattern	Transitional pattern
Abernathy & Utterback (1975)	Product/process innovation	Fluid pattern	Specific pattern	Transitional pattern
Peters & Waterman (1982)	"Pillar of structure"	Entrepreneurship	Stability	Breaking old habits
Huseman & Alexander (1979)	Coordination	By feedback	By plan	By lateral interaction
Mintzberg (1979)	Coordinating mechanism	Standardization of skills and outputs	Standardization of work; direct supervision	Mutual adjustment
Goldhar & Jelinek (1983)	Manufacturing technology	Independent tools and methods	Dedicated systems	Flexible systems; progammable systems
Miller & Friesen (1984)	Adaptive device	Formal structural	Information processing	Interpersonal
Etzioni (1961)	Control/involvement	Utilitarian/remunerative	Coercive/alienative	Normative/moral
Hirschman (1970)	Response to decline	Exit	Loyalty	Voice
Ackoff (1974)	Organizing problem	Environmentalization	Self-control	Humanization
Friend, Power, & Yewlett (1974)	Planning uncertainty	About operating environment	Of policy	About related choices
Trist (1976)	Planning philosophy	Disjointed incrementalism	Comprehensive planning	Adaptive planning
Schwartz & Ogilvy (1979)	Order:chaos relation	Anarchy	Hierarchy	Heterarchy

hence Ouchi's (1984) M-form organization bears less resemblance to basketball than do his H-form and U-form patterns to baseball and football, respectively. Neither is basketball the *sum* of baseball and football; thus, for instance, Miles and Snow's (1978, 1984) "analyzer" type is less like a basketball-organization than their "prospector" and "defender" types are like baseball- and football-organizations, respectively. In abstract terms, c is neither $(a + b)/2$ nor $a + b$. This distinction has relevance both for issues expressed along one dimension (such as the endless centralization versus decentralization debate) and for those expressed along two dimensions (as in a 2 $\times$ 2 or 3 $\times$ 3 matrix) because it suggests the importance of considering new options outside the single continuum or dual continua.

References

Abernathy, W. J., and Utterback, J. (1975). "A Dynamic Model of Product and Process Innovation." *Omega* 3 (6): 639–57.

Ackoff, R. L. (1974). *Redesigning the Future*. New York: Wiley.

Etzioni, A. (1961). *A Comparative Analysis of Complex Organizations*. New York: The Free Press.

Friend, J. K., Power, J. M., and Yewlett, C. J. (1974). *Public Planning: The Inter-Corporate Dimension*. London: Tavistock.

Galbraith, J. R. (1973). *Designing Complex Organizations*. Reading, Mass.: Addison-Wesley.

Goldhar, J. D., and Jelinek, M. (1983). "Plan for Economies of Scope." *Harvard Business Review* 61 (6): 141–48.

Greiner, L. E. (1972). "Evolution and Revolution as Organizations Grow." *Harvard Business Review* 50 (4): 37–46.

Herbst, P. G. (1976). *Alternatives to Hierarchies*. Leiden, Holland: Martinus Nijhoff.

Hirschman, A. O. (1970). *Exit, Voice, and Loyalty*. Cambridge, Mass.: Harvard University Press.

Huseman, R. C., and Alexander, E. R. III (1979). "Communication and the Managerial Function: A Contingency Approach." In *Readings in Organizational Behavior: Dimensions of Management Actions*. Edited by R. C. Huseman and A. B. Carroll. Boston: Allyn & Bacon.

Lawrence, P. R., and Dyer, D. (1983). *Renewing American*

Industry. New York: The Free Press.

Miles, R. E., and Snow, C. C. (1978). *Organizational Strategy, Structure, and Process.* New York: McGraw-Hill.

——. (1984). "Designing Strategic Human Resources Systems." *Organizational Dynamics* 13 (1): 36–52.

Miller, D., and Friesen, P. H. (1984). *Organizations: A Quantum View.* Englewood Cliffs, N.J.: Prentice-Hall.

Mintzberg, H. (1979). *The Structuring of Organizations.* Englewood Cliffs, N.J.: Prentice-Hall.

Ouchi, W. G. (1979). "A Conceptual Framework for the Design of Organizational Control Mechanisms." *Management Science* 25 (9): 833–48.

——. (1980). "Markets, Bureaucracies, and Clans." *Administrative Science Quarterly* 25 (1): 129–41.

——. (1984). *The M-Form Society: How American Teamwork Can Recapture the Competitive Edge.* Reading, Mass.: Addison-Wesley.

Peters, T. J., and Waterman, R. H. Jr. (1982). *In Search of Excellence: Lessons from America's Best-Run Companies.* New York: Harper & Row.

Porter, M. E. (1980). *Competitive Strategy: Techniques for Analyzing Industries and Competitors.* New York: The Free Press.

——. (1985). *Competitive Advantage: Creating and Sustaining Superior Performance.* New York: The Free Press.

Scott, W. R. (1981). *Organizations: Rational, Natural, and Open Systems.* Englewood Cliffs, N.J.: Prentice-Hall.

Segal, M. (1974). "Organization and Environment: A Typology of Adaptability and Structure." *Public Administration Review* 34: 212–20.

Schwartz, P., and Ogilvy, J. (1979). *The Emergent Paradigm: Changing Patterns of Thought and Belief.* Menlo Park, Calif.: SRI International.

Thompson, J. D. (1967). *Organizations in Action.* New York: McGraw-Hill.

Trist, E. L. (1976). "Action Research and Adaptive Planning." In *Experimenting with Organizational Life.* Edited by A. W. Clark. London: Plenum.

Vancil, R. F. (1978). *Decentralization: Managerial Ambiguity by Design.* Homewood, Ill.: Dow Jones–Irwin.

APPENDIX 2

SPORTS' PAY STRUCTURES

According to Michael Janovsky in *The New York Times* (September 2, 1984, p 8E), average player salaries in 1983 were as follows:

- Major League baseball $289,194
- NFL football $126,500
- NBA basketball $305,000

The first thing that is striking is how close the baseball and basketball figures are to each other, and how far they are from the average football salary. Although there are myriad possible explanations for this disparity (team size, player mobility, and popularity of the sport, among others), it does reflect the fact that both baseball and basketball are more player-oriented sports than football.

In March 1983, *Sport* magazine first published an annual list of the one hundred highest paid athletes in professional sports. Taken together, the 1983 and 1984 lists include 208 athletes, 172 of whom are from baseball, football, or basketball. After averaging the two years and accounting for the number of players in each sport, we see that baseball had the highest proportion of players in this category—about one in ten. Basketball was not far behind, with about one in fifteen, whereas football had less than one in two hundred. The following chart shows the distribution of this "top 86" relative to the number of players in each sport. Baseball is truly for the star player.

Now consider hierarchy. Using *Sport*'s 1983 and 1984 lists of the top ten salaries in each sport, we find that high pay is less evenly distributed among different positions in football than in the other two sports. The top twenty salaries in baseball are spread among seven of the sport's nine positions (excluding designated hitter); basketball's top twenty include all three positions—with as many forwards represented as centers. In football, however, nineteen of the top twenty-two salaries went to offensive players who handle the ball—quarterbacks, running backs, and pass receivers; in fact eleven of the twenty-two were quarterbacks. Not one offensive lineman, defensive lineman, or defensive back made either list. This pattern clearly reflects football's hierarchical character.

DISTRIBUTION OF "TOP 86" PLAYER SALARIES—
Baseball, Football, and Basketball
During 1983 and 1984

	MAJOR LEAGUE BASEBALL	NFL FOOTBALL	NBA BASKETBALL
Number of players among top 86 (average for two-year period)*	63	4**	19
Number of players in league†	650	1,372	276
Percentage of players in league among top 86	9.7	Less than 1	6.9

*Source: *Sport* magazine's "The Sport 100" (March 1983; March 1984).
**This figure includes two players from the USFL.
†Based on number of teams in league × roster size (baseball = 26 × 25; football = 28 × 49; basketball = 23 × 12).

Further evidence of this bias is provided by a March 1984 *Sport* listing of the six highest paid professional coaches, irrespective of sport. The top four were all from football, with number five from baseball and number six from basketball. It is instructive to compare the salary of the highest paid coach (manager) in each sport with the corresponding average player salary. We find that in baseball and basketball the highest paid manager/coach made only slightly more (1.2 times as much in baseball; 1.1 times as much in basketball) than the average player in those sports. In football, by contrast, the highest paid head coach made more than four times as much as the average player. Football is unequivocally a coach's sport.

Finally, basketball has a more even pay distribution (stars: nonstars) then either baseball or football based on the average "top 10" salary as a multiple of the average salary for the rest of the league. The details are shown in the chart below.

AVERAGE PLAYER SALARIES
in Relation to "Top Ten" Player Salaries and Highest Paid Coaches' Salaries

	MAJOR LEAGUE BASEBALL	NFL FOOTBALL	NBA BASKETBALL
Number of players in league	650	1,372	276
Average league salary*	$289,194	$126,500	$305,000
Total league salaries	$187,976,100	$173,558,000	$84,180,000
Total "Top Ten" salaries**	$13,540,000	$6,337,292†	$10,964,750
Total league salaries less total "Top Ten" salaries	$174,436,100	$167,220,708	$73,215,250
Average "Top Ten" salary	$1,354,000	$633,729	$1,096,475
Average league salary exclusive of "Top Ten"	$272,556	$122,776	$275,245

Average "Top Ten" salary as multiple of average salary for rest of league	5.0	5.2	4.0
Salary of highest paid coach (manager) in league	$333,333	$540,000	$325,000
Salary of highest paid coach (manager) as multiple of average league salary for players	1.2	4.3	1.1

*Source: *The New York Times* (September 2, 1984).
**Source: *Sport* magazine's "The Sport 100" (March 1983; March 1984).
†This figure includes the salaries of two players from the USFL.

Although it is hazardous to generalize from this top-end sample to the overall pay structure of each sport, the patterns are fascinating—and highly suggestive for business.

NOTES

Introduction

PAGE

1 "Turning the workplace": Andrew S. Grove, *High Output Management* (New York: Random House, 1983), p. 171.

1 the three major team sports: Combined professional and collegiate attendance in the U.S. during 1983 was 78.1 million for baseball, 54.4 million for football, and 41.7 million for basketball. The fourth most popular team sport was ice hockey, which drew 20.3 million (*U.S. News & World Report*, August 13, 1984, p. 26).

1. The Corporate Team

6 "Baseball is a team game": Pete Rose, quoted by Tom Callahan, "Savoring the Extra Innings After 40," *Time* (July 26, 1982), p. 55.

6 "The game's not over": Yogi Berra, quoted by Kevin Nelson, *Baseball's Greatest Quotes* (New York: Fireside/ Simon & Schuster, 1982), p. 190.

7 Football involves about twice as many: In football there are 22 players on the field at any one time (11 offensive versus 11 defensive); in baseball there are anywhere between 10 (9 on defense plus the batter) and 13 (when the bases are loaded).

7 Apart from turnovers: Actually transitions represent a

184

fourth component. Placekicking—of extra points after touchdowns, and of field goals—is the third component.

8 "A football team is a lot like": George Allen, quoted in Studs Terkel, *Working* (New York: Pantheon/Random House, 1972), p. 388.

8 Football-equivalents: The concept of long-linked technology is treated at length in James D. Thompson, *Organizations in Action* (New York: McGraw-Hill, 1967).

11 In the other sports: Thomas Boswell generalizes this fact by declaring that "In baseball, all moments are not of equal value, or even equal potential," in *How Life Imitates the World Series* (New York: Penguin Books, 1983), p. 71.

11 This theory argues that: *Ibid.*

11 "in world diplomacy and baseball": Peter Pascarelli, "POWER: The World Series Ticket," *Inside Sports* (November 1983), p. 48.

12 "Why do teams": Bill James, *The Bill James Baseball Abstract, 1984* (New York: Ballantine Books, 1984), pp. 246–47.

12 But it has three or four: If a team has failed to gain a first down after three tries, it may use the fourth down to punt the ball away.

12 "If football . . .": Fran Tarkenton, *Playing to Win* (New York: Harper & Row, 1984), p. 68.

12 "don't go for 15": *Ibid.*, p. 69.

13 "statistically speaking": Bud Wilkinson, *Sports Illustrated Football: Quarterback* (New York: Sports Illustrated, 1976), p. 80.

13 Scoring in baseball: There are, of course, exceptions to these tendencies. For example, Walter Alston's Los Angeles Dodgers in the 1960s were notorious for eking out close wins by improbably combining singles, sacrifices, stolen bases, and other incremental plays. Alternatively, the NFL's Los Angeles (formerly Oakland) Raiders have always been known as a "big-play" team.

14 "I never understood": The following account is taken from Robert W. Keidel, "Baseball, Football, and Basketball: Models for Business," *Organizational Dynamics* (Winter 1984), p. 11; and Robert W. Keidel and Michael J. Umen, "Winning Plays in the R&D Game," *Pharmaceutical Executive* (February 1984), pp. 42–44.

2. Filling Out the Lineup Card: Baseball

17 "Baseball is the American": J. G. Taylor Spink, quoted in Nelson, *Quotes*, p. 16.

17 "Baseball is almost": Bill Veeck, quoted in Lee Green, *Sportswit* (New York: Harper & Row, 1984), p. 27.

17 "Whoever wants to know": Jacques Barzun, quoted in Nelson, *Quotes*, p. 13.

18 it had become "America's...": Stuart Berg Flexner, *Listening to America* (New York: Simon & Schuster, 1982), p. 37.

19 "a baseball game follows": Stanley Cohen, *The Man in the Crowd: Confessions of a Sports Addict* (New York: Random House, 1981), p. 180.

19 "What I thought scouting": Gary Nickels, quoted in Kevin Kerrane, "Diamonds in the Rough," *Sports Illustrated* (March 19, 1984), p. 79.

20 *Sports Illustrated*: Dan Jenkins, quoted in *The Philadelphia Inquirer*, December 2, 1984, p. 2E.

20 "We are operating exactly": Yohan Cho, quoted by Myron Magnet, "Acquiring Without Smothering," *Fortune* (November 12, 1984), p. 26.

21 "I think the competition": Mary Kay Ash, *Mary Kay* (New York: Harper & Row, 1981), p. 19.

21 "The New York Yankees": Mary Kay Ash, *Mary Kay on People Management* (New York: Warner Books, 1984), p. 109.

21 "INTERVIEWER: What's the secret": Earl Weaver, quoted in Nelson, *Quotes*, p. 151.

22 "I have nothing against": Earl Weaver (with Terry Pluto), *Weaver on Strategy* (New York: Collier Books/Macmillan, 1984), p. 58.

22 He was able ... to weave: Earl Weaver (with Barry Stainback), *It's What You Learn After You Know It All That Counts* (New York: Fireside/Simon & Schuster, 1982), pp. 266–67.

22 "I still think it was": Bill James, *The Bill James Baseball Abstract* (New York: Ballantine Books, 1983), p. 166.

22 "Baseball is pitching": Earl Weaver, quoted in Boswell, *Life Imitates*, p. 60.

22 Consider Julien J. Studley: This example is taken from

John A. Byrne, "Think You're Tough? Try Selling," *Forbes* (December 17, 1984), pp. 205–206.

23   "Sometimes I feel like": *Ibid.*, p. 206.

23   Sportswriter Jimmy Cannon: Jack Cannon and Tom Cannon, eds., *Nobody Asked Me, But . . . The World of Jimmy Cannon* (New York: Penguin Books, 1983), p. 28.

23   "of all team sports": John Updike, "Hub Fans Bid Kid Adieu," *The New Yorker* (October 22, 1960); reprinted in Howard Siner, ed., *Sports Classics* (New York: Coward-McCann, 1983), p. 200.

23   Of the three sports: Baseball is the only one of the three sports in which the umpires (officials) outweigh the players. According to the research staff at the National Baseball Hall of Fame in Cooperstown, New York, the average weight of major league umpires at the start of the 1983 season was 207.8 pounds (personal communication).

23   "Any deviation from the 'usual'": Marvin Cohen, *Baseball the Beautiful* (New York: Links Books, 1974), p. 72.

24   Conglomerates clearly have a lot: The following material relies heavily on Kenneth N. M. Dundas and Peter R. Richardson, "Implementing the Unrelated Product Strategy," *Strategic Management Journal 3* (1982): 287–301.

24   Operating units "on the team": Excluded from my definition of *conglomerate* are two varieties in which the operating units are tightly controlled from above. The first type has a massive headquarters staff that constantly audits and challenges unit managers; this type is exemplified by ITT under former chief executive officer (CEO) Harold Geneen. The second type divides operating units into neat categories based on whether they are cash-users and/or cash-producers. Under such a "portfolio" system, unit actions can be highly interdependent financially, and their behavior is often orchestrated by senior management at headquarters, much like that of football-organizations.

24   These units are likely: This is not to say that such units are totally independent of each other. Clearly, they compete for corporate resources and in some cases, compete fiercely. But apart from this vital area, units enjoy considerable operating freedom. Dundas and Richardson, "Implementing" (p. 297), cite the following reasons for operating unit independence from each other: "First, the

capital allocation and performance evaluation processes are made easier. More importantly, when problems arise, they are easier to spot and deal with. In the limit, if a division is viewed as expendable, the divestment decision affects only a clearly identifiable business unit."

24 "almost every act": Boswell, *Life Imitates*, p. 246.

24 "Other sports have": *Ibid.*, p. 75.

24 "Only in baseball can a team": Branch Rickey, quoted in Bob Chieger, *Voices of Baseball* (New York: Atheneum, 1983), p. 4.

24 "The key to running": Royal Little, "Conglomerates Are Doing Better than You Think," *Fortune* (May 28, 1984), p. 50.

25 "You run the show": "How Bob Pritzker Runs a $3 Billion Empire," *Business Week* (March 7, 1983), p. 65.

25 "How Bill Farley could *swing*": Advertisement in *Forbes* (October 24, 1983), p. 74.

26 According to Bill James: Quoted by Daniel Okrent, "He Does It By the Numbers," *Sports Illustrated* (May 25, 1981), p. 45.

26 "When the Baltimore Canyon": Daniel D. Holt, "How Amoco Finds All That Oil," *Fortune* (September 8, 1980), p. 56.

26 "He lets you run": *Ibid.*, p. 54.

26 "[Amoco] likes to drill": *Ibid.*, p. 51.

26 In fact, the company: *Ibid.*, p. 52.

26 "The company's biggest problem": *Ibid*.

27 "There's no training": Robert Levering, Milton Moskowitz, and Michael Katz, *The 100 Best Companies to Work for in America* (Reading, Mass.: Addison-Wesley, 1984), p. 55.

27 "The kind of people": *Ibid.*, p. 54.

27 Trammell Crow himself: Quoted by G. Bruce Knecht, "Equitable's Player in the Real Estate Sweepstakes," *The New York Times*, July 1, 1984, p. 7F.

27 William Jovanovich: Quoted by Evan Hunter, "Why Authors Are Singing the Mid-List Blues," *The New York Times Book Review*, April 8, 1984, p. 12.

27 William Morrow's Lawrence Hughes: *Ibid*.

27 "In this business, we basically back": William R. Hambrecht, quoted in "Betting Big on a Computer System for Managers," *Business Week* (March 26, 1984), p. 134.

28   "When the San Francisco Giants": Michael Moritz, "Arthur Rock: 'The Best Long-Ball Hitter Around,'" *Time* (January 23, 1984), p. 55.

28   "There are only a few rules": Don Gamache, quoted by Maria Fisher, "The Genius Within," *Forbes* (March 12, 1984), p. 189.

28   "They earned the title": Advertisement in *Newsweek* (August 11, 1980), p. 6.

29   the term *basic research*: George F. Mechlin and Daniel Berg, "Evaluating Research—ROI Is Not Enough," *Harvard Business Review* (September–October 1980), p. 94.

29   "One of the things that people": Arno Penzias, quoted by Rosalind Williams, "Are Scientists Different?" *The New York Times Book Review*, October, 14, 1984. p. 15.

29   "Mauch lives the game": Thomas Boswell, *Why Time Begins on Opening Day* (Garden City, N.Y.: Doubleday, 1984), p. 96.

29   Earl Weaver's response: *Ibid.*

29   "Our goal is to be seen": Richard Gelb, quoted in "Bristol-Myers Bucks the Odds in Search of a Blockbuster Drug," *Business Week* (October 29, 1984), p. 140.

30   Such isolation may be appropriate: It may be appropriate, that is, to a point. Beyond the factory, isolation leads to implosion, as happened with U.S. automakers in the early 1970s when they failed to appreciate the strength of the Japanese challenge.

30   *Individual-based service*: Excluded here are approaches to service that effectively "industrialize" the process. See, for example, Theodore Levitt's articles, "Production-Line Approach to Service," *Harvard Business Review* (September–October 1972); and "The Industrialization of Service," *Harvard Business Review* (September–October 1976). Richard B. Chase, in "Where Does the Customer Fit in a Service Operation?" *Harvard Business Review* (November–December 1978), describes the contrast in terms of "high-contact" and "low-contact" systems. Industrialized service (low-contact/low-individual-discretion) will be treated in Chapter 3 under the rubric *system-based* service.

30   Two implications follow: The following points are elaborated by Peter K. Mills and Dennis J. Moberg in "Perspectives on the Technology of Service Operations,"

Academy of Management Review (July 1982), pp. 470–71.

31 "Behind locked doors": Levering, et al., *Best Companies*, p. 46.

31 "A manager's job": Bill James, "How They Play the Game," *Sport* (July 1984), p. 52.

31 Citicorp chairman Walter Wriston: Quoted in "What Made Reed Wriston's Choice at Citicorp," *Business Week* (July 2, 1984), p. 25.

32 "Reed would bet the bank": Daniel Hertzberg, "Citicorp Names John S. Reed as Its Chairman," *The Wall Street Journal*, June 20, 1984, p. 3.

32 "in a practical sense": Irving Shapiro, quoted by Leslie Wayne in "Citi's Soaring Ambition," *The New York Times*, June 24, 1984, p. 8F.

32 "I never even hear": Jerry Reinsdorf, quoted in "Jerry Reinsdorf Pulls a Double Play in Chicago," *Business Week* (October 10, 1983), p. 53.

32 According to *Fortune*: Gary Hector, "A Go-Go Insurer Adds Zest to Life," *Fortune* (March 5, 1984), p. 52.

32 "What Dee has done": "The Iconoclast Who Made Visa No. 1," *Business Week* (December 22, 1980), p. 44.

32 "he adamantly refuses": *Ibid.*, p. 46.

33 "I looked at it": Gerald Hannahs, quoted by Barbara Ettorre, "Don't Let the Slam Dunks Get to You," *Forbes* (July 18, 1983), p. 82.

33 "looking for people who": Levering, et al., *Best Companies*, p. 69.

33 "When you ride alone": Advertisement in *Forbes* (November 21, 1983), pp. 22–23.

34 "In most corporations": "Schlumberger: The Star of the Oil Fields Tackles Semiconductors," *Business Week* (February 16, 1981), p. 60.

34 "We don't think in terms": Andrew A. Anspach, quoted by Jeremy Main in "Toward Service Without a Snarl," *Fortune* (March 23, 1981), p. 66.

34 "Baseball is not precisely": Jim Murray, quoted in Chieger, *Voices*, p. 7.

3. Preparing the Game Plan: Football

36   "[I]t's a world in itself": Peter Dexter, "Don Shula in Perspective," *Esquire* (September 1983), p. 82.

36   "The game proceeds": David Harris, "Pete Rozelle: The Man Who Made Football an American Obsession," *The New York Times Magazine*, January 15, 1984, p. 14.

36   "It is not just violence": Michael Oriard, "Why Football Injuries Remain a Part of the Game," *The New York Times*, November 20, 1983, sec. 5, p. 2.

37   American football's origins: The following brief history is taken from Flexner, *Listening*, pp. 233–61.

37   "When you talk about the functions": John Ralston, quoted by Jack Clary, *The Gamemakers* (Chicago: Follett Publishing/National Football League Properties, Inc., 1976), p. 200.

39   "to outline each day's work": *Ibid.*, p. 50.

39   "Don can look at the schedule": *Ibid.*, p. 231.

39   "in our business": Lee L. Morgan, quoted in "Caterpillar: Sticking to Basics to Stay Competitive," *Business Week* (May 4, 1981), p. 76.

40   Joy's chairman, Andre R. Horn, "believes": "Joy Manufacturing: Out to Double in Size as It Predicts a 1990s Boom in Capital Goods," *Business Week* (April 9, 1984), p. 61.

40   Carl Peterson, president: Personal interview, March 6, 1984.

40   The NFL's regular season: The United States Football League (USFL)'s season consists of 18 games.

40   Moreover, in the postseason: There is still another difference, with professional teams. A baseball game that is tied at the end of nine innings goes into extra innings; a basketball game tied at the end of regulation play goes into a five-minute overtime period. In each case, both teams have the opportunity to score. By contrast, a football game that is tied when time runs out goes into "sudden death," in which the first team to score wins. Thus, it is entirely possible that one of the two teams in sudden death never has the opportunity to be on offense.

40   "no more than a list": Sam DeLuca, *The Football Hand-*

book (Middle Village, N.Y.: Jonathan David, 1978), p. 372.

40   For example, San Francisco: "The Computer Scores Big on the Gridiron," *Business Week* (October 24, 1983), p. 185.

41   "we can use up to": Woody Widenhofer, quoted by Paul Zimmerman, "Pete, the Way They Play Today Stinks," *Sports Illustrated* (December 12, 1983), p. 34.

41   "People say he's a patterned coach": Paul Wiggin, quoted by Clary, *Gamemakers*, p. 35.

41   On his part, Vince Lombardi: Quoted by Robert W. Wells, *Vince Lombardi: His Life and Times* (Madison, Wis.: Madison House, 1971), p. 143.

41   "Over the years, however": *Ibid.*, p. 146.

42   "Players talk about individualism": Tom Landry, quoted by Clary, *Gamemakers*, p. 103.

42   The Dallas Cowboys': Bob St. John, *The Man Inside . . . Landry* (New York: Avon Books, 1981), p. 126.

42   "Our team never will be": John Madden, quoted by Clary, *Gamemakers*, p. 117.

42   A 1983 study reported: Subrata N. Chakravarty, "Character Is Destiny," *Forbes* (October 10, 1983), p. 123.

42   "an inbred, promote-from-within": Paul Gibson with Barbara Rudolph, "Playing Peoria—to Perfection," *Forbes* (May 11, 1981), p. 60.

43   "People went to work for Kodak": Subrata N. Chakravarty and Ruth Simon, "Has the World Passed Kodak By?" *Forbes* (November 5, 1984), p. 190.

43   "The Southerners are naturally": Forrest McDonald, quoted by Frank Deford, "I Do Love the Football," *Sports Illustrated* (November 23, 1981), p. 102.

43   Prior to the 1982 strike: Personal interview with Irv Cross, August 23, 1982.

43   Many football-organizations exhibit: This definition of *vertical integration* is similar to that provided by Michael Porter in *Competitive Strategy: Techniques for Analyzing Industries and Competitors* (New York: Free Press, 1980), p. 300.

44   Cooper Industries, Inc.: "Cooper Industries: Pulled Through the Slump by Two Bold Buys, It Goes Hunting for New Acquisitions," *Business Week* (July 23, 1984), p. 136.

44   "Caterpillar goes out of its way": "Caterpillar," p. 77.

45   The nation's largest chemical company: "Du Pont's Costly Bet on Conoco," *Business Week* (July 20, 1981), p. 52.

45   [Andrew] "Carnegie [who] adopted a strategy": Paul Lawrence and Davis Dyer, *Renewing American Industry* (New York: Free Press, 1983), p. 60.

45   Consider the 1984 merger: E. Bradley Jones, "Communication to Stockholders," April 13, 1984, pp. 8–10.

46   For our purposes, long-linked: For a more detailed review of the different types of systems, see Elwood S. Buffa and William H. Taubert, *Production-Inventory Systems: Planning and Control* (Homewood, Ill.: Irwin, 1972). A shorter overview of different manufacturing systems is found in J. T. Black, "Cellular Manufacturing Systems Reduce Setup Time, Make Small Lot Production Economical," *Industrial Engineering* (November 1983), pp. 36–48.

46   "No longer was it to coordinate": William J. Abernathy, Kim B. Clark, and Alan M. Kantrow, *Industrial Renaissance* (New York: Basic Books, 1983), p. 33.

46   "the use of families": *Ibid.*, p. 35.

47   "strictly in terms": *Ibid.*, p. 39.

47   "he saw that the sheer magnitude": *Ibid.*, p. 70.

47   *Line balance* has to do: See Buffa and Taubert, *Production-Inventory Systems*, pp. 309–14, for a more complete definition.

48   But even these decisions: There are, to be sure, variations in player dependence based on platoon (defensive players tend to be less disciplined than their offensive counterparts) and position. For a provocative essay on this subject, see Arnold J. Mandell, "A Psychiatric Study of Professional Football," *Saturday Review* (October 5, 1974), pp. 12–16.

48   "There are a lot of times": Paul Brown, quoted by Clary, *Gamemakers*, p. 39.

48   "An offensive lineman": Bill Curry, quoted in DeLuca, *Football Handbook*, p. 48.

48   "There's nothing like having control": Billy Joe DuPree, quoted by Roy Rowan, "Fran Tarkenton, Corporate Quarterback," *Fortune* (January 21, 1985), p. 121.

48   "I think about what I've seen": DuPree, quoted by Joseph P. Kahn, "The Biggest Little Businessman in Texas," *Inc.* (June 1983), p. 100.

49   "two qualities stand out": *Ibid.*, p. 97.

49   "the critical path is the bottleneck": Ferdinand K. Levy, Gerald L. Thompson, and Jerome D. Wiest, "The ABCs of the Critical Path Method," *Harvard Business Review* (September–October 1963), p. 99.

50   "Through painstaking attention": Theodore Levitt, "Production-Line Approach," *Harvard Business Review* (September–October 1972), p. 46.

50   "The substitution of technology": *Ibid.*, p. 50.

50   Thus Coca-Cola's push: Anne B. Fisher, "The Ad Biz Gloms onto 'Global,'" *Fortune* (November 12, 1984), p. 80.

50   "The shaver company's chairman": *Ibid.*

50   An example from retail: This example is taken from Jay Gissen, "Nice Number, 40,000," *Forbes* (November 21, 1983), p. 292.

51   Or consider the programming: This account is taken from Walter Roessing, "What You *Didn't* Know About the Olympics," *Sky* (Delta Airlines' Inflight magazine) (May 1984), pp. 12–20.

51   "He can take his'n": Bum Phillips, quoted in Green, *Sportswit*, p. 187.

4. Managing the Flow: Basketball

52   "The game is simple": Pete Axthelm, *The City Game* (New York: Penguin Books, 1982), p. x.

52   "the thinking parts": Neil D. Isaacs and Dick Motta, *Sports Illustrated Basketball* (New York: Harper & Row, 1981), pp. 110–11.

52   "The game is unified action": Jack Ramsay, with John Strawn, *The Coach's Art* (Forest Grove, Oreg.: Timber Press, 1978), p. 69.

53   Basketball is, in the view: Bob Ryan, *The Pro Game: The World of Professional Basketball* (New York: McGraw-Hill, 1975), p. 43.

53   Unlike baseball or football: Glenn Dickey, *The History of Professional Basketball* (New York: Stein & Day, 1982), p. 3.

53   Basketball began as: Zander Hollander, *The Pro Basketball Encyclopedia* (Los Angeles: Corwin Books, 1977), p. 5.

53   In fact, the average player: The precise figure for 1982

was 6'6⅔", *Hoop*, The Official NBA Program Magazine (1982).

53   A field goal is attempted: According to NBA rules, a team has twenty-four seconds to get off a shot; otherwise the ball is turned over to the opponent.

53   "In each split second": Bill Russell and Taylor Branch, *Second Wind: The Memoirs of an Opinionated Man* (New York: Random House, 1979), p. 126.

54   Elkman views the process: Personal interview with Don Tuckerman, July 2, 1984.

55   Consider too, how a: The following contrast is taken from Ramsay, with Strawn, *Coach's Art*, p. 139.

56   The Donnelly Committee makes: John Simmons and William Mares, *Working Together* (New York: Knopf, 1983), p. 199.

56   One Donnelly employee: Quoted in "Participative Management at Work," an interview with John F. Donnelly, *Harvard Business Review* (January–February 1977), p. 119.

56   "Scouting reports": Isaacs and Motta, *basketball*, p. 111.

57   "'Keep it simple'": Bob Cousy, *The Killer Instinct* (New York: Random House, 1975), quoted by Ray Fitzgerald in *Champions Remembered* (Brattleboro, Vt.: Stephen Greene Press, 1982), p. 51.

57   "Auerbach would introduce a play": Fitzgerald, *Champions*, p. 80.

57   "In the 1961–62 season": Tommy Heinsohn, "Winning's Not Easier the 2d Time Around," *The New York Times*, May 6, 1984, p. 2S.

57   "The tempo, the essential beat": Gail Goodrich, with Rich Levin, *Gail Goodrich's Winning Basketball* (Chicago: Contemporary Books, 1976), p. 79.

57   He does this by calling: The only NBA coach whose substitution rotation is not determined by the flow of the game is Hubie Brown, who bases his system on the clock, Bruce Newman, "The Gospel According to Hubie," *Sports Illustrated* (October 31, 1983), p. 107.

58   "It was the first time": Ryan, *Pro Game*, p. 184.

58   "distinction between": Douglas Strain, quoted in Levering, et al., *Best Companies*, p. 102.

58   "Spring Fling gives many": Harry Quadracci, quoted by Ellen Wojhan, "Management by Walking Away," *Inc.* (October 1983), p. 68.

59 "company built by employees": *Ibid.*, p. 76.

59 In football each (offensive) play: Because defense is re-active, it cannot be choreographed so tightly. Still, defenses are planned and often subject to complex decision rules established by the coach.

59 "The toughest thing about managing": Paul Owens, quoted in *Sports Illustrated* (February 8, 1984), p. 8.

59 "Spending 82 games plus": John Bach, quoted by Michael Rozek, "What Does a Coach Do, Anyway?" *Sport* (March 1984), p. 36.

60 "I was very upset": Kareem Abdul-Jabbar and Peter Knobler, *Giant Steps* (New York: Bantam Books, 1983), p. 254.

60 "An exceptional player is simply": Bill Bradley, "You Can't Buy Heart," *Sports Illustrated* (October 31, 1977), p. 104.

60 "The entire Eclipse Group": Tracy Kidder, *The Soul of a New Machine* (New York: Avon Books, 1981), p. 120.

60 In his epilogue, Kidder: *Ibid.*, p. 288.

61 "I'm not taking anything away": Red Auerbach, quoted by Fitzgerald (*Champions*, p. 70), from Red Auerbach and Paul Sann, *Winning the Hard Way* (Boston: Little, Brown, 1966).

62 "One man alone can't": Bill Bradley, quoted by Richard O'Connor, "An Eye for the Main Ingredients," *The New York Times*, June 17, 1984, p. 2S.

62 "a player can play": Bradley, "You Can't Buy Heart," p. 105.

62 "Teams develop when talents": *Ibid*.

62 "professional basketball had not": David Halberstam, *The Breaks of the Game* (New York: Ballantine Books, 1983), p. 19.

63 "the technology lends itself": Michael Wolff, "Whatever Happened to 'Participative' Management?" *IEEE Spectrum* (February 1979), p. 61.

63 "Creativity comes from": James Treybig, quoted by Levering, et al., *Best Companies*, p. 330.

63 Not only do most employees: *Ibid.*, p. 331.

64 "Tandem now posts": Myron Magnet, "Managing by Mystique at Tandem Computers," *Fortune* (June 28, 1982), p. 86.

64 According to a programmer: *Ibid.*, p. 87.

64 When they come on board: *Ibid.*

64 "between the claims": *Ibid.*, p. 88.

64 "When the general idea": Renn Zaphiropoulos, quoted in "It's Not Lonely Upstairs," an interview with Renn Zaphiropoulos, *Harvard Business Review* (November–December 1980), p. 112.

65 "The trouble with the pyramid": *Ibid.*

65 Instead, they work in a large room: Levering, et al., *Best Companies*, p. 338.

65 "From the beginning": Kenneth Olsen, quoted by Harold Seneker, "Mid-Life Crisis," *Forbes* (May 21, 1984), p. 33.

65 Japan's NEC Corporation: This account is taken from Michael Porter, *Competitive Advantage: Creating and Sustaining Superior Performance* (New York: Free Press, 1985), pp. 403, 408, and 412–13.

65 "identifying and exploiting": *Ibid.*, p. 413.

65 Even in international advertising: Advertisement, *Business Week* (January 14, 1985), inside front cover.

66 "Now they had found a way": Eric L. Trist, *The Evolution of Socio-Technical Systems*, Ontario Quality of Working Life Centre, Occasional Paper no. 2 (June 1981), p. 8. For more detailed accounts of Trist's pioneering work, see E. L. Trist and K. W. Bamforth, "Some Social and Psychological Consequences of the Longwall Method of Coal-Getting," *Human Relations* 4 (1951): 3–38; and E. L. Trist, G. W. Higgin, H. Murray, and A. B. Pollock, *Organizational Choice* (London: Tavistock Publications, 1963).

67 The work flow at Topeka: The following description of Topeka is based on Richard E. Walton, "Establishing and Maintaining High Commitment in Work Systems," in John R. Kimberly, Robert H. Miles, and Associates, *The Organizational Life Cycle* (San Francisco: Jossey-Bass, 1980), pp. 208–90.

67 Richard Walton of Harvard, *Ibid.*, p. 220.

67 "In essence, our approach": Pehr G. Gyllenhammar, "How Volvo Adapts Work to People," *Harvard Business Review* (July–August 1977), p. 107.

68 Skilled trades workers: Michael Brody, "Toyota Meets U.S. Auto Workers," *Fortune* (July 9, 1984), pp. 54–56.

68 Early reports suggest: "How GM's Saturn Could Run Rings Around Old-Style Carmakers," *Business Week*

(January 28, 1985), pp. 126, 128.

69 "IBM designers worked": "How the PC Project Changed the Way IBM Thinks," *Business Week* (October 3, 1983), pp. 86, 90.

69 "One thing that characterized us": Alan Ladd, Jr., quoted in "When Friends Run the Business," interviews with Alan Ladd, Jr., Jay Kanter, and Gareth Wigan, *Harvard Business Review* (July–August 1980), pp. 88–89.

69 "One thing that has made": *Ibid.*, p. 91.

69 Wigan echoes this sentiment: *Ibid.*, p. 100.

69 "It's a small culture": *Ibid.*, p. 99.

70 "the making of a film": Eileen Morley and Andrew Silver, "A Film Director's Approach to Managing Creativity," *Harvard Business Review* (March–April 1977), p. 64.

70 "There were so many incredibly intelligent": Mark McNamara, quoted in *USA Today*, August 17, 1983, p. 2C.

70 "At every level, ads": Stephen Fox, *The Mirror Makers: A History of American Advertising and Its Creators* (New York: Morrow, 1984), p. 253.

72 "The prima donnas": Bill Caudill, quoted by Levering, et al., *Best Companies*, p. 57.

72 "Each group forms almost": *Ibid.*

72 "There's less politicking here": *Ibid.*, p. 99.

72 A prototypical basketball-organization: At the time, the company was called Hope's Windows and was part of a larger corporate entity, Roblin Industries, Inc.

5. Sports Hybrids

74 "the holy trinity": Michael Novak, *The Joy of Sports* (New York: Basic Books, 1976), p. 34.

74 "organization structures can either be": Peter Drucker, "New Templates for Today's Organizations," *Harvard Business Review on Management* (New York: Harper & Row, 1975), p. 631.

75 In one sense a baseball-organization: "Emerson Electric: High Profits from Low Tech," *Business Week* (April 4, 1983), pp. 58–62.

75 "Superachievers are rewarded": *Ibid.*, p. 61.

75 the successful Emerson manager: *Ibid.*, p. 60.

75   If, as *Business Week*: *Ibid.*

75   "You need an ability": Charles Knight, quoted by Marshall Loeb, "A Guide to Taking Charge," *Time* (February 25, 1980), p. 82.

75   "Knight is a tremendously conservative": "Emerson Electric," p. 62.

76   "Before McDonald's puts an item": John Koten, "Fast-Food Firms' New Items Undergo Exhaustive Testing," *The Wall Street Journal*, January 5, 1984, p. 25.

76   "McDonald's had to line up": *Ibid.*

76   *Grinding It Out*: Ray Kroc with Robert Anderson, *Grinding It Out: The Making of McDonald's* (New York: Berkley Books, 1978).

76   several new product ideas: Koten, "Fast-Food," p. 25.

77   a New Jersey-based firm: Lucien Rhodes, "The Importance of Being Arthur," *Inc.* (April 1982), pp. 66–77; and Sylvia Nasar, "Good News Ahead for Productivity," *Fortune* (December 10, 1984), p. 49.

77   A-P-A's philosophy: Rhodes, "Importance," p. 66.

77   "Every man chosen right": *Ibid.*, p. 72.

77   According to chief engineer August Pagnozzi: *Ibid.*, p. 77.

78   "It's not that I don't trust them": *Ibid.*

78   The differences between these two types: This chart is a composite drawn from (1) Dale Zand's contrast of authority/production and knowledge/problem ("collateral") organizations in *Information, Organization, and Power* (New York: McGraw-Hill, 1981), p. 63; and (2) Rosabeth Moss Kanter's contrast of maintenance and parallel organizations in *The Change Masters* (New York: Simon & Schuster, 1983), p. 407.

78   In most cases, however: By contrast, QWL is increasingly being built into organizational structure in new facility designs like the General Foods/Topeka and Volvo/Kalmar examples discussed in Chapter 4; these organizations more closely resemble basketball than they do a football/basketball hybrid.

79   Boeing Company illustrates: The following account is taken from Jay Galbraith, *Designing Complex Organizations* (Reading, Mass.: Addison-Wesley, 1973), pp. 133–34.

80   Still another type of collateral-organization: This and other applications of the group executive office concept are

discussed by N. R. Kleinfield, "When Many Chiefs Think as One," *The New York Times*, October 28, 1984, pp. 1F, 12–13F.

80   "It is an enabling and facilitating": *Ibid.*, p. 13F.

80   "Few people would fly": Henry Mintzberg, *The Structuring of Organizations* (Englewood Cliffs, N.J.: Prentice-Hall, 1979), p. 332.

80   "Unlike many other airlines": "Delta: the World's Most Profitable Airline," *Business Week* (August 31, 1981), p. 72.

81   "We do, of course, encourage": *Ibid*.

81   Perhaps the most dramatic evidence: Henry Eason, "Keeping Good People," *Nation's Business* (July 1984), pp. 37–39.

82   In 1982, 3M's average plant: Frederick C. Klein, "Some Firms Fight Ills of Bigness by Keeping Employee Units Small," *The Wall Street Journal*, February 5, 1982, p. 1.

82   Thus, 25 percent of sales: Lee Smith, "The Lures and Limits of Innovation," *Fortune* (October 20, 1980), pp. 86–94.

82   "When you put too many fences": 3M, "In the Search for New and Better Ideas, 3M Hears You," n.d., p. 2.

82   But they collect no royalties: Levering, et al., *Best Companies*, pp. 222–23.

83   "At 3M, listening": 3M, "In the Search," p. 4.

83   "that somewhere in 3M": Smith, "Lures and Limits," p. 91.

83   "He did it by inviting": Max De Pree, "Theory Fastball," *New Management*, 1, 4 (1984): 29.

83   "there is one more commitment": *Ibid.*, p. 30.

84   "Nothing is being *given*": *Ibid.*, p. 32.

84   "If you are a person who needs": Levering, et al., *Best Companies*, p. 128.

84   Gore describes its structure: Lucien Rhodes, "The Un-Manager," *Inc.* (August 1982), p. 34.

84   "We don't manage people": *Ibid.*, p. 36.

85   Gore estimates that his firm's productivity: Stanley W. Angrist, "Classless Capitalists," *Forbes* (May 9, 1983), p. 124.

85   A waterline decision involves: Rhodes, "Un-Manager," p. 34.

85   Consider General Motors' Inland Division: The follow-

ing account is taken from Robert W. Keidel, *Quality of Working Life in the Private Sector: An Overview and a Developmental Perspective* (Washington, D.C.: U.S. Office of Personnel Management, 1980), pp. 24–26.

87 "Several Emerson insiders": "Emerson Electric," p. 62.

87 In 1981, a good year: William Serrin, "The Way That Works at Lincoln," *The New York Times*, January 15, 1984, p. 4F.

87 "Encircled by the machines": Gene Bylinsky, "America's Best-Managed Factories," *Fortune* (May 28, 1984), p. 21.

87 Defects discovered by customers: Maryann Mrowca, "Ohio Firm Relies on Incentive-Pay System to Motivate Workers and Maintain Profits," *The Wall Street Journal*, August 12, 1983, p. 23.

88 To meet this commitment: Robert Zager, "Managing Guaranteed Employment," *Harvard Business Review* (May–June, 1978), p. 106.

88 According to Robert Zager: *Ibid.*, pp. 111–12.

88 "Lincoln Electric places": *Ibid.*, p. 115.

88 There are no break periods: With this exception: Smokers get a ten-minute break during the first shift, and during the second shift, when they are allowed to smoke—"a policy suggested by employees during the 1940's. This is the only time anyone may smoke—production workers or executives," Serrin, "The Way That Works," p. 4F.

88 "You have perhaps heard": William Baldwin, "This Is the Answer," *Forbes* (July 5, 1982), p. 52.

89 "While some scattered companies": Serrin, "The Way That Works," p. 4F.

6. The Right Team

90 With few exceptions, a player: Perhaps the major exception is the pitcher-catcher relation. The Phillies' Steve Carlton, for instance, insisted on having Tim McCarver as his catcher while McCarver was his teammate.

90 "Baseball players are the weirdest": Peter Gent, quoted in Green, *Sportswit*, p. 28.

90 "I've never seen a good player": Joe Morgan, quoted by Larry Linderman, "*Sport* Interview: Joe Morgan," *Sport* (June 1984), p. 22.

90   "The pro coach does not often": DeLuca, *Football Hand-book*, p. 240.

91   "In a game they beat": Vince Lombardi, quoted by Wells, *Lombardi*, p. 117.

92   As baseball author Charles Einstein: Charles Einstein, *Willie's Time* (New York: J.B. Lippincott, 1979), p. 345.

92   Consultant Stanley Davis: Stanley M. Davis, *Managing Corporate Culture* (Cambridge, Mass.: Ballinger, 1984), p. 8.

92   "Operations . . . is the new buzzword": Susan Fraker, "Tough Times for MBAs," *Fortune* (December 12, 1983), p. 71.

93   "Trade a player a year": Branch Rickey, quoted in Nelson, *Quotes*, p. 70.

93   "It's a lot more fun": Roland Hemond, quoted in Chieger, *Voices*, p. 213.

93   League standings are calculated: Glen Waggoner, ed., *Rotisserie League Baseball* (New York: Bantam, 1984).

94   The Cowboys' Tom Landry: Gary Cartwright, "Tom Landry: God, Family, and Football," in John Thorn, ed., *The Armchair Quarterback* (New York: Scribner's, 1982), p. 51.

94   "an Eagles player could never": Personal interview with Irv Cross, August 23, 1982.

94   "For all their talent": John Madden with Dave Anderson, *Hey, Wait a Minute, I Wrote a Book!* (New York: Villard, 1984), p. 183.

94   "It's easy to look at": *Ibid.*

95   "To me, the best trade": Red Auerbach, "Let's Make a Deal: Red Auerbach Talks Trade," *Sport* (November 1984), p. 46.

95   "The greatest single advantage": Arch Patton, "When Executives Bail Out to Move Up," *Business Week* (September 13, 1982), p. 13.

95   Similarly, conglomerate baseball-organizations: Except in cases like LTV's 1984 acquisition of Republic Steel, which was then merged with LTV's Jones & Laughlin Steel Corp. In this example a baseball-organization (LTV) tried to combine two football-organizations. The results, at least as of late 1984, were not very encouraging. (See, for instance, Thomas F. O'Boyle and Mark Russell, "Steel Giants' Merger Brings Big Headaches, J&L and Repub-

lic Find," *The Wall Street Journal*, November 30, 1984, pp. 1, 20.)

96   "It's tough to ignore": Scott M. Smith, quoted by Laurie P. Cohen, "Raytheon Is Among Companies Regretting High-Tech Mergers," *The Wall Street Journal*, September 10, 1984, p. 1.

97   A 1983 study of the performance: Chakravarty, "Character Is Destiny," pp. 114–23.

97   In fact, in every case: The one exception is the Oakland (now Los Angeles) Raiders, where John Madden, head coach since 1969, was replaced in 1979 by Tom Flores. But continuity was present even here: Flores had been Madden's assistant since 1972, and before that had been a Raiders player.

97   In the view of Ralph Saul: The following account is taken from Brian P. Sullivan, "Bringing the Entrepreneur's Spirit to Insurance," *The Philadelphia Inquirer*, May 7, 1984, p. 3D.

97   "a constant infusion": *Ibid*.

98   It is significant that: For football and basketball, colleges and universities have long served as functional equivalents of baseball's minor-league farm team system. With respect to scouting, the differences between baseball's and football's methods mirror the differences between the sports. Baseball's Major League Scouting Bureau was established in 1974 as a means of pooling resources among the various teams. As of 1984, however, eleven of the twenty-six major league teams did not belong. This group included the Orioles, Dodgers, and Phillies—three of baseball's top four teams over the past decade. Why do they go it alone? Probably, individualism and the fear of sharing information. In contrast, only two of the twenty-eight NFL teams did not belong to one of three football scouting combines in 1984. One of the two teams, the 49ers, had withdrawn because its owner's father owned a team in the rival USFL; the other team, the Raiders, has a baseball-like aversion to sharing information, Paul Zimmerman, *The New Thinking Man's Guide to Pro Football* (New York: Simon & Schuster, 1984), p. 297.

98   what they see: Ironically, although many baseball experts preach the virtues of continuity in a team's scouting operation, turnover among scouts often resembles that among

managers and players. Kevin Kerrane ventures that "the twenty-year scout has probably worked for at least three organizations so far, and been let go (the euphemism for fired) once because his club hired a new scouting director who brought in some friends," Kevin Kerrane, *Dollar Sign on the Muscle*: *The World of Baseball Scouting* (New York: Beaufort Books, 1984), p. 3.

98   "It isn't the quantity": Boswell, *Time Begins*, p. 66.

98   An obvious baseball-organization: Scott McMurray, "Salomon's Innovative, Risky Style Creates Profits and Some Problems," *The Wall Street Journal*, September 17, 1984, p. 37.

98   In the same compensation league: Levering, et al., *Best Companies*, p. 53.

98   "*before* they ask": Robert C. Wood, "Every Employee an Entrepreneur," *Inc.* (March 1983), p. 107.

98   "I think it's because people": Robert N. Noyce, quoted in "Creativity by the Numbers," an Interview with Robert N. Noyce, *Harvard Business Review* (May–June 1980), p. 124.

99   "The first real superstar": Russell and Branch, *Second Wind*, p. 111.

99   "Investors in Kaiser Steel": Andrew C. Brown, "The Asset Play at Kaiser Steel," *Fortune* (May 3, 1982), p. 129.

100 "players who jell together": Bradley, "You Can't Buy Heart," p. 106.

100 If Red Auerbach was right: Frank Deford, "A Man for All Seasons," *Sports Illustrated* (February 15, 1982), p. 61.

100 Consider Hewlett-Packard Company: Susan Fraker, "High-Speed Management for the High-Tech Age," *Fortune* (March 5, 1984), p. 66.

101 superbroker Richard F. Greene: Michael Blumstein, "The Man Who 'Constantly Prospects,'" *The New York Times*, July 29, 1984, p. 6F.

101 That same year, Merrill Lynch: Scott McMurray, "Brokerage Firms Push Salespeople to Produce More or Face Penalties," *The Wall Street Journal*, June 19, 1984, p. 31.

101 Management experts Raymond Miles and Charles Snow: Raymond E. Miles and Charles C. Snow, "Designing Strategic Human Resources Systems," *Organizational*

Dynamics (Summer 1984), p. 49. Miles and Snow's own term for what I call a football-organization is *defender*.

101 "There are only three levels": Levering, et al., *Best Companies*, p. 331.

102 "product plans, which are mapped out": Lee L. Morgan, former CEO, quoted in "Caterpillar," *Business Week* (May 4, 1981), p. 76.

7. The Right Game

104 Strengths of a Baseball-Organization: As we saw in Chapter 2, the players on a baseball team are relatively independent performers; they are "loosely coupled." It is therefore not surprising that a baseball design incorporates several strengths and weaknesses that resemble "potential functions and dysfunctions of loose coupling," as articulated by Karl Weick, "Educational Organizations as Loosely Coupled Systems," *Administrative Science Quarterly* 21 (1976): 1–19.

104 "When you're as diversified": Corporation president, quoted by Richard F. Vancil, *Decentralization: Managerial Ambiguity by Design* (Homewood, Ill.: Dow Jones-Irwin, 1978), p. 124.

106 Richard B. Madden, CEO: "Madden: A Washington Point Man for the Elite," *Business Week* (January 21, 1985), p. 68.

106 Allied Corporation: The following account is taken from Earl C. Gottschalk, Jr., "Allied Unit, Free of Red Tape, Seeks to Develop Orphan Technologies," *The Wall Street Journal*, September 13, 1984, p. 31.

106 "don't look ahead": *Ibid*.

107 Part of the corporation's reason: This account is taken from Carrie Dolan, "Tektronix New-Venture Subsidiary Brings Benefits to Parent, Spinoffs," *The Wall Street Journal*, September 18, 1984, p. 33.

107 "We'll never be completely able": *Ibid*.

108 "Xerox brought together": Charles Simonyi, quoted by Thomas J. Lueck, "Once a Prodigy, Xerox Faces Midlife Crisis," *The New York Times*. September 30, 1984, p. 8F.

109 "Managers are pitted against": "Corporate Culture: The

Hard-to-Change Values that Spell Success or Failure," *Business Week* (October 27, 1980), p. 148.

109　"People say there are": Chris Armstrong, quoted by Trish Hall, "Demanding PepsiCo Is Attempting to Make Work Nicer for Managers," *The Wall Street Journal*, October 23, 1984, p. 31.

109　*Macro:* Frank P. Davidson, with John Stuart Cox, *Macro: A Clear Vision of How Science and Technology Will Shape Our Future* (New York: Morrow, 1983).

109　"the study, preparation": *Ibid.*, p. 73.

110　"Mature individuals have learned: *Ibid.*, p. 246.

110　*The Mythical Man-Month*: Frederick P. Brooks, Jr., *The Mythical Man-Month: Essays on Software Engineering* (Reading, Mass.: Addison-Wesley, 1982).

110　"the entire system": *Ibid.*, p. 37.

110　"The bearing of a child": *Ibid.*, p. 17.

111　"As long as we demand": Mintzberg, *Structuring*, p. 347.

111　LTV Corporation claims: Advertisement, *The Wall Street Journal*, May 21, 1984, p. 19.

111　model for streamlining operations: For an early discussion of this perspective—that is, the potential value of routinizing lower-level choices—see Winston White, *Beyond Conformity* (New York: Free Press of Glencoe, 1961). A current treatment can be found in Paul A. Strassmann, *Information Payoff: The Transformation of Work in the Electronic Age* (New York: The Free Press, 1985).

112　"incremental errors": Ian Lustick, "Explaining the Variable Utility of Disjointed Incrementalism: Four Propositions," *The American Political Science Review* (June 1980), p. 348.

112　"safety equipment and procedures": *Ibid.*, p. 345.

112　"The cure": Ray Holton, "Rescuing a Dying Company Dependent on Steel Industry," *The Philadelphia Inquirer*, June 4, 1984, p. 3D.

113　"No surprises!": There is some irony here, because actual football teams certainly do try to surprise each other. As Yogi Berra once put it, in describing baseball: "It ain't like football. You can't make up no trick plays," quoted in Chieger, *Voices*, p. 105.

113　"The president is the only executive": Vancil, *Decentralization*, p. 38.

114   "[Such organizations] work best": Mintzberg, *Structuring*, p. 346.

114   For example, Timken Company: "Why Timken's 'Stability' Will Save Its Bottom Line," *Business Week* (May 17, 1982), p. 108.

114   In the language of organizational ecology: For an elaboration of this point, see Karl Weick's essay, "Management of Organizational Change Among Loosely Coupled Elements," in Paul S. Goodman and Associates, *Change in Organizations* (San Francisco: Jossey-Bass, 1982), pp. 375–408.

115   "Sears will be able": "The New Sears," *Business Week* (November 16, 1981), p. 142.

115   Synergy, as noted: Strictly speaking, synergy means that the whole *differs* from the sum of its parts; thus, in negative synergy, the whole is less than this sum.

116   "*Invention* is the process": Everett Rogers, "Re-Invention During the Innovation Process," in Michael Radnor, Irwin Feller, and Everett Rogers, eds., *The Diffusion of Innovations: An Assessment*, Center for the Interdisciplinary Study of Science and Technology, Northwestern University, July 1978, unnumbered.

116   "Progress comes as much": Russell L. Ackoff, *Redesigning the Future* (New York: Wiley, 1974), p. 91.

116   "to produce innovation, more complexity": Kanter, *Change Masters*, p. 148.

116   this design is closer to a tent: The tent metaphor is developed at length in Bo L. T. Hedberg, Paul C. Nystrom, and William H. Starbuck, "Camping on Seesaws: Prescriptions for a Self-Designing Organization," *Administrative Science Quarterly* 21 (1976): 41–65.

116   "Human resources units": Miles and Snow, "Human Resources Systems," *Organizational Dynamics* (Summer 1984), p. 45.

117   The intensive interaction: If each individual or unit must interact with every other, the degree of pairwise interaction required is given by the formula, $n(n-1)/2$. On an actual basketball team of five players, this means that there can be ten different pairwise exchanges. But on an eleven-man football team, the number of possible pairwise exchanges is fifty-five. And as this figure does not include interactions involving more than two players at a time, it is obvious that the size of a unit is a serious

constraint. Small wonder, then, that significantly less back-and-forth interaction is involved in either baseball or football than in basketball.

117 "A billion-dollar corporation": Roger von Oech, quoted in "Can Apple's Corporate Counterculture Survive?" *Business Week* (January 16, 1984), p. 82.

117 Companies like Apple: Sara Riner, "The Airline That Shook the Industry," *The New York Times Magazine*, December 23, 1984, p. 18.

117 Henry Mintzberg, among others, calls "adhocracy": Mintzberg (in *Structuring*) borrows this expression from Alvin Toffler, *Future Shock* (New York: Random House, 1970). The term had been used informally before that by behavioral scientist Warren Bennis.

117 Manned Spacecraft Center: William Litzinger, Albert Mavrinac, and John Wagle, "The Manned Spacecraft Center in Houston: The Practice of Matrix Management," *International Review of Administrative Sciences* (1970), p. 7.

118 "The company looks to": Charles F. Allison, quoted by N. R. Kleinfield, "When Many Chiefs Think as One," *The Wall Street Journal*, October 28, 1984, p. 12F. The more effective model of a group executive office, according to Allison, is one in which each member's responsibilities are spelled out (Kleinfield, p. 1F).

119 In vivid contrast: The following account is taken from Steven Flax, "The Toughest Bosses in America," *Fortune* (August 6, 1984), pp. 20–21.

119 "Ackman didn't recognize": *Ibid.*, p. 21.

119 Another instructive case: This account is taken from "What Undid Jarman: Paperwork Paralysis," *Business Week* (January 24, 1977), pp. 67–68.

120 "Jarman's style": *Ibid.*, p. 68.

120 the example of Jerry Dempsey: This account is taken from "A 'Nuts-and-Bolts Guy' Is Out at Borg-Warner," *Business Week* (December 19, 1983), pp. 108–110.

120 "Jerry is a nuts-and-bolts guy": *Ibid.*, p. 110.

120 "The job of [the top] executive": *Ibid.*

121 Moving from a regulated-monopoly: The following account is taken from Jeremy Main, "Waking up AT&T: There's Life After Culture Shock," *Fortune* (December 24, 1984), pp. 66–74.

121 "used to issue tomes": *Ibid.*, p. 70.

121   Exxon is a well-known: This account is taken from Leslie Wayne, "A Pioneer Spirit Sweeps Business," *The New York Times*, March 25, 1984, p. F13.

121   "when the giant oil company": *Ibid.*

121   Diamond Shamrock acquired: This account is taken from Myron Magnet, "Help! My Company Has Just Been Taken Over," *Fortune* (July 9, 1984), p. 48.

122   "Diamond Shamrock boasted": *Ibid.*

123   Consider the behavior: This example involves personal acquaintances of the author.

123   As one professor remarked: This tendency to overcontrol faculty is all too common throughout U.S. education. Robert Reich generalizes: "Increasingly America's educational curriculum is planned and monitored by professional administrators and delivered by teachers whose low salaries and tedious, repetitive jobs are coming to resemble those of production workers in a traditional American factory" (*The Next American Frontier* [New York: Penguin Books, 1984], p. 215). The same tendency can be identified *within* educational administrations. A study commission recently found the State University of New York (SUNY) to be "an extreme example of what not to do in the management of public higher education," and "the most overregulated university in the nation." The root cause? The wrong model: SUNY was originally designed "to function as a state agency, like New York's prisons, rather than as a quasi-independent entity, the status of institutions like the University of California" ("SUNY Red Tape," *Time* [January 28, 1985], p. 77).

124   Textron, the original conglomerate: The following account is taken from "Textron: Shaking Up the Divisions to Enliven a Sluggish Conglomerate," *Business Week* (May 26, 1980), pp. 88, 92–93.

124   "We want new managers": *Ibid.*, p. 92.

125   The Arp experience: The following account is taken from Craig R. Waters, "Raiders of the Lost Arp," *Inc.* (November 1982), pp. 38–44.

125   "It was difficult to tell": *Ibid.*, p. 42.

126   "Among the three of them": *Ibid.*, p. 44.

126   "I don't have to go through": Karen Tolland, quoted by Erik Larson and Carrie Dolan, "Large Computer Firms Sprout Little Divisions for Good, Fast Work," *The Wall Street Journal*, August 19, 1983, p. 17.

126 "We were under tremendous": Karen Tolland, quoted in "Two Lessons in Failure from Silicon Valley," *Business Week* (September 10, 1984), pp. 78, 83.

126 "In the old days": Harold Seneker, "Mid-Life Crisis," *Forbes* (May 21, 1984), p. 34.

127 "Under the old organization": Bro Uttal, "Delays and Defections at Hewlett-Packard," *Fortune* (October 29, 1984), p. 62.

127 Acme-Cleveland, an old-line: The following account is taken from Ralph E. Winter, "Acme-Cleveland Is Making Risky Changes to Survive in New Machine-Tool Industry," *The Wall Street Journal*, May 17, 1984, p. 33.

127 "This company was *geared"* : *Ibid*.

128 "When market conditions led": Bela Gold, "CAM Sets New Rules for Production," *Harvard Business Review* (November–December 1982), p. 89.

128 Johnson and Johnson (J & J) is: This account is taken from "Changing a Corporate Culture," *Business Week* (May 14, 1984), pp. 130–38.

128 "we would be headed toward": *Ibid*., p. 131.

128 "a sea change": *Ibid*., p. 133.

128 Xerox Corporation is: The following account is taken from Dennis Kneale, "Xerox Takes New Marketing Tack to Improve Poor Computer Sales," *The Wall Street Journal*, May 9, 1984, p. 31.

129 "Getting machines . . . to work": Advertisement, *The Wall Street Journal*, March 5, 1984, pp. 16–17.

129 "They understand how to fit": Paul Stieman, quoted by Kneale, "Xerox Takes New Marketing Tack," p. 31.

130 "a disciplined phalanx": Daniel Hertzberg, "Merger of Two Insurers into Cigna Corp. Brings Discord, Layoffs, and Profit Drop," *The Wall Street Journal*, July 29, 1983, p. 36.

131 "the companies had two very distinct": John R. Cox, quoted by Myron Magnet, "Help!" *Fortune* (July 9, 1984), p. 47.

131 "only last year did the company": *Ibid*., pp. 47–48.

8. Taking Stock of Your Company

133 "all work is done": "Automaking on a Human Scale," *Fortune* (April 5, 1982), p. 89.

134 "The lesson: if hand labor": Bylinsky, "America's Best Managed Factories," p. 21.

134 "Academic prestige depends upon": Frederick Terman, quoted by Everett M. Rogers and Judith K. Larsen, *Silicon Valley Fever* (New York: Basic Books, 1984), p. 36.

134 "a small faculty group": *Ibid.*

134 "The Name of the Game": Advertisement, *The Wall Street Journal,* November 20, 1984, p. 13.

134 "Listening to Bryan plot": Barry Stavro, "Grinding It Out," *Forbes* (March 11, 1985), p. 126.

135 Harnischfeger planned: Porter, *Strategy,* pp. 36–37.

135 "the conceptual integrity": Brooks, *Man-Month,* p. 46.

135 People Express tells: Advertisement, *The New York Times,* May 15, 1983, p. F43.

135 "Getting involved from the beginning": Michal Lawrence, quoted by Sara Delano, "Managing the Right Side of the Brain," *Inc.* (December 1982), p. 88.

136 According to *Business Week*: "The New Entrepreneurs," *Business Week* (April 18, 1983), p. 80.

139 "the name of the game": Joseph T. Brophy, quoted in "Office Automation Restructures Business," *Business Week* (October 8, 1984), p. 120.

139 "Employees have access": *Ibid.*

140 "network of more than": *Ibid.,* p. 125.

140 "Employees are paid": Steven Flax, "Toughest Bosses," *Fortune* (August 6, 1984), p. 20.

140 People Express exemplifies: This account is taken from Peter Nulty, "A Champ of Cheap Airlines," *Fortune* (March 22, 1982), pp. 127–34.

140 "This is a very democratic": *Ibid.,* p. 134.

141 "except for some hourly manufacturing": Levering, et al., *Best Companies,* p. 335.

141 Publix Super Markets, Inc.: *Ibid.,* p. 284.

141 most gain-sharing programs: the best-known gain-sharing programs are (1) Scanlon plans (which compare sales dollars produced to payroll dollars); (2) Rucker plans

(which compare production value-added—roughly, sales less purchases—to payroll dollars); and (3) "Improshare" plans (which compare operating performance to historical or estimated time standards; Improshare is a proprietary program devised and registered by Mitchell Fein, a New Jersey-based consultant).

141 Still other top-management teams: For an interesting essay on office layout alternatives, and the advantages of a "linked-dispersion" model (a baseball/basketball equivalent), see Fritz Steele, "The Ecology of Executive Teams: A New View of the Top," *Organizational Dynamics* (Spring 1983), pp. 65–78.

142 "It takes a certain type": Quoted by Charles Kaiser, "Simon & Schuster Sets Fast Pace in Publishing—And Violates Taboos," *The Wall Street Journal*, September 26, 1984, p. 1.

142 "I went to work": "Tony," quoted by Adam Smith, "If 'Smokestack America' Shrinks, Can Psychology Cure the Depression?" *Esquire* (April 1984), p. 69.

143 a prevailing belief: Smith, "Lures and Limits," p. 91.

143 "Shaub always did a lot": Richard J. Censits, quoted by Damon Darlin, "Road Can Be Bumpy When New Chief Acts to Enliven His Firm," *The Wall Street Journal*, September 17, 1984, p. 10.

144 "I had long believed": Harold Geneen, with Alvin Moscow, *Managing* (Garden City, N.Y.: Doubleday, 1984), pp. 41–42.

145 "Their management team": Walter B. Wriston, quoted in "The Golden Plan of American Express," *Business Week* (April 30, 1984), pp. 118–19.

145 flexibility in developing from the outside: Of course, American Express—or any other baseball-like company—could stretch its managerial capacities too thin by acquiring too many companies too fast. But such an organization still has more leeway in going the acquisition route than a more tightly joined football-organization.

145 Ed Carlson, former CEO: Richard Tanner Pascale and Anthony G. Athos, *The Art of Japanese Management* (New York: Simon & Schuster, 1981), p. 166.

145 John G. McCoy, chairman: This account is taken from Bernard Wysocki, Jr., "The Chief's Personality Can Have

a Big Impact—For Better or Worse," *The Wall Street Journal*, September 11, 1984, pp. 1, 12.

145   "Hire people who are exceptional": *Ibid*.
145   "a management team fashioned": This quotation, and the following account, are taken from Monica Langley, "ITT Chief Emphasizes Harmony, Confidence and Playing by Rules," *The Wall Street Journal*, September 13, 1984, pp. 1, 23.
145   "If I were concerned": *Ibid*., p. 23.
146   "Failure for us": John Sculley, quoted in "Corporate Counterculture," p. 82.
146   "it looks more like": Mary Williams Walsh, "Company-Built Retreats Reflect Firms' Cultures and Personalities," *The Wall Street Journal*, August 16, 1984, p. 27.
146   "Arthur Andersen places": *Ibid*.
146   The guiding concept: *Ibid*.
146   "its willingness to risk": Scott McMurray, "Salomon's Style," *The Wall Street Journal*, September 17, 1984, p. 31.
146   "They're very tough": *Ibid*.
147   "in the ball park": Alan W. Livingston, telephone interview, May 22, 1984.
147   "We have to get people": Jack Welch, quoted by Howard Banks, "General Electric—Going with the Winners," *Forbes* (March 26, 1984), p. 102.
147   "For me, that idea": Jack Welch, "Competitiveness from Within—Beyond Incrementalism," Hatfield Address at Cornell University, April 26, 1984.
147   "Ninety-nine percent": Geneen, with Moscow, *Managing*, p. 94.
147   "we lay the cards": Shelby H. Carter, Jr., quoted by Robert L. Shook, *Ten Greatest Salespersons: What They Say About Selling* (New York: Barnes & Noble, 1980), p. 81.
148   every plant employee wears: "New Corporate Elite," *Business Week* (January 21, 1985), p. 71.
148   "I never saw anybody": Fred Lynn, quoted by Stephen Kindel, ed., "The Hardest Single Act in All of Sports," *Forbes* (September 23, 1983), p. 181.
148   "hitting a baseball": *Ibid*., p. 180.
149   "a great place for self-starters": Levering, et al., *Best Companies*, p. 301

149   "There's instant prestige": *Ibid.*, p. 108.

149   executives at Timken Company: "Timken's 'Stability,'"
        p. 107.

149   "a split at the bottom": This expression is used by Eric
        L. Trist in his essay, "A Socio-Technical Critique of
        Scientific Management," in D. O. Edge and J. N. Wolfe,
        eds., *Meaning and Control* (London: Tavistock Publi-
        cations, 1973).

149   "have been going downhill": Quoted in "Caterpillar,"
        p. 80.

149   "There's an intensity": Nick Larsen, quoted in Rogers
        and Larsen, *Fever*, p. 137.

150   "working conditions—competition": *Ibid.*, p. 152.

150   "Working 90 hours": "Corporate Counterculture," p. 82.

153   the following diagram: This diagram is an adaptation of
        the Maxwell "color triangle," whose vertices are red,
        blue, and green; any mix of colors (of lights) can be
        described by a point inside the triangle, *Van Nostrand's
        Scientific Encyclopedia,* 5th ed. (New York: Van Nos-
        trand Reinhold, 1976), p. 615. Pascale and Athos (*Jap-
        anese Management*, p. 119) have used the same schematic
        device, which they call the "executive triangle," in con-
        trasting the interdependence patterns of American and
        Japanese executives.

153   any organization should strike a balance: For a more
        detailed discussion of this trade-off, see Robert W. Kei-
        del, "QWL Development: Three Trajectories," *Human
        Relations 35* (1982): 743–61.

154   senior management teams: Richard F. Vancil and Charles
        H. Green, in "How CEOs Use Top Management Com-
        mittees" (*Harvard Business Review*, January–February
        1984, pp. 65–73), describe two contrasting models of
        top-management team behavior vis-à-vis the rest of the
        organization: General Electric (baseball-like) and IBM
        (football-like).

155   the institute has recently had to tighten: "Battelle: Out-
        growing a Stubborn Loyalty to the 'Rust Bowl,'" *Busi-
        ness Week* (September 10, 1984), p. 70.

155   organizations do have considerable choice: Clearly, the
        generic business functions of sales and manufacturing
        parallel baseball and football, respectively. But as we
        have seen, there are nonbaseball approaches to selling
        (for example, Xerox's football pattern as described by

Shelby Carter, and that company's basketball pattern as evidenced by "Team Xerox"); and nonfootball approaches to manufacturing (such as E. T. Wright's baseball pattern and General Foods/Topeka's basketball pattern). Similarly, different industries mirror different sports, yet exhibit significant variations within. Thus, for example, the automobile industry—historically a football prototype—contains examples of both baseball (Porsche) and basketball (Volvo/Kalmar).

155 a value like loyalty: In fact there is strong sentiment in some quarters that loyalty comes at the expense of dependence and mediocrity. See, for example, Jeanne Dorin McDowell, "Job Loyalty: Not the Virtue It Seems," *The New York Times*, March 3, 1985, sec. 3, p. 1.

156 "You sit in front": Tony Nathan, quoted by Bill Lyon in *The Philadelphia Inquirer*, February 1985, sec. E, p. 1.

156 situations that do call for a football style: Paradoxically, a football style may be effective when team members are new or immature, and lack the capacity to "play" baseball or (especially) basketball. Thus, Harry Quadracci puts new employees at Quad Graphics through a harsh regimen: "They're raw recruits, and as far as we're concerned, they're in boot camp for about two years. . . . It's authoritarian all the way, until they've proven they're adult enough to handle a participative management style" (quoted by Ellen Wojhan, "Walking Away," p. 72). But the danger in using a football style in this manner is that the style may become entrenched—and only reinforce dependent behavior.

9. It's a Whole New Ballgame

157 "The guy was in command": Bruce Entin, quoted in "A New Pac-Man," *Time* (July 16, 1984), p. 50.

157 "Leadership is demonstrated": Steven Flax, "Toughest Bosses," *Fortune* (August 6, 1984), p. 20.

157 "from superb to pathetic": *Ibid.*, p. 19. According to Flax, "The median return on shareholders' equity over the past five years for seven of the ten companies for which data are available ranged from 7.3% . . . to 18.1%.

... That compares with the median for the *Fortune* 500 of 13.8%."

157   "glee and delight": Charles Kaiser, "Simon & Schuster," *The Wall Street Journal*, September 26, 1984, p. 24.

157   *Life and Death:* Paul Solman and Thomas Friedman, *Life and Death on the Corporate Battlefield* (New York: New American Library, 1982); *Corporate Combat:* William E. Peacock, *Corporate Combat* (New York: Facts on File Publications, 1984).

157   "How to run all over": Advertisement, *The Wall Street Journal*, October 5, 1984, p. 6.

158   "smothered the enemy": William S. Knudsen, quoted by John S. DeMott, "Manufacturing Is in Flower," *Time* (March 26, 1984), p. 51.

158   coming of postindustrial society: The term *postindustrial society* was coined by David Riesman in "Leisure and Work in Post-Industrial Society," in E. Larrabee and R. Mayershon, eds., *Mass Leisure* (Glencoe, Ill.: The Free Press, 1958). The term became more widely accepted through Daniel Bell's essay. "Twelve Modes of Prediction," in J. Gould, ed., *Penguin Survey of the Social Sciences* (London: Penguin Books, 1965); and Bell's book, *The Coming of Post-Industrial Society* (New York: Basic Books, 1973).

158   when, for the first time, more people: John Naisbitt in *Megatrends* (New York: Warner Books, 1982) puts the year at 1956.

158   According to MIT's David Birch: David Birch, quoted by Garry Emmons, "David Birch: Putting the Numbers to Work," *Harvard Business School Bulletin* (April 1984), p. 54.

158   American jobs will increasingly lie: Rogers and Larsen, *Fever*, p. 132.

158   societies that preceded it: These "societies" parallel the three "tidal waves of change in history" discussed by Alvin Toffler in *The Third Wave* (New York: Morrow, 1980).

158   "military images restrict": Karl Weick, *The Social Psychology of Organizing*, 2d ed. (Reading, Mass.: Addison-Wesley, 1979), p. 51.

159   "Those who have ever played": Bradley, "You Can't Buy Heart," p. 114.

159   "Winning isn't everything": This quotation is commonly

attributed to Vince Lombardi; according to Lee Green (*Sportswit*, p. 57), however, it belongs to former Vanderbilt football coach Red Sanders.

159 "Our competition is our own sense": Edwin P. Land, quoted by H. Igor Ansoff, *Strategic Management* (London: Macmillan, 1979), p. 125.

160 This is the quaintness: George Carlin, on NBC's "Late Night with David Letterman," May 7, 1984.

161 "the most-played game": Frederick C. Klein: "Star Wars: Competition Across National Boundaries," *The Wall Street Journal*, January 4, 1983, p. 28.

161 coordinate themselves as a unit: In fact, just as the game of soccer is gaining legitimacy in the U.S., so is a more soccerlike (or basketball-like) approach to military doctrine itself—at least in certain quarters. Brigadier General Donald R. Morelli, special assistant to the commanding officer of the Army's Training and Doctrine Command, uses sports to illustrate the new direction. Reports Deborah Shapley in *The New York Times Magazine* (November 28, 1982, p. 40): "General Morelli likes to show a slide of a soccer match and one of a football game. The Army, he argues, should stop thinking of battle as a football game, in which players assume fixed positions, and start emulating soccer, in which play shifts rapidly from one part of the field to another and players decide independently what to do."

161 in his book, *The Game*: Ken Dryden, *The Game* (New York: Times Books, 1983), pp. 222–36.

161 "Once, when we were losing": Joe Montana, quoted by Kenny Moore, "To Baffle and Amaze," *Sports Illustrated* (July 26, 1982), p. 70.

161 "play as controlled as any": Bill Walsh, quoted by Zimmerman, *New Thinking Man's Guide*, p. 250.

162 "Few fans will understand": Jean S. Fugett, Jr., "The Fear Factor in Pro Football's Contract Talks," *The New York Times*, September 5, 1982, p. 2S.

162 "You've got to meet the bogey": Ann Crump, quoted by William Serrin, "Computers Divide AT&T and Its Workers," *The New York Times*, November 18, 1983, p. 1.

162 "The higher the emphasis": Robert Karasek, quoted by Michael Uhl, "Technostress," *Forbes* (July 2, 1984), p. 158.

162 "minimal critical specifications": P. G. Herbst, *Socio-*

Technical Design: Strategies in Multidisciplinary Research (London: Tavistock Publications, 1974).

163   "Industrial management has gone back": Wickham Skinner, "Boosting Productivity Is the Wrong Focus," *The Wall Street Journal*, March 15, 1982, p. 26.

163   "for most top-performing companies": Peters and Waterman, *Excellence*, p. 193.

164   "The Focused Factory": Wickham Skinner, "The Focused Factory," *Harvard Business Review* (May–June 1974), pp. 113–21.

164   "The problem," according to: John A. Endee, quoted in "Small Is Beautiful Now in Manufacturing," *Business Week* (October 22, 1984), p. 153.

164   monthly *profit* of $280,000: *Ibid.*, p. 156.

165   the Data Entry Systems Division: The following account is taken from Eugene Linden, "Let a Thousand Flowers Bloom," *Inc.* (April 1984), pp. 66–70.

165   "One consequence of all this": *Ibid.*, p. 68.

165   "Baseball gives you": Joe Garagiola, quoted in Nelson, *Quotes*, p. 186.

165   "Do for yourself": Gaylord Perry, quoted in Chieger, *Voices*, p. 155.

165   "As modern technology": Edward E. David, quoted by Ronald Alsop, "Many Young Scientists Are Choosing Industry Over College Careers," *The Wall Street Journal*, May 31, 1984, p. 1.

165   "If someone wanted to research": *Ibid.*

165   "a great painter": *Ibid.*, p. 22.

165   "To survive, once fiercely": "Reshaping the Computer Industry," *Business Week* (July 16, 1984), p. 84.

166   "We'll see a substantial surge": Bobby Ray Inman, quoted by William H. Inman, "Ex-Spy Seeks High-Tech Supremacy," West Chester (Pa.) *Daily Local News*, January 12, 1985, p. 15.

166   "a severe housing shortage": Rogers and Larsen, *Fever*, p. 199.

166   "the greedy, self-serving": *Ibid.*, p. 201.

167   "Most major airlines": Donald Burr, "People Express Grows Bigger Without Getting Fat," *The Wall Street Journal*, January 7, 1985, p. 24.

167   "Anyone who isn't studying": D. Daryl Wyckoff, quoted by Sara Riner, "Airline," *The New York Times Magazine*, December 23, 1984, p. 18.

167   JIT: For a lucid examination of how the Japanese employ
       JIT techniques, see Richard J. Schonberger, *Japanese
       Management Techniques* (New York: The Free Press,
       1982).

167   "The thing about Red": K. C. Jones, quoted by George
       Vecsey, "Talking About Arnold," *The New York Times*,
       January 6, 1985, p. S3.

168   "discrete products will ideally flow": J. T. Black, "Cel-
       lular Manufacturing," *Industrial Engineering* (November
       1983), p. 36.

168   "Each increase in self-regulating": Larry Hirschhorn, *Be-
       yond Mechanization: Work and Technology in a Post-
       industrial Age* (Cambridge, Mass.: MIT Press, 1984),
       pp. 82–83.

168   how the different jobs all fit together: Harley Shaiken
       generalizes this point in terms of automated production
       systems in his article, "The Automated Factory: The View
       from the Shop Floor," in *Technology Review* (Massa-
       chusetts Institute of Technology, January 1985), p. 18:
       "Manufacturing systems never seem to break down at
       machine-tool shows, but I have visited automated fac-
       tories that were down a third or more of the time. The
       cause is not hard to discover. Reducing human input often
       means instituting complex technologies that are prone to
       trouble. To put it another way, the drive to eliminate
       uncertainties arising from human influence only winds
       up creating mechanical and electronic uncertainties. Thus,
       despite the vision of total automation, workers must in
       the end play critical roles in operating, as well as unjam-
       ming and repairing, computer-based production sys-
       tems."

169   "Many executives who talk about": Douglas McGregor,
       The Human Side of Enterprise (New York: McGraw-Hill,
       1960), pp. 228–29.

169   "We spend a lot of time": Renn Zaphiropoulos, quoted
       in "Upstairs," *Harvard Business Review* (November–
       December 1980), p. 124.

169   An even better example: I have worked with James River
       Graphics as a consultant since 1983.

169   Hirschhorn estimated: Hirschhorn, *Beyond Mechaniza-
       tion*, p. 120.

170   "Some new scientific fields": Tohru Moto-oka, quoted
       by Steve Lohr, "The Japanese Challenge," *The New York*

Times Magazine, July 8, 1984, p. 41. John P. McKelvey, a professor of physics at Clemson University, puts the case for collaboration even more strongly: "It is less easy now than it was 50 or 100 years ago for technologists like Edison—or scientists like Einstein, I might add—to assert their independence. Experimental high-energy physics, for example, requires an incredibly complex grid of technologies, including electronics, nuclear technology, magnetics, cryogenics, new materials, high vacuum, and advanced computers," "The Driven and the Driver," *Technology Review* (January 1985), p. 47.

170   "small groups are": Peters and Waterman, *Excellence*, p. 126.

170   relevance of basketball-style teamwork: The exact nature of "basketball" at the top levels of a major corporation will differ from that at lower levels. Typically, senior managers find it difficult to collaborate in a sustained manner because of the time pressures and travel demands under which they operate. Neither are they readily able to exchange tasks because the tasks tend to require highly specialized skills—particularly in science-based organizations.

Calvin Pava has addressed these issues in his book *Managing New Office Technology: An Organizational Strategy* (New York: The Free Press, 1983). Pava advocates different sociotechnical designs for nonroutine, mixed, and routine work; these alternate designs thus apply to different organizational levels. Specifically, "discretionary coalitions" fit top management; "product-line/market segment teams" fit middle management; and "work groups" fit the work system level. In his Afterword, Eric Trist places Pava's argument in historical perspective and shows how important it is that, in my idiom, basketball be played throughout the organization.

170   *Small Is Beautiful*: E. F. Schumacher, *Small Is Beautiful: Economics as if People Mattered* (New York: Harper & Row, 1973).

170   a new generation of computers: The new generation will constitute the fifth. First-generation computers were based on vacuum tubes; second-generation, transistors; third-generation, integrated circuits, and fourth-generation, very-large-scale integrated circuits. But since the 1940s, when mathematician John Von Neumann developed "the

basic scheme of the stored-program computer, the essential blueprint of operation for computers has not changed. The computer . . . executes arithmetic calculations one at a time before going on to the next calculation" (Steve Lohr, "Challenge," *The New York Times Magazine*, July 8, 1984, p. 39). Fifth-generation computers will be able to carry out many calculations simultaneously.

171   "When something goes down": Rod Zilles, quoted by Levering, et al., *Best Companies*, p. 246.

171   "We're able to diversify": George Mischenko, quoted by Ray Holton, "A Scrappy New Foe of Big Steel," *The Philadelphia Inquirer*, March 18, 1984, p. 2D.

172   "One consistent request": Robert M. Adams, quoted by Frederick Klein, "Ills of Bigness," *The Wall Street Journal*, February 5, 1982, p. 16.

172   "He's passed a point": "Growing Pains at People Express," *Business Week* (January 28, 1985), p. 91.

172   "is one of designing corporations": Russell L. Ackoff, *Creating the Corporate Future*, (New York: Wiley, 1981), p. 152.

173   The most general baseball/basketball model: My concept builds on Herbert Simon's notion of "nearly decomposable systems" as articulated in *The Sciences of the Artificial*, 2d ed. (Cambridge, Mass.: MIT Press, 1981), pp. 209–17; it is also similar to Terence Deal and Allan Kennedy's "atomized organization," as discussed in *Corporate Cultures* (Reading, Mass.: Addison-Wesley, 1982), pp. 177–86; and to Michael Porter's "new organizational form" (an amalgam of autonomy and interrelationships), as described in *Competitive Advantage*, pp. 414–15.

173   "It's a whole new ball game": David M. Wood, quoted in "A Scramble to Supply 'The Total Solution,'" *Business Week* (October 8, 1984), p. 138.

173   "lost not only their jobs": "'Suddenly, the World Doesn't Care If You Live or Die,'" *Business Week* (February 4, 1985), p. 98.

174   "These people were so damn loyal": *Ibid.*

Appendix 2: Sports' Pay Structures

180   lists include 208 athletes: In the 1983 list, eleven players
       tied for number 98, so 108 players were included. The
       1983 list was compiled from 1982–83 data for football
       and basketball, and 1983 data for baseball; the 1984
       list was based on 1983–84 data for basketball and 1983
       data for baseball and football.

181   nineteen of the top twenty-two salaries: In the 1984 list,
       three players tied for 9, so a total of 22 players appeared
       on the two years' lists.

182   average "top 10" salary: In terms of actual dollars dif-
       ference (average "top 10" salary *minus* average league
       salary excluding the "top 10"), basketball ($821,230)
       falls between baseball ($1,081,444) and football
       ($510,953).

INDEX